995
NET

Program Behavior:
Models and
Measurements

ELSEVIER COMPUTER SCIENCE LIBRARY

Operating and Programming Systems Series
Peter J. Denning, *Editor*

Halstead	A Laboratory Manual for Compiler and Operating System Implementation
Spirn	Program Behavior: Models and Measurements
Halstead	Elements of Software Science (in prep.)
Franta	The Process View of Simulation (in prep.)

OPERATING AND PROGRAMMING SYSTEMS SERIES

Program Behavior: Models and Measurements

Jeffrey R. Spirn

The Pennsylvania State University

ELSEVIER
NEW YORK OXFORD AMSTERDAM

Elsevier North-Holland, Inc.
52 Vanderbilt Avenue, New York, New York 10017

Elsevier Scientific Publishing Company
335 Jan Van Galenstraat, P.O. Box 211
Amsterdam, The Netherlands

© 1977 by Elsevier North-Holland, Inc.

Library of Congress Cataloging in Publication Data
Spirn, Jeffrey R
Program behavior: models and measurements
(Operating and programming systems series)
Bibliography: p.
Includes index.
1. Computer programs—Evaluation. I. Title.
QA76.6.S68   001.6'42   77-3646
ISBN 0-444-00219-7
ISBN 0-444-00220-0 pbk.

Manufactured in the United States of America

To Judith

Publisher's Note

Camera-ready copy for this book, which was supplied to us by Dr. Spirn, was printed on the IBM 370 at The Pennsylvania State University under the control of the ROFF360 text formatting program that was originally written by Alan Demers and Leonard Vanek.

This procedure has enabled us to bypass the usual typesetting process, thereby accelerating the date of publication of the book. We are indebted to Dr. Spirn for the opportunity to share in this new and developing text-editing technology.

Contents

Preface		ix
1	**On Modeling**	1
	1.1 Introduction	1
	1.2 Why Do We Model?	1
	1.3 Programs in Execution	7
	1.4 What Effects Should Be Modeled?	8
	1.5 Philosophies in Modeling	11
	1.6 Locality—The Basic Principle	16
2	**Paging Issues**	18
	2.1 Hardware Review	18
	2.2 Thrashing	22
	2.3 Paging Algorithms	23
	2.4 Properties of Memory Reference Locality	45
3	**Models for Memory Reference Behavior**	56
	3.1 Some Extrinsic Program Models	56
	3.2 Intrinsic Models of Locality	84
	3.3 On the Optimal Paging Algorithm for the GLM	95
4	**The LRU and Related Stack Models**	98
	4.1 Paging in Simple Stack Models	98
	4.2 The LRU Stack Model (SLRUM)	111
	4.3 Extensions to the LRU Stack Model	132
5	**Tools for Measurement and Validation**	143
	5.1 What Should We Validate?	143
	5.2 Measurement of Working Set Behavior	145
	5.3 Other Criteria for Validation	165
	5.4 Practical Issues of Reference String Measurement	166
	5.5 Stack Distance Validation	169
6	**Two Modeling Examples**	207
	6.1 Modeling the Page Fault Process	207
	6.2 A Semi-Markov Page Fault Model	209

	6.3	A Markovian Distance String Model	224
	6.4	Summary	252
7	The State of the Art	253
	7.1	Review of the Models	254
	7.2	Measurement and Validation	258

Appendix: Working Set Statistics of the LRU Stack Model 260

Bibliography 264

Index 272

Preface

The study of program behavior has lately increased in intensity. There have been many recent research papers on the subject, and even a special issue of *IEEE Computer* (November, 1976), not to mention frequent applications of existing program models in system analysis and simulation. But to my knowledge, there is no up-to-date attempt to draw the concepts together into a survey of the field. I do not claim that all aspects of program behavior receive adequate coverage here, but this book does attempt to meet this need.

There are probably good reasons why there has been no previous book on this subject—the field is hardly stabilized, and the current best models are still deficient in many ways. When teaching a rapidly changing technical discipline, it is usually thought desirable to emphasize the basic mathematical techniques that will not be made obsolete by advancing technology. Here, quite a lot of space is devoted to the methodology of measurement and statistical characterization (or, in effect, "how to create and validate your own program behavior model"). These techniques will outlive many current models. On the other hand, one should not underestimate the difficulties in actually applying the techniques herein to a new model.

This book is intended for two principle classes of readers: those interested in applying program behavior models in their systems modeling efforts, and those interested in program behavior, per se, for research or study purposes. I have attempted to survey the current state of the art in modeling and in measuring programs. Some results are new, having never before been published, but more of them are gathered from the computer science and the statistical literature. The subtitle *Models and Measurements* indicates a primary theme—that models require measurements for their validation, and conversely, that measurements require models for their interpretation and application. Program behavior is largely an empirical study.

The organization of the book is as follows: Chapter 1 motivates program behavior modeling and measurement, and introduces several philosophical distinctions to be used later. The principle of locality, the most basic program behavior effect, is also introduced. Chapter 2 deals with those features of paging and paging systems relevant to later discussions: hardware, paging, algorithms, and a more detailed examination of the properties of locality. Chapter 3 presents several basic models, and chapter 4 elaborates on one of the most important models—the LRU stack model and its extensions. Chapter 5 covers techniques for program measurement and model validation, including an introduction to spectral analysis, with many examples. Some of the more advanced of these techniques are applied in chapter 6 to two sophisticated program models. Finally, the various models and measurement methods are summarized in chapter 7.

Several algorithms are presented, particularly in chapter 5, but also elsewhere. The algorithms are coded in what might be called "Pidgin PL/1"; anyone familiar with PL/1 (or any structured language) should have no trouble understanding them.

This book should be suitable as a supplementary text for a graduate course in operating systems or performance evaluation. However, the average computer science student may have difficulty with chapters five and six. This is not a serious drawback, since there is easily enough material in chapters 1–4, unless a whole course is to be taught on the subject of program behavior. To follow the first four chapters, one should have had some prior exposure to random variables, plus understanding of inductive proof and (preferably) knowledge about paging systems and algorithms. An intuitive feel for the meaning of Fourier transforms and convolution is recommended before trying to read the latter part of chapters 5 and 6. For those lacking this additional background, the beginning of chapter 5, at least through section 5.2.1, is still highly recommended. Finally, the appendix assumes familiarity with generating functions, but this can be skipped, if desired, with no later difficulty.

The following people have provided valuable comments on the manuscript: Hussein Badr, G. Scott Graham, and Gerald S. Shedler (who gave very detailed suggestions on two successive drafts of the text). An anonymous referee was also very helpful. But most of all, I am greatly indebted to Peter J. Denning, without whose constant help this book might never have appeared at all. Many of the ideas and insights within are his. In spite of a busy schedule, he has spent a great deal of time helping to beat this thing into shape.

The first draft of this book was written while I was visiting at the Electrical Engineering Department of the University of Hawaii. The text was originally typed on their BCC-500 computer. It was later revised on the PDP-10 of the Electrical Engineering Department of the Pennsylvania State University. Teddi Potter provided essential typing help on a tight schedule. Judith Spirn helped to edit the manuscript. The assistance of everyone mentioned above is greatly appreciated.

Chapter 1
On Modeling

1.1 Introduction

This chapter introduces the uses and properties of program models. The modeling of systems is a reasonably well developed discipline (c.f. [4, 20]), but that of programs is less well understood. We shall argue that programs must also be modeled for performance studies of systems. A program does many things which might be of interest to model: it references memory, issues input/output requests, generates various kinds of interrupts, acquires and releases resources, and so on. We will review aspects of behavior in section 1.4. Although in later chapters we shall consider only memory reference behavior, this is primarily because little is known about other behavioral aspects, and not because they are unimportant. Nevertheless, we will show that memory reference behavior has important implications in the design of efficient virtual memory systems.

In section 1.5, we shall classify program models according to their philosophy and appropriate use. Finally, we will conclude the chapter by introducing the phenomenon of locality, the central effect in almost any aspect of a program's behavior.

1.2 Why Do We Model?

Any effort to build or improve an operating/computer system requires an experimental environment in which to test and compare design alternatives. The most accurate such environment is the system itself; however its use is often impractical. For one thing, the system exists only on paper initially. We can, however, test these alternatives in a model of the system. Likewise, a model of an already existing system can be employed to test proposed modifications without inconvenience to system users. Often the model will be invoked for deciding questions of basic underlying policy, followed by minor tuning of parameters in experiments with the actual system (perhaps based on so-called "benchmark" sample job loads).

The two prevalent techniques for studying system models are simulation and analysis. The technique to be used usually determines the level of detail (simulation models tend to be more detailed) and the method of presentation (as described below). Thus, we shall speak informally of "simulation models" and "analytic models", even though both forms are conceptually the same type of mathematical abstraction of the system.

Simulation models are generally programmed using a language (SIMSCRIPT, GPSS, etc.) specifically designed for this purpose. For example, arrival of terminal requests to a time-sharing system is often nearly a Poisson process (c.f. Coffman and Denning [20]). Noting that the time between events of a Poisson process is an exponentially distributed random variable, successive values of which are independent, the following SIMSCRIPT-like program simulates the arrival process:

```
event arrival
   create terminal_request
   enter terminal_request into arrival_queue
   cause event arrival after
           exponential(arrival_rate) time
end
```

This program creates a new terminal request, puts it in a queue, and schedules the following arrival. Complicated systems can in this way be simulated, often with surprisingly few program steps.

In analytic models, mathematical relations indicating known aspects of system operation are postulated, from which new relations are derived. These new relations often specify some measure of goodness of performance. For example, Coffman and Ryan [21] showed analytically that dynamic memory allocation --- continual adjustment of the memory space assigned to each task --- yields improved memory utilization as compared with static (fixed) allocation. Analytic models have been proposed for terminal-system interactions, processor scheduling, peripheral device scheduling, virtual memory management, and many other areas (c.f. [20] for a

1.2 Why Do We Model?

survey). Many of these deal with rather general system concepts; others may be created for specific designs in more detail. Recent advances, especially in analysis of networks of queues ([4] and others) facilitate the latter goal. While they are undoubtedly less detailed (therefore usually less accurate) than simulation models, analytic models often have the advantage of providing _insight_ rather than long tables of numbers[1]. Simulations can be performed only so many times to evaluate a limited range of circumstances, but analysis can guide intuition and yield summary system behavior over a continuum of parameter values. One must also take great care that simulation experiments are properly designed, or their predictions may be statistically invalid. A methodology for the testing of design alternatives might be as follows: 1) Use analytic models to choose among basic alternatives, followed by 2) Build a simulation model to compare more detailed, often system-specific alternatives and to find initial good estimates of critical system parameters, and lastly 3) Fine tune the parameters under benchmark or production system operation. It is sometimes possible to combine steps 1 and 2 above, yielding hybrid models which are more detailed than analytic, yet less costly in computer time than pure simulation.

Each step above requires assumptions about user programs in execution on the system[2]. Certainly, a business-oriented system design in which I/O speed is of prime importance will probably manage inefficiently a user load consisting of large numeric problems. Often, however, exact behavior of the user programs receives inadequate attention.

In analysis, the program behavior assumptions are often made for mathemtical tractability, rather than based on actual program characteristics. But the analysis is often dependent on quite detailed probabilistic assumptions. For example, figure 1.1 shows a classical queueing process (called the _M/G/1 queue_) which can be used as a model of certain

---

1) paraphrasing Richard Hamming

2) We use the term "user program" loosely --- it might include compilers, editors, and certain other operating system routines which compete with user-written programs for system resources.

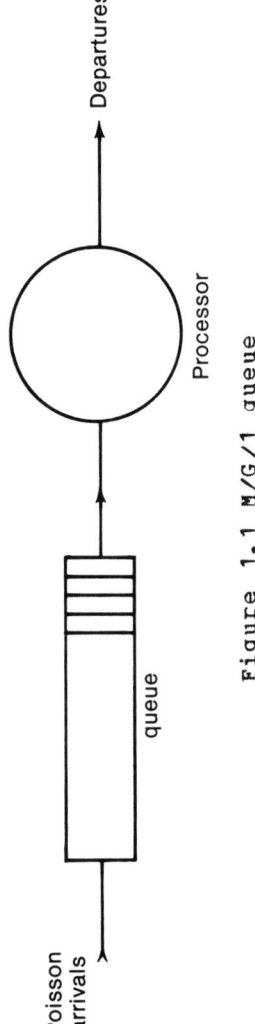

Figure 1.1 M/G/1 queue

1.2 Why Do We Model?

important system functions. Requests for processing arrive to the queue in a Poisson stream with rate λ requests per unit time. Basically, this means that arrivals are completely random --- given that an arrival occurs during some interval, it is equally likely to be anywhere in the interval. If the processor is idle when the request arrives, the request commences processing immediately; otherwise the request must wait its turn (on a first-come-first-served basis) in the queue. Processor service times are independent random variables $s_1, s_2, \ldots$ having a common probability distribution:

$$F_s(x) = Pr[s_i \leq x] .$$

The processing time mean and variance are, respectively:

$$\bar{s} = \int_0^\infty x \, dF_s(x)$$

$$\sigma_s^2 = \int_0^\infty (x-\bar{s})^2 d\, F_s(x)$$

The Pollaczek-Khintchine formula (c.f. [20]) shows that the **mean total waiting time** $\bar{W}$ of a request, from its arrival until its departure, is:

$$\bar{W} = \frac{2\bar{s} + \lambda(\sigma_s^2 - \bar{s}^2)}{2(1 - \lambda\bar{s})} \qquad (1.1)$$

We see that as basic a performance statistic as the mean waiting time depends on both the mean and the variance of the processing time distribution. Thus, if the model of figure 1.1 is used to represent programs executing on a central processor, more than just the mean execution time is needed for accurate analysis. In fact, this particular model is atypically _independent_ of execution time statistical detail --- in many cases analysis will depend upon the _entire probability distribution_ of program behavior measures.

There is a similar difficulty in simulation models. Such models usually include queues, thus implicitly invoking relations like (1.1). Other simulation model topologies will also yield results which depend significantly on detailed properties of the individual user programs.

The form and level of detail required of a program model obviously depend on the application. Since analysis usually requires omission of fine detail, we do not often expect it to yield quantitative predictions of system behavior. Commonly, it is used to make qualitative, _relative_ predictions of _comparative_ performance among design alternatives. For example, we shall use program models to prove analytically that certain virtual memory management strategies are optimal. Accurate _numerical_ prediction of the performance of each strategy will of course depend on the accuracy of the program model. It will also depend to some extent on system details that we shall ignore (for instance: shared pages, cost of rewriting a page to external memory, inaccuracies in implementation of certain paging algorithms, etc.) The analysis may actually be capable of fair numeric prediction (as has been occasionally demonstrated), but it is more often used for comparison only. Note that although _strict_ accuracy in program modeling may be unnecessary, _poor_ accuracy can invalidate even comparative performance analysis.

Detailed simulations, on the other hand, can be limited in accuracy only by their program models (and other external input), at least in theory. Many simulation efforts avoid this limitation by using programs as models of themselves. A few selected programs are _traced_; that is, their interesting behavioral interactions during an interval of execution are recorded (say on a tape). This tape, or several such tapes, is used to drive the simulation. While this is a reasonable approach, it has drawbacks. First, the trace tapes are expensive to prepare. Moreover, if the system is not already operational they may be generated elsewhere, leaving their

1.2 Why Do We Model?

validity open to question. Second, the user program mix cannot be manipulated conveniently --- only the several available tapes in some combination can be used. Third, detailed statistics of the traced programs may not be known, making it difficult to relate predicted system performance to the properties of the user programs executing within. Fourth, processing of large amounts of input data may significantly slow down (and increase the computation cost) of the simulation. Fifth, the tapes may not be long enough to allow simulation of long real times, since thousands or millions of data items may be accumulated during the trace of only a few seconds of a program's execution. Most of these difficulties can be overcome if a program behavior model of acceptable accuracy is available. A program model for simulation purposes could be more detailed than a model intended primarily for use in analysis, but if it is **excessively** complex it will significantly affect the simulation speed.

The essential point is that program behavior models of varying complexity (and presumably varying degrees of approximation to reality) are needed as a basis for a spectrum of system and sub-system models, whether analytic, simulation, or hybrid. Of course, we have discussed only guidelines, not rules, for model usage --- some analyses have used sophisticated models (c.f. Shedler and Tung [83]) and some simulations relatively simpler ones (c.f. Opderbeck and Chu [72]).

1.3 Programs in Execution

In order to be precise in our following discussions, we must take a short diversion to define notions of program execution. Technically, a **program** is a sequence of instructions as written by a programmer. When we discuss "program behavior", we really mean programs **in execution** on a processor. Processor scheduling should not be a part of this behavior, and we can effectively ignore processor switching effects by postulating a clock, the **virtual time** clock, which runs only while the given program is executing (we shall be more specific later). A program in execution timed by a virtual clock has frequently been termed a "process", but the definitions of the term in the various literature have often been contradictory and confusing. Thus, following [20], we introduce the term task, defined as a program in execution in virtual time. By "program" we mean any logical computational unit whose processing is subject to ordinary system interaction: for example, the performing of an edit command such as deletion of a line of text, or a single compilation of a FORTRAN program, or an entire matrix inversion in a matrix inversion routine. We shall thus discuss "task measurements" and "task models". Because of its prevalence in the literature, we have used the term "program behavior", and we shall continue to use it. However, the term is imprecise since we are concerned with programs in execution. The reader is invited to substitute the term "task behavior" if this makes the meaning clearer.

1.4 What Effects Should Be Modeled?

Any type of interaction between tasks and their parent systems is a candidate for modeling. Some interactions of importance, such as terminal think times or batch program submissions, are not really properties of tasks, but of people. Think time at a terminal, for example, is determined by psychology, environment, and certainly many other nebulous factors. The only general statement we can make is that the distribution of think times must have a very long tail. Although the mean might plausibly be less than a minute, delays measured in hours are not at all uncommon. Without an underlying theory of "people behavior", the best approach to modeling such an effect is to measure an empirical distribution. Such measurements for think time have been reported [23, 80, 82].

Other aspects of program behavior are explicitly determined by the way programmers use certain operations or techniques. The most obvious example is input/output. By its nature, input tends to be accepted near the beginning of a task, while output tends to be generated towards the end. Other than this, an empirical study of tasks would undoubtedly show a preponderance of certain patterns, depending on

1.4 What Effects Should Be Modeled?

the type of I/O (input or output), the device accessed, and perhaps the programming language. To model an I/O request in simulation or analysis, three items of information are necessary:

1) **When** will the request occur?
2) **Which** device will be accessed?
3) **How long** will it take to complete the request?

Question 3) is usually determined by the answers to 1) and 2), in the sense that the physical properties of the device (including access time statistics) are known. Thus, a task model for input/output must answer the questions "when?" and "which?". Unfortunately, very little confirmed basis exists for proposing a model. Measurements which have been reported [54, 82], while providing statistical characterization in various ways, do not usually provide sufficient information to imply a model for use in analysis or simulation. Once preliminary experimentation and physical intuition indicate a proposed model, measurements can be designed to confirm or reject the proposal. Thus, we shall suggest a model having some intuitive appeal, but it must be stressed that **no attempt has been made to validate it experimentally**. For this reason, we present it only as a **first example** to indicate what may be required of a model.

As the basis for the model we hypothesize that there are three primary modes of task access to a file: either a) All accesses occur near the start of execution, or b) All accesses occur near the end of execution, or c) Accesses occur at independent and identically distributed intervals throughout the lifetime of the task. Mode a) is typical of some (but not all) input files, mode b) is typical of some output files, and mode c) is typical of some input, some output, and probably most scratch files and permanent data bases. Thus, we describe the i-th file by three probabilities:

$$p_{ai}, p_{bi}, p_{ci}$$

and by three probability distribution functions:

$$F_{ai}(n), F_{bi}(n), F_{ci}(\tau)$$

where p_{ai}, p_{bi}, and $p_{ci}=1-p_{ai}-p_{bi}$ are respectively the probabilities of access modes a), b), and c) above. Distributions $F_{ai}(n)$, $F_{bi}(n)$, and $F_{ci}(\tau)$ describe the detailed behavior given the mode. If mode a) or b) is selected, n accesses (n chosen according to the applicable distribution) will be made at the beginning or at the end of the task. If mode c) is selected, the time between the i<u>th</u> and (i+1)<u>th</u> accesses is a random variable τ chosen according to the distribution $F_{ci}(\tau)$.

In general, a model will include <u>parameters</u>, which are variables that can be adjusted to fit the model form to specific situations. Appropriate parameter values can be determined by experiment (usually a byproduct of the model validation procedure, as we shall see). To use the above model we must choose values for two independent access model probabilities and for three distribution <u>functions</u>, so that very many individual scalar parameters must be determined. For this reason, the model may be inconvenient to use. Generally speaking, a model having few parameters has the advantages of conceptual simplicity and clarity, compact form, and easier experimental parameter estimation. We shall term a model <u>parsimonious</u> if it has few parameters, after Box and Jenkins [13]. A model should have some parameters, however, so that it can be adapted to the inevitable wide range of observed program behavior.

There is another part of a task's behavior, which will be of primary importance in the following chapters. These are task-system interactions not <u>explicitly</u> controlled by the programmer, but which are nevertheless implicit in the program. Such effects are at too fine a level of detail to be of concern to the programmer. As a simple example: when using a high level language, one generally has no knowledge of index register usage. The effect we shall study in detail is <u>memory reference</u> behavior --- specifically, the combined sequence of instruction fetch and data fetch/store addresses emitted by a task. This is of great importance in <u>virtual memory systems</u>, in which statistical prediction of future memory references is a prerequisite for efficiency. However, it has application in systems with other memory designs. For example, accesses to an <u>interleaved main memory</u> do not

1.4 What Effects Should Be Modeled?

all take the same amount of time --- the time to complete the kth access depends on the memory addresses of access numbers k,k-1,...,k-n+1, for some n (called the degree of interleaving) which is a physical property of the memory. Thus, a model of memory reference patterns would be required to model access times of such a memory.

Although we shall concentrate on memory reference behavior, with particular application to virtual memory, it should be understood by now that this is not the only important aspect of task behavior. We avoid other aspects only because little is known about modeling them except perhaps qualitatively. The realization has come recently that even those parts of task operation, such as input/output, which are under complete programmer control are poorly understood in a statistical sense. It was the popularization of multiprocessing that coincided with complex problems in managing system resources, hence sophisticated operating and computer systems. We hope that the work described here will provoke interest into investigation of other aspects of program behavior.

1.5 Philosophies in Modeling

1.5.1 Intrinsic and Extrinsic Models

There are several ways to classify task models (or in fact, models of almost any physical process in time). One distinction is in the location of an observer of the task. Suppose we wish to model some recurring event in time, for instance the issuance of input/output requests. At one extreme, the pure empiricist would record events of some real task or tasks, and derive statistics of interest. He might tell us, for example, that with probability 0.3 the time between two successive requests will exceed one second. Not wishing to bother with "theoretical" analysis, he will report his data without inquiring into the internal mechanisms which account for it. This is often termed black box analysis --- characterization of data emitted from a "box" without any idea of its contents. A pitfall is that the data will sometimes be dominated by spurious effects which have nothing to do with the effects of interest.

Thus, a careless radio-astronomer might conclude from black box analysis that some stellar body emitted the top forty rock and roll hits. As a more relevant (and plausible) example, one might attempt to measure the times between interesting events in typical tasks by recording the _system-wide_ event times, making the assumption that this would be an overall average of the several active tasks in the system (for an instance of this, see section 3.1.2). However, the overall effect would not be a simple average on many modern systems, due to the complex methods of scheduling tasks for processing. Thus, any conclusions drawn from such a measurement may be heavily influenced by processor and device scheduling algorithms.

At the other extreme from pure empiricism, a strict formalist would postulate a mathematical task model (based perhaps on physical intuition), but he would make no attempt to determine by experiment if his model corresponds to reality. Thus, the real-world relevancy of his analysis remains questionable. Extensive experimentation must be performed with any task model before it can be sufficiently trusted to influence questions of system design.

Clearly, a synthesis of the two approaches is needed. Models should have both a physical and an experimental basis. Yet there are still two valid approaches in modeling, depending on the initial orientation of the modeler. Either a) one can postulate an intuitively appealing model and design experiments to validate it, or b) one can measure data and use physical intuition as a check on the results. In the first instance the mathematical structure is the model, whereas in the second instance the measurement is the model.

As an example of approach a), consider a task having two distinct main loops, called LOOP1 and LOOP2. If we wish to model the sequence of memory reference addresses, it seems reasonable to consider the task to have _two states_ S_1 and S_2, depending on whether the task is in LOOP1 or LOOP2, respectively. We may then suppose that there are distinct probability distributions for the two states, governing the choice of next memory reference. Since we attempt in this manner to model the _internal_

1.5.1 Intrinsic and Extrinsic Models

mechanism of the task, we shall refer to this kind of model as an intrinsic program behavior model. Of course, it will be necessary to confirm its validity experimentally.

Now consider the same task, but modeled from approach b). We measure the memory references emitted by the task, observing two modes of behavior. A description of the empirical behavior constitutes the model. We term a model of this kind an extrinsic program behavior model, since it is from the point of view of an external observer of the task. Examination (perhaps even analysis) of the program code would be required to support the validity of the conclusions.

1.5.2 Descriptive and Generative Models

This classification refers to the appropriate application of a model. Some models can emit streams of data simulating some aspect or aspects of program behavior. For instance, a memory reference model might be used to generate a stochastic sequence of memory addresses. A schematic of such a model, termed a generative model, appears in figure 1.2. Clearly, a generative model is an algorithm for simulating task-like time sequences when driven by a random input. This is the type of model needed in system simulation work; it also adapts to analysis if the emitted data can be mathematically described. A simple example for memory reference sequences is the independent reference model (section 3.2.2). In this model, successive reference addresses are chosen independently according to a fixed probability mass function $\{p(k)\}$, $k=0,1,2,\ldots$, where $p(i)$ is the probability of reference to address i. However, we shall discuss generative models considerably more sophisticated than this one.

A descriptive model, on the other hand, provides statistical characterization of the behavior (or expected behavior) of interest with no direct simulation capability. One example of a descriptive memory reference model is a probability mass function $\{p(k)\}$ giving the probability of reference to each address. (Many times it is possible to suggest a typical form for such a function --- this reduces the

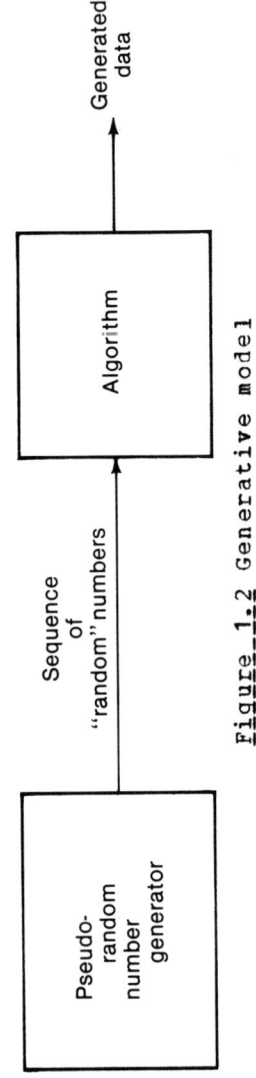

Figure 1.2 Generative model

1.5.2 Descriptive and Generative Models

number of parameters.) Of course, we can infer a generative model from this by assuming successive references to be statistically independent and identically distributed. It will usually be possible to create a generative model from a descriptive model by the inclusion of additional assumptions. Thus it might be said that a descriptive model is really an incompletely specified generative model. It can equally well be said that a generative model is really a descriptive model, to which are added assumptions that are often the most tenuous part of the model. Intrinsic models are usually generative and extrinsic models usually descriptive, but there are many exceptions.

1.5.3 Functional Models

By *functional modeling* we mean that only those statistical features having importance in applications of the model are reproduced. For example, with respect to the system model of figure 1.1, a functional model of task processing time need only reproduce the mean and variance. This would suffice for accurate mean waiting time prediction. Further detail, as in ability to predict higher moments, would be irrelevant in this case; the task model should be as simple as possible consistent with accurate duplication of the mean and variance. We observe the corollary principle of *program model - system model matching*: one should choose the least complex program model which reproduces the statistics considered in a given system model.

Any program behavior model is bound to be functional for some applications, and not for others. Our intention for each model is to indicate those statistical features reproduced by the model, and those not. This is one reason we shall have not a single model, but a *range* of several models, all attempting to reproduce memory reference behavior. There is an obvious trade-off between model simplicity and reproduced statistical detail.

1.6 Locality --- the Basic Principle

In general, it has been observed that a good predictor of a task's immediate future behavior is its immediate past behavior. We call this the _principle of (extrinsic) locality_. For example, Jalics and Lynch [54] determined in their measurements of a PDP-10 system that the peripheral device accessed by the (k+1)_th_ input/output request was nearly always the same device accessed by the _kth_ request. (Note that this effect is largely ignored in the input/output model proposed in section 1.4, although the model may still be _functionally_ valid.) We term this "extrinsic" locality, because it characterizes future external measurement in terms of past measurement.

Correspondingly, we define _intrinsic locality_ as follows: Assume that a task has some finite set of _states_ $S_1, \ldots, S_n$. The states are not detailed micro-states in the classical finite automaton sense. Rather, each state can be thought of as a logical interval of task activity (such as a loop or subroutine) during which the behavior of interest remains statistically invariant. An _intrinsic locality model_ consists of a state transition mechanism and a characterization of the behavior within each state. Note a subtle difference in implication as compared with extrinsic locality: expected immediate past and future behavior will now agree _only during the holding time of a given state_. The assumption of extrinsic locality is that future behavior is always best estimated by past behavior, due to the ignorance of internal state transitions.

Thus, extrinsic locality is specified by an external measurement, whereas intrinsic locality is specified by a state. Since knowledge of the state gives the better prediction of behavior, we shall often refer to the intrinsic state as the "true" locality, and the extrinsic measurement as the "estimated" (intrinsic) locality. This has further intuitive appeal, since the intrinsic locality reflects "what the task is doing", rather than merely the behavioral result of doing it.

Since we shall be concerned primarily with memory reference behavior, we shall use the term "locality" in a convenient, more restricted sense to mean _memory reference locality_. The extrinsic locality will thus

1.6 Locality --- the Basic Principle

denote the <u>set of addresses</u> (actually, as we shall see, pages) referenced recently by a task, and the intrinsic locality will denote the set of addresses likely to be referenced while the task remains in its current state. To avoid confusion with the <u>principle</u> of locality, we shall often refer to the extrinsic or intrinsic <u>locality set</u>.

The above "definitions" of intrinsic and extrinsic locality are rather fuzzy. We will clarify the issue when we present specific intrinsic locality models, and specific extrinsic measurement techniques.

Chapter 2
Paging Issues

2.1 Hardware Review

Since we are concerned with modeling the memory reference behavior of tasks, with particular application to virtual memory systems, we review now some concepts of these systems. Further discussions on some of these issues can be found in the article by Denning [30] and in the books by Coffman and Denning [20], and by Wilkes [89].

The common implementations of virtual memory are by either <u>segmentation</u> or <u>paging</u>, or both. We shall work within the context of paging, but many of the results are extendable to segmented systems as well. A <u>page</u> is a fixed size block of contiguous instructions and/or data, generally 2^p words long for p typically about 10. An n-bit (virtual) memory address can be divided into two parts --- a <u>page number</u> and a <u>word number</u>, as follows:

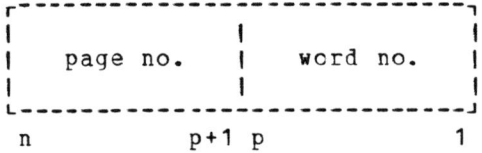

```
 ┌─────────────────────────────────┐
 │                │                │
 │   page no.     │   word no.     │
 │                │                │
 └─────────────────────────────────┘
   n            p+1 p            1
```

The high-order n-p bits denote the page number, and the low-order p bits denote the word number (the index of the word within the given page). For example, let p=10 and n=32. Since there are 32 bits in the address, there are 2^{32} possible unique addresses. Each page is 2^{10}=1024 words long. Page 0 contains addresses 0-1023; page 1 contains addresses 1024-2047;

2.1 Hardware Review

and so on. Note that a page is 2^p words[1] of <u>information</u> (program and/or data) rather than 2^p words of memory. A page retains its identity regardless of where it is stored.

Since few, if any, computers have 2^{32} words of main memory available for the pages of a task, not all pages can be in memory at the same time. The main memory consists of k <u>page frames</u>, each of which is capable of containing one page. At a given time, at most k pages of the several active tasks are scattered about in the page frames, in no particular order. Associated with each active task must be a map, or <u>page table</u>, which gives the storage location of each of the pages of the task. A typical page table appears in figure 2.1. The table is in the form of an array. The first entry is for page 0, the second for page 1, etc. Each entry in this example includes three flags, called <u>fault</u>, <u>use</u>, and <u>change</u>. The respective meanings of the flags are:

<u>fault</u> --- 0 if the page is in main memory
        1 if the page is not in main memory

<u>use</u> --- 0 if the page has not been referenced recently
      1 if the page has been referenced recently

<u>change</u> --- 0 if the page has not been modified (written into) recently
         1 if the page has been modified recently

If the fault flag is 0, a <u>page frame pointer</u> indicates the page frame holding the given page. If the fault flag is 1, the given page does not appear in main memory at all --- it can only be found in the <u>external memory</u> device (often a drum). In figure 2.1, we observe a page table for a task of six pages, 0-5. Pages 0, 1, 4, and 5 can be found in page frames 4, 16, 8, and 36, respectively. Pages 2 and 3 are available only from external memory. The purpose of

---

[1] This is not always true; a page might be only partially filled. Any empty space is usually at the end of the page. Strictly speaking, a page has <u>at most</u> 2^p words of information.

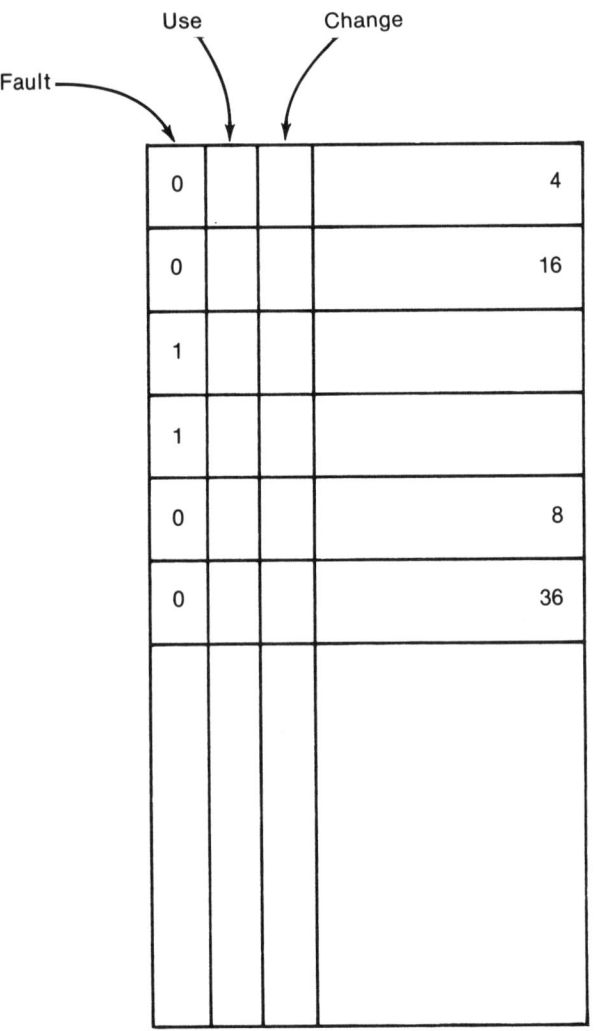

Figure 2.1 An example page table

2.2 Thrashing

will usually be multiprogrammed (shared among several tasks) --- equality would hold in a <u>uniprogrammed</u> system, in which the processor is always available to the given task.

Relation (2.1) may be used to illustrate an instance of <u>thrashing</u> [29], defined to be the sudden collapse of system performance when the page fault rate rises above a critical threshhold. Figure 2.2 shows the time to complete a single reference in a uniprogrammed system, from relation (2.1). The critical value of page fault rate is about $f=1/D$. Below this value, we have $1>fD$ and the value of f has little effect on T. Once $fD>1$, however, T begins to become proportional to f and performance degrades sharply. In section 3.1.3, we will show how an overly high degree of multiprogramming can similarly cause a system to thrash by producing a high system page fault rate.

It is obviously of great importance to maintain the page fault rate below the thrashing level. Any scheme to reduce the rate aids in this objective. In our consideration of paging algorithms, we shall try to minimize the fault rate. A further objective is to control the system load to prevent the exceeding of the fault rate threshold. The working set algorithm [27, 28] is an example of a memory management scheme designed to accomplish this (section 2.3.3).

2.3 Paging Algorithms

The paging algorithm is responsible for fetching and managing pages in main memory. A <u>prepaging algorithm</u> tries to anticipate future references of a task (and bring in pages before they are referenced) in an attempt to reduce page fault waiting time. However, such predictions are difficult to make accurately, so nearly all virtual memory systems use <u>demand paging</u> algorithms, which bring pages into main memory only when they are referenced. Once in memory, a page remains until the paging algorithm decides to remove it; once removed, it will not reenter main memory until it is next referenced.

Let $N = \{0,1,2,...,n-1\}$ be the set of pages of a

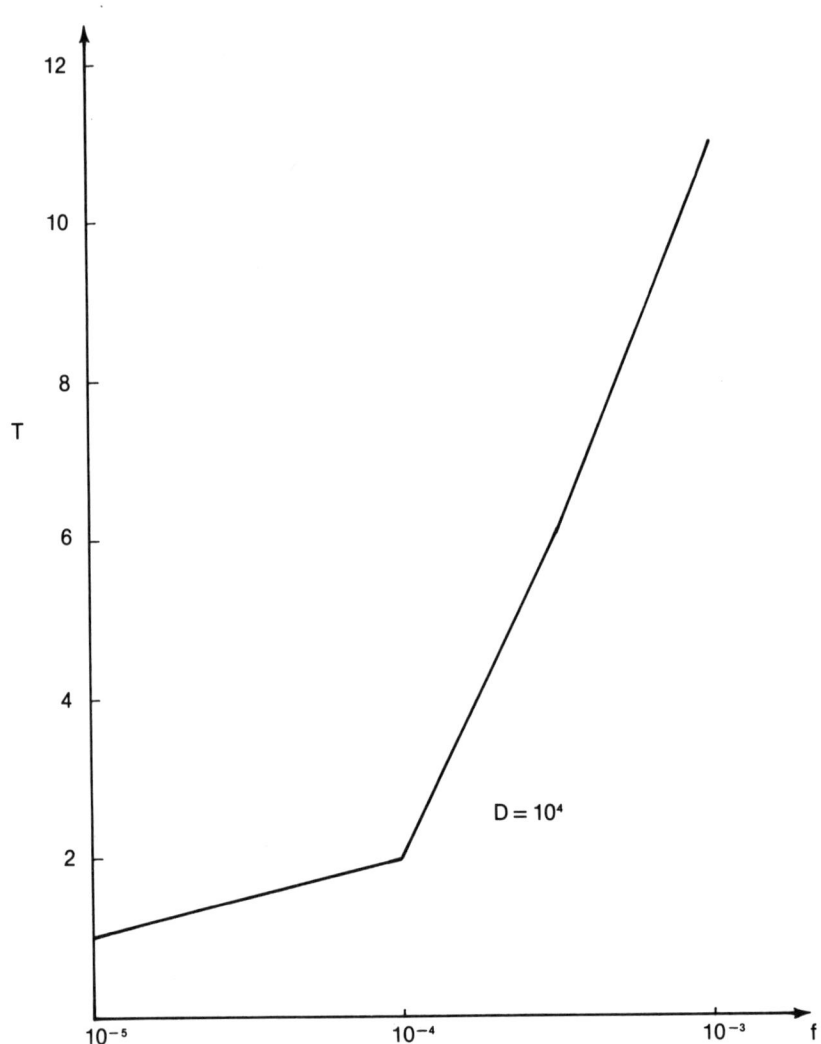

Figure 2.2 Real time tc complete one reference as a function of the page fault rate

2.3 Paging Algorithms

task, and let $M(t) = \{0,1,2,...,m(t)-1\}$ be the set of page frames in main memory allocated to the task. We shall assume that n is constant with $1 \leq m(t) < n$. We call $m(t)$ the memory allocation of the task at time t. Often, we shall assume $m(t)=m$, a constant; this is called fixed allocation. When $m(t)$ is allowed to vary with time, this is variable or dynamic allocation. As a matter of analytical convenience, we shall assume that every page in N is referenced at least once in the interval of interest --- this is no loss of generality, since if some page is not referenced we simply delete it from N.

We shall use $|A|$ to denote the size (number of members) of any set A, and $\bar{A}$ ("A complement") to denote the set N-A. Thus, $|M(t)|=m(t)$ and $|\bar{M}(t)|=n-m(t)$. The symbol $\emptyset$ will denote the empty set. Finally, if x is a page, we shall use the simplified notation A+x to denote the set $A \cup \{x\}$, and A-x to denote the set A-$\{x\}$.

Before proceeding, we must clarify our measures of time. We shall deal with two types of time measures. Real time is our usual notion of time --- the period between one o'clock and two o'clock is one hour of elapsed real time. However, real time is an inconvenient measure for most of our discussions, because a task may not execute continuously during any given real time period. Not only will delays occur due to page faults, but even if the task is ready to execute, another task may instead have control of the central processor. Let us postulate a clock that runs only when a given task is actually executing. Our unit of time will be one memory reference, so that if the clock has made t ticks during some period, the task will have generated t memory references (regardless of page faults) during the period. Elapsed time as indicated on this special clock will be called virtual time; it is running time as seen by the task. In this book, all uses of "time" (unless otherwise qualified) will mean virtual time.

Let the memory references of a task be $r(1)r(2)r(3)...r(K)$, where $r(t) \in N$ is the page referenced at virtual time t. Note that we only care which page --- not which word --- is referenced. A sequence of references in some virtual time interval $r(t)r(t+1)...r(t+k)$ is called a reference string. We shall use S(t) to denote the __set of pages in main memory just after the reference at time__ t (the S stands for "storage"). For all t, we have S(t) ⊆ N and |S(t)|≤m(t) (there may be empty page frames). We shall often use S(0) to indicate the initial content of memory, before the first reference. However, since it may not always be clear which pages should be loaded into memory at time zero, we shall often assume S(0)=∅, an empty initial memory.

In like manner, L(t) will denote the __locality set__ just after the reference at time t, with L(t) ⊆ N and |L(t)|≤n. We shall usually assume the initial locality L(0) to be non-empty. Recall that the locality set is the set of pages currently "in use" by the task --- a more precise definition will depend on the intrinsic model or extrinsic measurement under consideration.

We are now ready to make a formal definition of demand paging, which will be useful in later chapters. The definition of a __strict demand paging algorithm__ gives S(t+1) as a function of S(t):

$$S(t+1) = \begin{cases} S(t) & \text{if } r(t+1) \in S(t) \\ S(t)+r(t+1)-Z(t+1) & \text{if } r(t+1) \notin S(t) \end{cases} \quad (2.2)$$

where Z(t+1), the __replaced page set__, is a (possibly empty) subset of S(t). In other words, if no page fault occurs, the memory content is unchanged. If r(t+1)∉S(t), a page fault, then the missing page is brought into memory, replacing the set of pages Z(t+1). For many of the cases we shall consider, |S(t)|=m (a constant) for all t, so that Z(t) consists of exactly one page z(t), the __replaced page__. Since demand paging algorithms do not try to anticipate memory references, such algorithms are distinguished (for our purposes) solely by their means of choosing Z(t) or z(t).

Often, we shall allow a less stringent definition than (2.2), defining a demand paging algorithm to be any which __fetches__ pages on demand. Pages may be removed from memory at any time in this case. For a __loose demand paging algorithm__:

$$S(t+1) = \begin{cases} S(t)-Z(t+1) & \text{if } r(t+1) \in S(t) \\ S(t)+r(t+1)-Z(t+1) & \text{if } r(t+1) \notin S(t) \end{cases} \quad (2.3)$$

2.3 Paging Algorithms

We will make a small exception to our policy of considering only demand paging algorithms. Many demand-paged systems preload an initial estimate of a task's locality when the task commences an interval of execution. This (hopefully) prevents an initial spurt of page faults, as would occur if the memory were originally empty. For some external memories, in particular drums and disks, it may take less total time to preload the pages all at once than to load them individually on demand. We shall consider such initial preloading in some of our analysis. Thus, when a task commences an interval of execution, we assume that an initial set of pages $S(0)$ is preloaded. Ideally, we might expect that $S(0)=L(0)$, but in practice $S(0)$ will be only a (perhaps rough) estimate of the initial locality.

2.3.1 Paging Cost and Optimalty

The choice of paging algorithm can have a significant effect on the page fault behavior of a task. To compare algorithms, we must define a measure of cost. One that we shall use is the **page fault rate of some task** under control of the paging algorithm.

If we were considering prepaging algorithms, we might define the cost to be the total rate of page fetches from external memory, whether due to page faults or in anticipation of them. The following proposition shows that our restriction to demand paging does not force us to adopt high cost paging algorithms:

<u>Proposition 2.1</u> (Mattson, Gecsei, Slutz, and Traiger [67]) Among the set of all optimal prepaging algorithms for a given reference string will be at least one algorithm which fetches pages on demand. In other words, there is a demand algorithm which fetches no more pages than any prepaging algorithm.

This result is intuitively reasonable, since prepaging merely causes page fetches to occur earlier.

It does not eliminate them. If a page is replaced to make room for a prepaged page, that page might itself be referenced before the fetched page, in which case prepaging causes the cost to increase. Note, however, that prepaging *is* superior under some other cost measures. For example, it is often quicker to fetch k>1 pages at once from a drum than to make k separate fetches of one page each. Thus, using the cost measure *page waiting time*, it is possible that prepaging might be effective by fetching groups of pages at once. But because of the difficulty of anticipating the demands of a task, no prepaging algorithm has been shown to improve over demand paging in practice.

In one sense, an optimal demand paging algorithm is known; it is called OPT[3] [67, 10]. This algorithm replaces one page at each page fault. The page chosen for replacement is the one in memory which will not be referenced for the longest time --- the algorithm is assumed to have exact knowledge of all future references. OPT has been shown [67] to minimize the number of page faults generated in any virtual time interval by any reference string. Not even a prepaging algorithm can do better, in terms of the number of pages fetched from external memory.

Of course, it is not possible to know exactly all future references to be made by a task. Algorithms have been designed to look ahead a limited number of references, but both the overhead and the prediction error increase with the span of the lookahead. It is easy to construct examples of reference strings for which the lookahead required to implement OPT is arbitrarily long. Exact implementation of the algorithm is impossible, and although it could conceivably be approximated with limited lookahead, this has not been done with good success.

The page-fault-rate measure of cost, while simple and analytically convenient, is useful only for paging algorithms which keep a task's memory allocation fixed. If two paging algorithms have equal fixed

---

[3] A related algorithm called MIN was earlier proposed by Belady [7]. This was technically not a paging algorithm, but a means for determining the fewest possible number of page faults when processing a reference string with unlimited lookahead.

2.3.1 Paging Cost and Optimality

allocations m, the page fault rate is a reasonable way to compare them. However, if their allocations differ, the comparison is meaningless since all else being equal, fewer page faults ought to occur under the larger allocation. If the memory allocation varies under control of some paging algorithm, it can be similarly meaningless to try to compare its performance with some other algorithm by simply comparing page fault rates.

It would appear reasonable to compare the fault rates of two variable-space algorithms, provided that their _average_ memory allocations are the same. But one must be careful to define the meaning of "average" --- it has at least two interpretations. The _virtual-time-average_ allocation over reference string $r(1)...r(K)$ is the average of the memory sizes at each virtual time instant:

$$\bar{m} = \frac{1}{K} \sum_{t=1}^{K} m(t)$$

This type of average is convenient for some analysis, but since not all memory states have equal holding intervals in _real_ time, it is a somewhat unrealistic measure of memory usage. When a page fault occurs, say at reference $r(t)$, $m(t)$ page frames are tied up until the missing page is fetched[4]. Suppose that page faults occur at the times $0 < t_1 < t_2 < ... < t_j \leq K$. If the mean page wait time is D, then the _real-time-average_ allocation is:

---

4) Note that $m(t)$ is the allocation _after_ the page is fetched. Thus we are making the assumption that before a fetch is begun, a page frame must be assigned as an input buffer. If this is unrealistic, one could instead assume that $m(t-1)$ pages were allocated during the page wait.

$$\bar{m}_R = \frac{1}{K+jD} \left[\sum_{t=1}^{K} m(t) + D \sum_{i=1}^{j} m(t_i) \right]$$

Since D is typically about 10,000 in drum-oriented systems, the allocations at page fault times are heavily weighted in the average.

Using some notion of average memory size, cost measures can be proposed which allow comparison of variable-space paging algorithms. Suppose it costs b to keep a page in memory for one instant of virtual time, and suppose it costs d for each page fault. For a reference string of length K with j page faults, the total cost is:

$$C = bK\bar{m} + dj$$

where $\bar{m}$ is the virtual-time-average memory allocation. Using this cost measure, paging algorithms can be compared, even if their respective average allocations differ. An optimal (but physically unimplementable) paging algorithm similar to OPT is known for this cost measure [73, 33]. Let y(t) be the (virtual) time interval until the next reference to referenced page r(t). That is, r(t+y(t))=r(t), but r(t) does not appear anywhere in the string r(t+1)...r(t+y(t)-1). If r(t) is retained in memory until it is next referenced, this will cost b·y(t). On the other hand, if r(t) is removed from memory immediately after time t, it will cost d to fetch it again at its next reference (assuming it is again referenced). The optimal algorithm, called VMIN (for Variable-space MINimal cost) simply selects the lesser of the two costs. Specifically, at each time t it removes the page just referenced r(t) if

$$y(t) > T .$$

where T=d/b. Otherwise, r(t) is retained in memory. If page r(t) is never afterwards referenced, we define y(t) = ∞, so that r(t) is always removed in this case.

Typically, T is about 10,000 or 100,000, which is

2.3.1 Paging Cost and Optimality

the amount of lookahead which would be required to actually implement the VMIN algorithm. The OPT and VMIN algorithms cannot be implemented because they require foreknowledge of a prohibitively large number of future references.

Nevertheless, since a suboptimal page replacement can only affect later page fault behavior, some knowledge of future references is essential for intelligent paging. In the absence of exact foreknowledge, we turn to stochastic information, as supplied by a model. Using such information, we attempt to specify the _expected_ future behavior of a reference string, even if its _actual_ behavior is unknown. We assume that at a given time t, we have exact knowledge only of the references at times up to and including t. The problem is to use this knowledge to predict likely reference behavior after time t, in order to make low cost page replacements at page fault times. Hence, we shall concentrate on the class of _non-lookahead_ paging algorithms, in which the action taken at time t is not a function of the references $r(t+1)\,r(t+2)\ldots$.

Since we assume that future page reference behavior is unknown except in a stochastic sense, we must define optimality of a paging algorithm in terms of _expected_ (rather than actual) future page fault behavior. Let us define an optimal (fixed allocation) paging algorithm to be one which minimizes the _expected number of page faults_ of some (stochastic) reference string. Formally, let $C_k(S,t)$ be the _minimal expected cost_ (number of page faults) of page references $r(t+1)\,r(t+2)\ldots r(t+k)$, for a given task with main memory content S at time t. The minimization is over all demand paging algorithms having a fixed memory allocation of $m=|S|$. Note that $C_1(S,t)$ is just the probability of a page fault at time t+1, or

$$C_1(S,t) = \Pr[\,r(t+1) \notin S\,] \qquad (2.4)$$

Define $p(x,t)$ to be the _probability that page x is referenced at time t_; i.e., $p(x,t) = \Pr[r(t)=x]$. We can in principle compute $C_k(S,t)$ for any k by solving the following dynamic programming problem [1]:

$$C_0(S,t) = 0$$

(2.5)

$$C_{k+1}(S,t) = \sum_{x \in S} p(x,t+1) C_k(S,t+1)$$

$$+ \sum_{x \in \bar{S}} p(x,t+1) [1 + \min_{z \in S} C_k(S+x-z,t+1)]$$

If a page fault happens at time t+1 (when $x \notin S$), a cost of one is incurred. This is added to the cost expected in the remainder of the interval of measurement, after an optimal page replacement z is made. If no page fault occurs at time t+1 (when $x \in S$), no cost is incurred and the memory content remains unchanged.

The dynamic programming problem specified by (2.5) seems straightforward, but in practice it does not have an easy solution unless the set of probabilities $\{p(x,t)\}$ is simple in structure. Part of our effort in modeling program behavior will be to find stochastic models which are robust enough to be good mirrors of reality, but which are nevertheless tractable under the formulation of (2.5). Note that a solution to this dynamic programming problem has a side benefit: it specifies minimal cost page replacements, and consequently an optimal realizable paging algorithm.

With respect to the OPT algorithm, we have noted that the page having the longest actual time until next reference cannot be determined in practice. However, for an intrinsic-locality task model, it is often possible to compute the page having longest _expected_ time until next reference. Following the OPT algorithm, the _expected forward distance criterion_ [85] (sometimes called the "informal principle of optimality" [1]) is a rule always to choose for replacement the page in memory having longest expected time until next reference. It is not necessarily optimal [1, 85], but it is undoubtedly a good heuristic. We shall later demonstrate that it _is_ optimal for certain intrinsic task models.

2.3.2 Stack Algorithms and Priority Algorithms

It can be shown that certain fixed-allocation paging algorithms are subject to anomalous behavior [9]. That is to say, increasing the memory allocation can actually increase the page fault rate of certain reference strings when using these algorithms. A class of paging algorithms, called stack algorithms, which avoids such undesirable behavior[5] has been studied by Mattson, Gecsei, Slutz, and Traiger [67]. At each instant of time, a stack algorithm defines a vector (the "stack") on some or all of the pages of a task. The stack at time t is $\underline{s}(t)=[s_1(t),\ldots,s_{n(t)}(t)]$, with $n(t) \leq n$, such that if the algorithm operates with memory allocation m, then the memory will contain exactly the set of pages

$$S(m,t) = \begin{cases} \{s_1(t),\ldots,s_m(t)\} & \text{if } m \leq n(t) \\ \{s_1(t),\ldots,s_{n(t)}(t)\} & \text{if } m > n(t) \end{cases}$$

at time t. The following inclusion property results: $S(m,t) \subseteq S(m+1,t)$ for all m and t. This implies that there cannot be anomalous behavior[6]. At each memory reference the stack will (in general) change, but $\underline{s}(t)$ is dependent only on the initial stack $\underline{s}(0)$ and the reference string $r(1)r(2)\ldots r(t)$ [7]. The stack is at all times independent of the memory allocation.

---

5) Stack algorithms also have another important property: the page fault rate of a reference string under such an algorithm can be efficiently measured for many memory sizes simultaneously. This was the original motivation for the study of this class of algorithms by Mattson, et. al.

6) Proof: Consider memory sizes m and m+i for i>0. If $r(t+1) \notin S(m+i,t)$, a page fault, then it must also be true (by the inclusion property) that $r(t+1) \notin S(m,t)$. Thus, every page fault in the larger memory matches one in the smaller memory. The fault rate in the smaller memory must be at least as large.

7) This is true for non-lookahead paging algorithms. For algorithms such as OPT, with lookahead, the dependence can be on the entire string $r(1)\ldots r(K)$, where $r(K)$ is the last reference made by the task.

Note that the stack need not contain all pages of a task, for the same reason that a memory of size n need not contain all n pages. For example, if we assume empty initial memory, then $\underline{s}(0)$ is the empty vector, and pages are added to the stack (and to memory) as they are first referenced. But page x must appear somewhere in stack $\underline{s}(t)$ if x appears in reference string $r(1)...r(t)$, since if the allocation is large enough page x will remain in memory once referenced. Likewise, stacks can only grow in size as new pages are referenced --- they never lose pages. In particular, if $\underline{s}(0)$ contains all pages of a task, then so will $\underline{s}(1)$, $\underline{s}(2)$, ..., $\underline{s}(K)$.

We define $s_1(t)$, the first element in the stack vector, to be the <u>top</u> of the stack, and $s_{n(t)}(t)$ to be the <u>bottom</u>. If i>j, we say that $s_i(t)$ is lower in the stack than $s_j(t)$.

The <u>stack distance</u> $d(t)$ is defined to be the position (or index in the stack) of $r(t)$ in stack $\underline{s}(t-1)$. If $r(t)=s_i(t-1)$ then $d(t)=i$, with $1 \leq i \leq n(t-1)$.

If $r(t)$ does not appear anywhere in $\underline{s}(t-1)$, then $d(t) = \infty$. If we are given an initial stack $\underline{s}(0)$ and a reference string $R=r(1)...r(K)$, then we can compute a <u>distance string</u> $D=d(1)...d(K)$, such that $d(i)$ is the stack distance of $r(i)$ in $\underline{s}(i-1)$, for all i. Since $\underline{s}(t)$ is a function only of $\underline{s}(0)$ and the reference string $r(1)...r(t)$, it is easily seen [20] that R can be reconstructed (to within a renaming of the pages) from D. Therefore, either D or R can be used to specify the sequence of memory references in an interval. One use of the distance string is to compute the cost of processing references for an arbitrary memory allocation m using the given stack algorithm: The cost of processing $D=d(1)...d(K)$ is the number of distances in D which exceed m. A more important use of the distance string for our purposes is in task modeling, since it can serve as an alternative to the reference string, as we shall see.

There is another class of paging algorithms, <u>priority algorithms</u> [67, 20], which is related to the class of stack algorithms. A priority algorithm defines at every instant of time a priority ranking on

2.3.2 Stack and Priority Algorithms

all pages of a task. We specify this ranking by means of a <u>priority list</u>, $\underline{PL}(t)=[x_1,\ldots,x_n]$, where x_1 is the highest priority page and x_n is the lowest priority page. As with our previous notation, $\underline{PL}(t)$ denotes the priority list just after $r(t)$ is made. The vector $\underline{PL}(t)$ is a strict ordering (there are no ties), and every page of the task is represented, whether or not it is in memory. The priority list is in general time-varying (although some non-trivial paging algorithms, such as Last-In-First-Out [20], have a fixed priority list), but as in the case of the stack, $\underline{PL}(t)$ is a function only of the reference string $r(1)\ldots r(t)$ [or $r(1)\ldots r(K)$ for lookahead algorithms], and the initial priority list $\underline{PL}(0)$. The priority list is at all times independent of the memory allocation.

A priority algorithm uses its priority list in the following way: If $r(t+1) \notin S(t)$, a page fault, then the page chosen for replacement is that page in $S(t)$ having lowest priority in $\underline{PL}(t+1)$[8]. A single priority list thus provides a means of computing page replacements for all possible memory allocations.

Priority and stack algorithms are similar in an important respect: They both maintain a single vector which is sufficient to specify the operation of the paging algorithm for all possible allocations. In fact, it has been shown [67, 20] that the two classes are essentially the same; every priority algorithm is a stack algorithm, and every stack algorithm is equivalent to some priority algorithm. The procedure for updating the stack at a given reference can be stated in terms of the priority list: Let $d(t+1)=i$. Then [20, 67]

---

8) In Coffman and Denning [20], the replacement was that page in $S(t)$ having lowest priority in $\underline{PL}(t)$, rather than in $\underline{PL}(t+1)$. For this reason, our proposition 2.3 disagrees with their theorem stating that $\underline{PL}(t)=\underline{s}(t)$ only for LRU.

$$s_j(t+1) = \begin{cases} r(t+1) & \text{if } j=1 \\ \max[\min(S(j-1,t)), s_j(t)] & \text{if } 1<j<i \\ \min[S(i-1,t)] & \text{if } j=i \\ s_j(t) & \text{if } j>i \end{cases}$$

where max and min are defined with respect to the priority list $\underline{PL}(t+1)$. (The highest priority page has maximum value.) Recall that $S(j,t)$, the contents of a memory of size j at time t, is the top j members of $\underline{s}(t)$.

We now briefly state some important properties of the stack that are implied by the above updating procedure. This is intended as a review; see Coffman and Denning [20] for details:

a) $s_1(t) = r(t)$ for all t.

b) If $r(t) = s_i(t-1)$, then $s_j(t) = s_j(t-1)$ for all j>i.

c) If $r(t) \neq x$ and $x = s_i(t-1)$, then $x = s_j(t)$ for some $j \geq i$.

Property a) says that the current reference is always at the top of the stack. Property a) can be quickly proven by noting that for an allocation of one page frame, we must have $S(1,t)=r(t)$ for all t. Property b) says that all pages below the referenced page in the stack retain their same positions after the stack is updated. If $r(t) = s_i(t-1)$, only the pages in $s_1(t-1),\ldots,s_i(t-1)$ may have different positions in $\underline{s}(t)$. Property c) says that an unreferenced page may never move up the stack.

As an example of a stack and priority algorithm, consider the <u>least</u> <u>recently</u> <u>used</u> (<u>LRU</u>) paging algorithm (we shall make extensive use of the properties of the LRU stack). This algorithm chooses for replacement that page in memory which has not been

2.3.2 Stack and Priority Algorithms

referenced for the longest period of time. The stack $\underline{s}(t)$ for the LRU algorithm consists of all pages of the task ordered by decreasing time of their most recent reference. Thus, $s_1(t)$ is the most recently used page (which is $r(t)$), $s_2(t)$ is the next most recently used page, and $s_n(t)$ is the least recently used page. Pages which have never been referenced are grouped together at the bottom of the stack in any arbitrary order[9].

The procedure for updating the LRU stack is conceptually quite simple. If $d(t)=i$, then $s_1(t)=r(t)$, and $s_j(t)=s_{j-1}(t-1)$ for all j such that $1<j\leq i$. Each entry in the stack above the point of reference is moved down by one position. See figure 2.3. Of course, pages below the point of reference do not move in the stack (stack property b).

We now demonstrate that the classes of stack algorithms and priority algorithms are _equivalent_. In particular, every stack algorithm A is equivalent to the priority algorithm whose pricrity list is identical to A's stack at every instant of time. Likewise, every pricrity algorithm satisfies the definition of a stack algorithm --- its memory contents can be written in stack vector form:

Proposition 2.2 (Mattson, et. al. [67]) Every priority algorithm is also a stack algorithm.

The idea of the proof is to show that the inclusion property $S(m,t) \subseteq S(m+1,t)$ holds at all times for every priority algorithm. This works because the priority list is independent of the memory allocation. We can use proposition 2.2 to prove:

---

9) Alternatively, they might be omitted from the stack. We choose to put them in the stack because it is convenient in the formulation of the LRU stack model (chapter 4).

38 PROGRAM BEHAVIOR: MODELS AND MEASUREMENTS

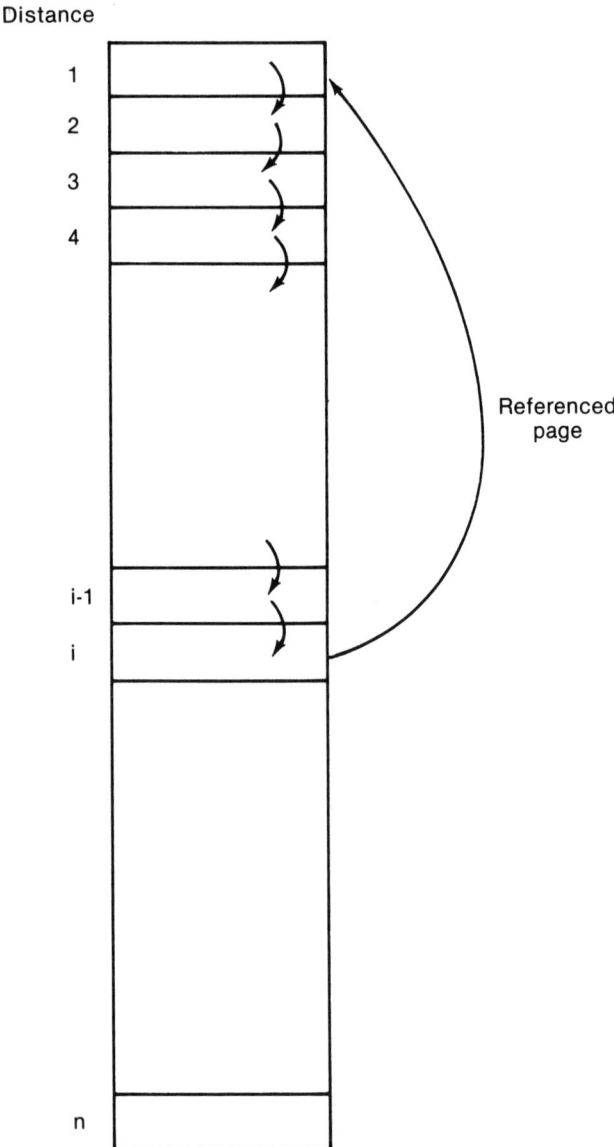

Figure 2.3 LRU stack updating procedure

2.3.2 Stack and Priority Algorithms 39

Proposition 2.3 Consider stack algorithm A with stack sequence $\underline{s}(0), \underline{s}(1), \ldots$ for a given reference string R, where $\underline{s}(0)$ contains all pages of the task. Let B be a priority algorithm with priority list sequence $\underline{PL}(0), \underline{PL}(1), \ldots$ such that $\underline{PL}(t) = \underline{s}(t)$ for all t. By proposition 2.2, B is a stack algorithm. Let B have initial stack $\underline{s}(0)$. Then algorithms A and B behave identically when processing R, for any memory allocation.

Proof Let $\underline{s}(B,t)$ denote the stack of priority algorithm B at time t. By assumption, A and B have the same initial stack, so $\underline{s}(B,0) = \underline{s}(0)$. Suppose $\underline{s}(B,t) = \underline{s}(t)$ at all times $1 \le t \le t'$. We shall show that $\underline{s}(B,t'+1) = \underline{s}(t'+1)$ by demonstrating that the page replaced at time $t'+1$ by the two algorithms is the same, for any choice of memory allocation m. From the inductive hypothesis, we have $S(m,A,t') = S(m,B,t')$, where $S(m,A,t')$ denotes the contents of a memory of size m at time t' under algorithm A; similarly for $S(m,B,t')$ and algorithm B. If $r(t'+1) \in S(m,A,t')$, neither algorithm will replace a page. If $r(t'+1) \notin S(m,A,t')$, then A will replace some page $z(t'+1)$ and B will also replace a page. Page $z(t'+1)$ is removed from $S(m,A,t')$, so it will be farthest down in $\underline{s}(t'+1)$ of all pages in $S(m,A,t')$. But $\underline{s}(t'+1)$ is the priority list of algorithm B, so the same page will be chosen by algorithm B for removal from memory.
□

The converse of proposition 2.3, that every priority algorithm is equivalent to a stack algorithm whose stack is identical to the priority list, is not strictly true. A priority list sequence can be arbitrary, but a stack sequence must satisfy certain constraints. However, from the above two propositions, it is clear that every priority algorithm is equivalent to another priority algorithm whose priority list matches its stack:

Corollary 2.4 Let B be a priority algorithm which generates stack sequence $\underline{s}(B,0), \underline{s}(B,1),\ldots$ for a given reference string R. Let B' be another priority algorithm with priority list sequence $\underline{PL}(B',0), \underline{PL}(B',1),\ldots$ such that $\underline{PL}(B',t) = \underline{s}(B,t)$ for all t. Then B and B' behave identically when processing R, for any memory allocation.

Proof Immediate from proposition 2.3, since B is a stack algorithm by proposition 2.2.
□

2.3.3 Examples of Paging Algorithms

For purposes of review, we shall define some demand paging algorithms. See Coffman and Denning [20] for more details. The first group of algorithms operate under a fixed memory allocation, so that these algorithms are methods for computing the page to replace at page fault times.

First-In-First-Out (FIFO): The page which has been in memory for the longest period of time is replaced. Formally, define a control state of the algorithm to be an ordering of the pages *in memory* by increasing time spent residing in memory. We write the control state as $[x_1,\ldots,x_m]$, where x_1 is the

page which was fetched into memory most recently, and x_m is the page which has resided in memory the

longest. Note that this is not a priority list in the sense of the previous section, since not all pages are represented; only those in memory appear. If $r(t+1) \notin S(t)$, a page fault, then page x_m is

2.3.3 Examples of Paging Algorithms

replaced and the new control state becomes $[r(t+1), x_1, \ldots, x_{m-1}]$. The control state changes only at page fault times.

It can be shown [20] that FIFO is not a stack algorithm.

OPT Algorithm: This was described in section 2.3.1. This is a stack algorithm, so we shall define the algorithm formally by specifying a priority list. The pages in the priority list are ordered by increasing <u>forward distance</u>, defined for page x at time t to be ψ-t, where ψ is the earliest time after t at which page x is referenced. Thus $\underline{PL}(t)=[x_1,\ldots,x_n]$, where x_1 is $r(t+1)$, which has the minimum possible forward distance of 1, and where x_n is that page having the longest time until next reference at time t. Pages which are never referenced after time t can be assigned a forward distance of infinity; they are grouped together in an arbitrary order at the end of the priority list. If $r(t+1) \notin S(t)$, a page fault, the page in $S(t)$ having lowest priority in $\underline{PL}(t+1)$ is replaced.

The priority list for this algorithm is time varying, and must be updated after every reference. Suppose $\underline{PL}(t)=[x_1,\ldots,x_n]$. Then $r(t+1)=x_1$, so that:

$$\underline{PL}(t+1) = [x_2,\ldots,x_i,x_1,x_{i+1},\ldots,x_n]$$

where i is chosen such that x_1 has a longer forward distance (from time t+1) than x_i, and a shorter forward distance (from time t+1) than x_{i+1}.

Least Recently Used (LRU): The page in memory which has not been referenced for the longest period of time is replaced. This is also a stack algorithm, so we shall define the algorithm by specifying a priority list. The priority list consists of the pages ordered by increasing backward distance. The backward distance of each page $x \in N$ at time t is defined to be $t-\psi'$, where ψ' is the latest time not after t at which x was referenced. Thus, for example, r(t) has a backward distance of zero. Pages which do not appear in the reference string r(1)...r(t) are assigned a backward distance of infinity.

The priority list for this algorithm is time varying, and must be updated at every reference. Suppose $PL(t) = [x_1, \ldots, x_n]$, and suppose $r(t+1) = x_i$. Then:

$$PL(t+1) = [x_i, x_1, \ldots, x_{i-1}, x_{i+1}, \ldots, x_n].$$

Other examples of stack algorithms are to replace the page which has been Least Frequently Used, or to replace the page which has been fetched most recently (Last-In-First-Out or LIFO). An oddity is that LIFO is a stack algorithm but FIFO is not (c.f. [20]). Stack algorithms can also be based on probabilistic information derived from intrinsic task models. For example, two stack algorithms are 1) replace the page least likely to be referenced next, and 2) replace the page with the longest expected time until next reference.

The following algorithms have variable (or dynamic) allocation. They cause their own allocations to change by replacing page sets Z(t) rather than pages z(t) at fault times, or by removing pages from memory at other than fault times (loose demand paging):

2.3.3 Examples of Paging Algorithms

Working Set Algorithm (WS): The *working set* $W(t,T)$ of a task at time t has been defined by Denning [27, 28, 36] to be the set of distinct pages in the T most recent references $r(t-T+1)...r(t)$. Parameter T is called the *window size*. The *working set algorithm* retains exactly the working set in memory at all times. Pages can leave the working set at other than page fault times, so this is a loose demand paging algorithm. Since $S(t)=W(t,T)$ at all times, a page is removed from memory only when it has not been referenced in T consecutive time instants.

VMIN Algorithm: This algorithm, defined in section 2.3.1, is essentially a "working set" on *future references* instead of on past references. Whereas in the WS algorithm, a page is replaced if its backward distance exceeds some T; in VMIN, a page is replaced if its forward distance exceeds T. Define the *VMIN set* $V(t,T)$ at time t recursively, as follows:

$$V(0,T) = \emptyset$$
$$V(1,T) = \{r(1)\}$$

and for $t \geq 1$:

$$V(t+1,T) = \begin{cases} V(t,T)+r(t+1) & \text{if } r(t) \in W(t+T,T) \\ V(t,T)+r(t+1)-r(t) & \text{if } r(t) \notin W(t+T,T) \end{cases}$$

The *VMIN algorithm* [73, 33] retains exactly the VMIN set in memory at all times, so that $S(t)=V(t,T)$ for all t. The choice of window size T was discussed in section 2.3.1.

Page Fault Frequency Algorithm (PFF): This is a recently proposed [18, 71, 72] adaptive algorithm which tries to maintain the page fault rate below a given maximum. P (the "page fault frequency") is a parameter. When a fault occurs, the length of the time interval since the previous fault is compared with 1/P. If the interval does not exceed 1/P, no page is replaced, so the allocation increases by one page. If the interval exceeds 1/P, those pages (if any) not referenced in the interval are removed from memory. In contrast to the working set algorithm, this is a strict demand algorithm, since pages may be removed from memory only at page fault times. Formally, suppose that $r(t+1) \not\in S(t)$, a page fault. Let $t' \leq t$ be the time of the most recent page fault preceding $t+1$. Then the replaced page set is:

$$Z(t+1) = \begin{cases} \emptyset & \text{if } (t+1)-t' \leq 1/P \\ S(t)-W(t,t-t') & \text{if } (t+1)-t' > 1/P \end{cases}$$

Recall that $W(t,T)$ is the set of distinct pages appearing in $r(t-T+1)...r(t)$. Since this is a strict demand paging algorithm, the sequence of memory states is defined in expression (2.2).

FIFO generally gives the poorest performance of the above algorithms, and in fact has been shown to exhibit anomalous behavior for certain reference strings [9], as we have noted. However, some systems use FIFO because of its relative ease of implementation.

OPT and VMIN are unimplementable, as we have noted, but they have been proposed as benchmarks against which to compare other algorithms. Suppose some algorithm under consideration for use in a system performs within, say, ten percent of one of these two algorithms. Then we can improve by at most ten percent, which may mean that any improvement is not worth additional effort. Of course, since OPT and VMIN require such a high degree of lookahead, they may not be sharp bounds on the best that can be achieved by a _practical_, non-lookahead algorithm.

Working Set and LRU have the limitation that it is necessary to keep a record of the time of the most recent reference to each page, for exact implementation. Few current computers have the hardware to do this. These algorithms are usually implemented in an approximate fashion by periodic examination of _hardware use bits_ (not to be confused with the page table use flags of section 2.1). These are single-bit registers, one per page frame. Whenever a memory reference is made, the hardware turns on the use bit for the referenced page frame. Those frames with use bits off are thus determined to have been accessed less recently than those with use bits on, but no finer ordering can be made.

2.3.3 Examples of Paging Algorithms

Periodically, the hardware use bits are examined and reset, and the corresponding use flags in the page tables are set, to give a similarly coarse ranking of the pages of a task by backward distance.

When a page is fetched into main memory, the copy in external memory is not normally erased. The external memory copy remains up to date as long as the page in main memory is not stored into (or _modified_). When a page is removed from main memory it must be re-written back to external memory if and only if it has been modified. Associated with each page frame is a single-bit register called the _change bit_, which is set by the hardware when a store operation is effected into the frame. The paging algorithm interrogates this bit to determine if an external memory re-write is necessary.

PFF has been proposed as an alternative to Working Set. It can be exactly implemented with use bits, and experiments [18, 71, 72] indicate its cost to be comparable to Working Set. However, it is less stable than WS --- it can, in fact, exhibit anomalies in behavior [44], when small changes in parameter P cause large changes in performance. It is possible that by decreasing (increasing) P, one could actually cause the page fault rate to increase (decrease), contrary to the intent of the algorithm. Since hardware to measure the working set exactly is not expensive [69], and since the working set can be successfully approximated with use-bit-only measurement hardware (c.f. [28]), the WS algorithm is probably the better choice.

2.4 Properties of Memory Reference Locality

Locality is a notion essential to paging systems. No overview of such systems is complete without discussing its properties. We have presented the concept of locality in general terms in chapter 1. Now we shall be specific to paging.

In its simplest form for page reference behavior, the term "locality" refers to the unequal distribution of page references in any given time interval. Some pages (those in the _locality set_) will be referenced frequently, whereas others will be referenced few times, if at all. Locality is the central property underlying successful paging algorithms; in fact, it is the property which allows paging systems to function at all without prohibitively high fault rates. Locality is not a provable attribute of programs, but is more a reflection of the way people write them. Numerous studies [7, 15, 17, 64, 65, 79, 87] have indicated that locality is to be found in the overwhelming majority of programs to at least some degree.

Denning and Schwartz [36] have indicated three properties which characterize the phenomenon of locality. While not exclusive, they are important points to consider in the design of program models. The first two properties are:

1) At almost all times, the locality, or favored set of pages, is only part of the total set of pages of a task.

2) At almost all times, the localities at times t and t+1 have many pages in common.

A task is considered to have a <u>high degree of locality</u> if L(t), the locality set at time t, is a small subset of the total set of task pages (statement 1), and if L(t) and L(t+1) are nearly always identical (statement 2).

The third locality property postulated by Denning and Schwartz has often failed to hold in practice. It is:

3) The localities at times t and t+k tend to become uncorrelated as k becomes large.

Let $w(t,T) = |W(t,T)|$ be the <u>working set size</u> at time t. Using a central limit theorem, it can be shown [36] that property 3) above implies $w(t,T)$ will be <u>normally distributed</u>. However, this is often refuted by measurements of real tasks [16, 45, 49, 75]. Apparently, real reference strings can exhibit dependence over very long intervals of time.

A further, intuitively reasonable property of importance in modeling (although not as fundamental as those above) is:

2.4 Memory Reference Locality

4) The size of the locality set tends to vary in time.

Since the working set is an extrinsic locality set, property 4) is implied by property 3) --- if the working set size is normally distributed, it will certainly vary in time. But even when locality sizes are not normally distributed, they will usually exhibit some sort of variation.

Properties 1) and 2) above do not **always** hold, only at "almost all times". Occasional disruptive behavior occurs when a task enters a new **phase** of execution. We expect tasks to have temporal breakpoints, on either side of which they perform distinct functions. A compiler, for example, might exhibit the following phases of execution: lexical analysis, syntactic analysis, semantic interpretation, etc. Some of these are so complex that they are themselves collections of several phases. The phases of a task can be seen graphically [52, 65] by recording successive extrinsic locality sets (working sets, for example). Every so often a sharp, almost disjoint change in membership occurs. This is clearly at variance with locality properties 1) and 2), which assume gradual change.

A well-known general method of treating processes of this type is to model behavior on two levels: **micro-behavior** and **macro-behavior** [35]. A **macro-model** considers only phase transitions --- each macro-state corresponds to a phase. A **micro-model** considers only behavior within a phase. A task's state at some time instant can then be characterized by knowledge of its phase (macro-state), and its detailed activity within the phase (micro-state). The complete intrinsic state is consequently given by the pair <micro-state, macro-state>.

Locality properties 1) and (especially) 2) refer to micro-behavior only. Close examination of property 2) reveals the difference between the holding time of a phase (or macro-state) and that of a locality set (or micro-state). Phases are delineated by abrupt changes of behavior, while within a single phase the locality set is allowed to change **slowly**. For example, consider a task which makes one pass through a large array. Each array page enters the locality set, remains there awhile, and finally departs after the last array element in the page is processed. The locality set changes gradually (in this case, one page at a time), but the task is clearly in only a single phase of execution.

Using the concepts of macro and micro behavior, we can make a prediction about the performance of the working set algorithm. We will now show that the optimality of VMIN implies that the working set algorithm is almost optimal for a task with long-lasting phases [33]. Let T be the size of the VMIN algorithm's forward window as determined in section 2.3.1, and let V(t,T) denote the set of pages in memory at time t under VMIN. Suppose all phases are at least h>T references long, and suppose that within a phase, every page in each locality set is referenced at least once during any interval of length T. Then for most t, the working set W(t,T) and the optimal V(t,T) are identical --- they are both the locality set. This fails to be true only when a page leaves the locality set, in which case VMIN will replace the page immediately, whereas WS will retain it for T additional references. Here, the working set algorithm has the same page fault rate as VMIN, but its mean allocation is larger because non-locality pages are not immediately removed. During the holding time of a phase, pages leave the locality set slowly, so working set's excessive allocation occurs largely at phase transitions. Assuming that the locality sets on either side of a phase transition are disjoint (this is the worst case), the virtual-time-average WS allocation will exceed that of VMIN by roughly $T\ell/h$ page frames, where ℓ is the mean locality set size. (We have neglected the additional increase in WS allocation due to intra-phase locality changes.) Of course, if the phase and/or locality transitions are frequent, the mean WS allocation will be much larger than that of VMIN.

In section 1.5.1, we discused the philosophies of extrinsic and intrinsic modeling. Corresponding to this are extrinsic and intrinsic definitions of locality. The most successful extrinsic definition is the working set. Using locality property 2) above, the working set defines the extrinsic locality at time t to be the set of pages referenced in the interval of length T immediately preceding t. The idea is that the pages recently in use are likely to still be in current use. But the working set algorithm performs sub-optimally at phase transitions, as we have seen, since locality property 2) is a micro-behavior effect

2.4 Memory Reference Locality 49

and does not hold across phase transitions.

Intrinsic locality is based on the internal function or state of the given task. For instance, as soon as a task enters a loop of many iterations, we might define the pages in the loop to be the intrinsic locality. The working set attempts by extrinsic measurement to estimate the "true" intrinsic locality. When the loop is first entered, the estimate will be poor, because the intrinsic locality changes instantaneously while the working set does not. It is not always easy (even possible) to measure the intrinsic locality of a task exactly, so we shall have to consider extrinsic estimation. For such estimation using the working set, the window size T should be large enough so that all pages in an intrinsic locality will nearly always be referenced in a window. On the other hand, T should be small enough so that more than one _locality transition_ (change of locality set) is unlikely in a window. Individual locality sets may change rapidly enough to make this difficult. In practice, window size T is usually about 10,000 or 100,000 references, spanning _entire phases_ rather than locality sets. But this can be considered a matter of definition --- one could simply define the intrinsic locality set to be all pages referenced in the current phase.

2.4.1 Spatial Locality

Madnick [66] has noted a second basic locality phenomenon, called _spatial locality_. This is based on word, rather than on page, references. If word w is referenced at time t, then words in the range w-i to w+i for some small i are likely to be referenced at times close to t, according to the notion of spatial locality.

Spatial locality is itself considered inherently in paging; if any word in a page is referenced, the whole page is fetched and made ready for use. The main effect of spatial locality on program behavior studies might be for small page sizes, where a reference to page x would increase the likelihood of references to pages in the range x-i' to x+i'. The implication would be to anticipate references to nearby pages. In systems which group pages into segments, there have been attempts to preload the entire segment when any page in the segment is referenced (this obviously works only for small segments). However, we shall not consider spatial locality further because its detailed characteristics are not known.

2.4.2 Program Restructuring for Locality Improvement

Since locality is the phenomenon which allows paging to occur with acceptable efficiency, it follows that if the degree of locality of a task can be improved, its performance in a virtual paging system will improve. Two approaches are: either a) pack the program code and data into as few pages as possible (i.e. --- compile tighter code, reformat the data, etc.), or b) rearrange the instructions and data so that individual localities occupy as few pages as possible. We shall consider alternative b), often termed program restructuring. Note that while the first alternative produces smaller programs, the second may not (in fact, the number of pages may increase) because parts of pages may be left empty by the reordering procedure.

As a simple example, consider three subroutines X, Y, and Z as follows:

Name	Length in Words
X	800
Y	1400
Z	1100

The page size is 1000 words. If the subroutines appear in name space ordered alphabetically as in figure 2.4a, then X, Y, and Z will span respectively 1, 3, and 2 pages. Thus, 3 pages may have to be in main memory for efficient execution of Y. If the routines are reordered as in 2.4b, the page span of Y drops to 2, and the average locality size will probably be smaller. Note the wasted space at the end of the second page.

2.4.2 Program Restructuring

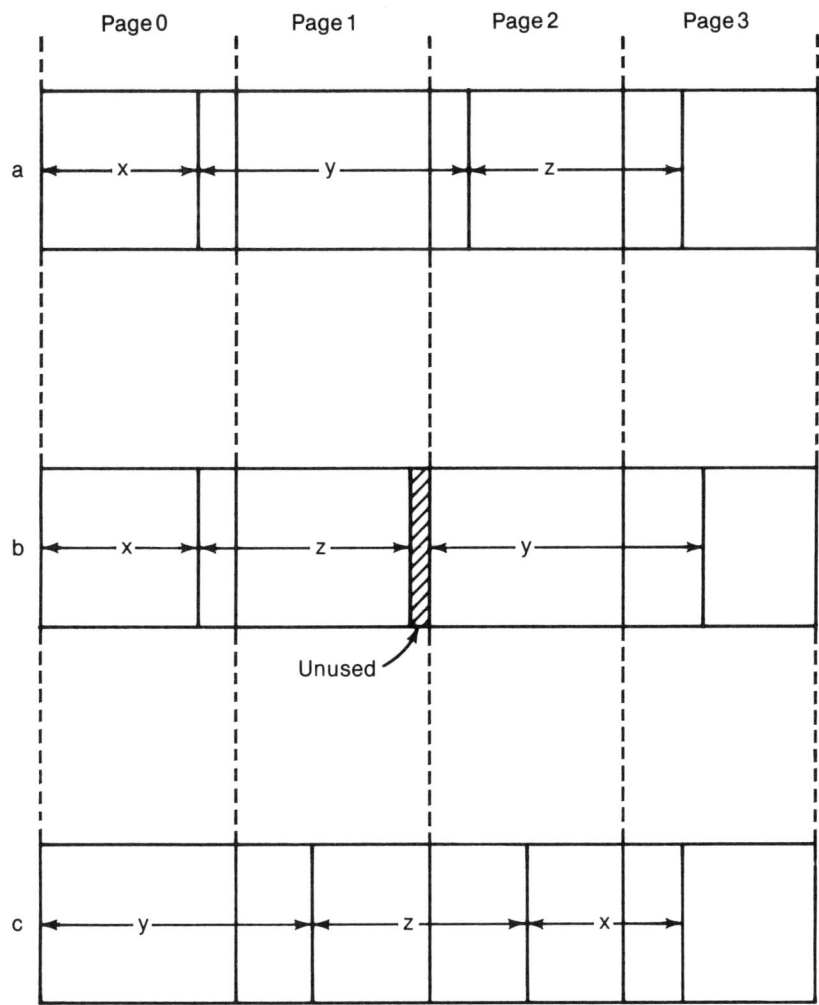

Figure 2.4 Three possible arrangements of a program in name space

If the programmer has a reasonably good idea of the localities in his program, he might specify them as part of a programming language. Define a **block** to be a logical program unit, such as a loop, short subroutine, array, etc. Blocks may be indicated by the programmer, or the compiler may calculate them from a flow analysis of the program (optimizing compilers do such flow analyses in any case). The compiler could attempt to rearrange the blocks to increase the degree of locality. In our example, we have assumed three blocks, routines X, Y, and Z, but in general a routine may consist of several blocks.

The simplest restructuring approach is to begin each block on a page boundary, guaranteeing that each will occupy the fewest number of pages. This is not a good scheme for several reasons: First, there will be much wasted space in the last page of each block, especially if the blocks are much smaller than pages. Second, a locality may consist of not one, but several blocks. In that case, we may actually increase the size of the locality set. Third, even if each block does happen to be a locality, we have made the locality sets disjoint. Every locality transition will require a completely new set of pages to be loaded into main memory.

A better method is to use the wasted space in the last page of a block to contain all or part of **neighboring** blocks; that is, blocks which tend to be used in adjoining time intervals. The reordering of figure 2.4b is excellent if X and Z tend to transfer control to one another frequently. For instance, if routine X calls routine Z, no page fault will occur. Figure 2.5a shows a possible **program graph** for this task. The vertices are blocks. The edges will, in general, denote either transfers of control or data references; however, in this example vertices corresponding to data blocks are omitted. According to this graph, the rearrangement of figure 2.4b is effective; apparently X and Z form a locality together, with Y a separate locality. A restructuring algorithm should use the **connectivity** information in the program graph, attempting to place neighboring blocks in overlapping page sets.

Now, consider figure 2.5b, which is another possible graph for this task. Blocks Y and Z now have the capability of transferring control to each other. The numbers on the edges of the graph are the counts

2.4.2 Program Restructuring

a)
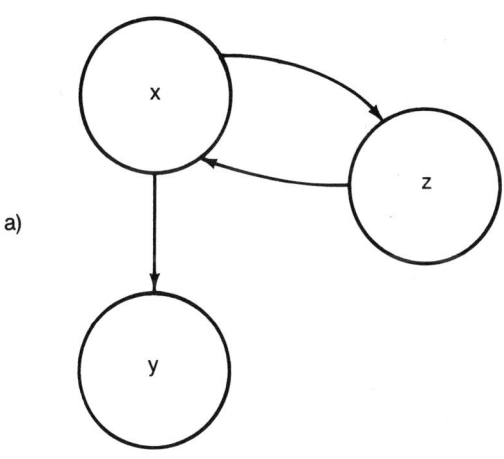

b)
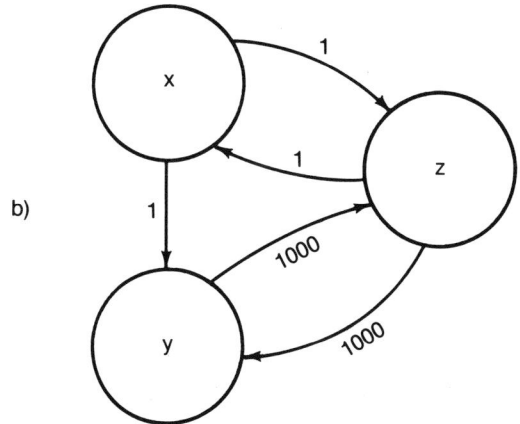

Figure 2.5 Two possible program graphs

of each control transfer during execution. Clearly, it is more important to combine blocks Y and Z than X and Z. Thus, the page assignment of figure 2.4c will be best for this task. In this assignment, the dominant locality of Y and Z together spans 3 pages, as compared to 4 pages in the other orderings. Block X also shares a page with Z (X calls Z), but this is a relatively minor consideration.

This example shows that the connectivity of the program graph is not enough to find a good assignment of blocks to pages. The _weight_ of each edge in the graph is crucial. The compiler cannot determine this information; neither, very often, can the programmer. The only reliable method is to measure the task as it executes. For frequently used tasks, in particular for system routines such as editors, compilers, etc., this is practical. It has been shown that restructuring according to measured edge weights reduces the page fault rate by as much as ten to one [52].

Hatfield and Gerald [52] base their restructuring technique on a measured _nearness matrix_ $B=[b_{ij}]$, where b_{ij} is the number of times a reference to block j immediately follows a reference to block i. This is an alternate way to represent the weighted program graph. In our current example, it is:

$$B = \begin{array}{c|ccc} & X & Y & Z \\ \hline X & - & 1 & 1 \\ Y & 0 & - & 1000 \\ Z & 1 & 1000 & - \end{array}$$

Hatfield and Gerald assumed that blocks were small compared to the page size, so that several blocks could be completely inserted into a single page. (This is, of course, not true in our example.) Under this assumption, the following heuristic was shown to yield good page assignments: Reorder the blocks in such a way that the large matrix entries fall close to the diagonal. Since entries on the diagonal would correspond to consecutive references to the same block (hence the same page), those near the diagonal correspond to consecutive references to blocks in nearby (perhaps the same) pages. The blocks are entered into the name space in the order which gives

2.4.2 Program Restructuring

the strongest diagonalization. Since this is a heuristic, and not usually optimal, the procedure can be iterated if measured page reference frequencies are available as feedback to the programmer.

Ferrari [39] has proposed the method of <u>critical working sets</u> (<u>CWS</u>) for use with working set memory management. Working set W(t,T) is called <u>critical</u> if $r(t+1) \notin W(t,T)$, a page fault. A <u>critical reference</u> is one causing a fault. The procedure is to measure the <u>CWS matrix</u> $C=[c_{ij}]$, where c_{ij} is the number of times a critical reference to block i occurs with a critical working set containing j. If restructuring were to place blocks i and j into the same page, then $c_{ij}+c_{ji}$ critical references would no longer be critical. Thus, we may assign weight c_{ji} to the edge of the program graph from i to j (this may entail adding new edges to the graph). Optimum graph clustering algorithms can then be used, to find the page assignment minimizing the sum of weights of edges between blocks in separate pages. Alternatively, a heuristic, such as that of Hatfield and Gerald, can be used. While the CWS method is not always optimal, experiments [39] have shown it to improve over Hatfield and Gerald's method when the memory is working set managed.

We have discussed only the reordering of program code, not data. If data is divided into blocks, such that there is no required positional arrangement among the blocks, it can often be treated in the same way (but instruction operand addresses will have to be changed). However, it is difficult to partition a large array or other data structure into blocks, because the elements must retain certain relative orderings. This kind of restructuring must usually be done by the programmer. For example, McKellar and Coffman [68] give efficient methods of organizing matrices. Alternatively, a change of algorithm to one making more local use of its data will achieve the same effect, as has been demonstrated for sorting algorithms by Brawn, Gustavson, and Mankin [14].

Chapter 3
Models for Memory Reference Behavior

3.1 Some Extrinsic Program Models

3.1.1 The Working Set Model

Recall that $W(t,T)$, the working set at time t, consists of the set of distinct pages in $r(t-T+1)...r(t)$. Let $w(t,T)$ denote the working set size (number of pages) of $W(t,T)$, and let $w(T)$ denote the virtual-time-average value of $w(t,T)$ over some specified time interval. Denning and others [27, 36, 20] have determined some important properties of the function $w(T)$, as follows:

A plot of $w(T)$ against T for a given task is called a working set curve; a typical one appears in figure 3.1. Here we have defined the working set with a zero-length window to be empty, so that $W(t,0)=\emptyset$ and $w(t,0)=0$. Note that the curve illustrated is concave (or concave down). By this we mean that any tangent to the curve lies entirely on or above the curve. For example, let T^o be the point of tangency; then

$$w(T) \leq w(T^o) + w'(T^o)[T-T^o], \quad 0 \leq T < \infty$$

where $w'(T)$ is the derivative with respect to T. This is shown pictorially in figure 3.1[1]. Denning has shown that all such curves are concave. Moreover, for all T, $w'(T) \leq 1$. One obvious consequence is that doubling the window size will less than double the mean working set size, but the implications of concavity are stronger. We shall examine this in detail in section 3.1.4.

---

1) Figure 3.1 is actually a simplification, since the working set is defined only for integer T. More realistically, the curve is piecewise linear, with straight line segments connecting the points at $T=0,1,2,...$ For such a curve, an equivalent definition of concavity is that the slopes of successive line segments do not increase.

3.1.1 The Working Set Model

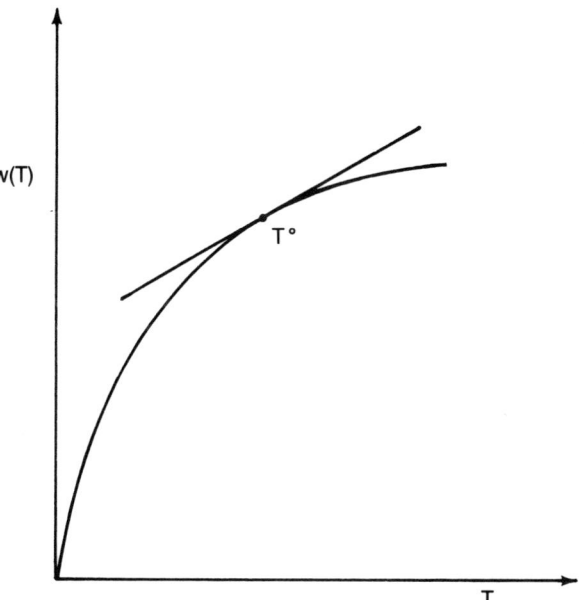

Figure 3.1 Example working set curve and tangent line

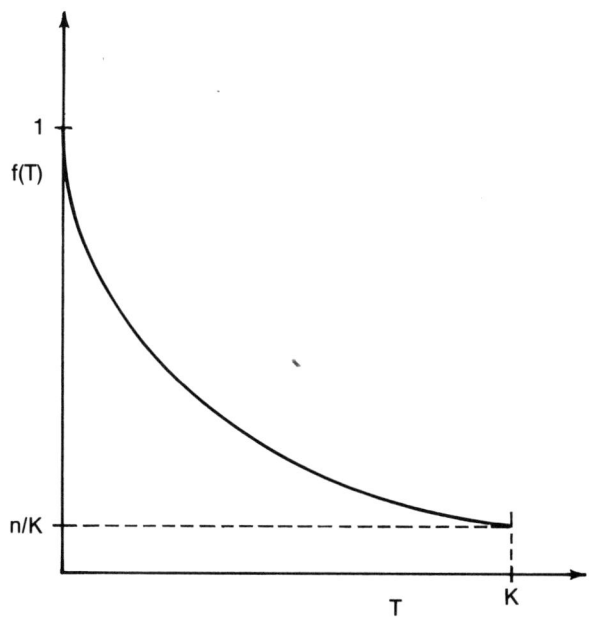

Figure 3.2 Example page fault rate curve

In a strict working set memory management policy, exactly the working set W(t,T) is in memory at time t. Let us denote by f(T) the _page fault probability_ (or _page fault rate_ per reference) under such a policy. This is simply the number of page faults divided by the number of references. Consider reference string R=r(1)r(2)...r(K). During the first T references, a window of length T falls partially before the start of R, so in such cases we define the working set to be the set of all distinct pages referenced since time zero. Summarizing:

$$W(t,T) = \begin{cases} \emptyset & \text{if } t \leq 0 \\ \text{all pages in } r(1)...r(t) & \text{if } 1 \leq t < T \\ \text{all pages in } r(t-T+1)...r(t) & \text{if } T \leq t \leq K \end{cases}$$

The average working set size is:

$$w(T) = \frac{1}{K} \sum_{t=1}^{K} w(t,T) \ .$$

Define the _page fault characteristic function_ $\nabla(t,T)$ to be:

$$\nabla(t,T) = \begin{cases} 1 & \text{if } r(t) \notin W(t-1,T) \\ 0 & \text{otherwise} \ . \end{cases} \quad (3.1)$$

We observe the following relation:

$$w(t+1,T+1) = w(t,T) + \nabla(t+1,T) \ , \quad 0 \leq t < K \quad (3.2)$$

since the windows of both working sets begin at the same time t-T+1 (or at time 1 if t<T). To find page fault rate f(T), we define:

$$f(T) = \frac{1}{K} \sum_{t=1}^{K} \nabla(t,T)$$

so that, using (3.2):

3.1.1 The Working Set Model

$$f(T) = \frac{1}{K}\sum_{t=1}^{K} w(t,T+1) - \frac{1}{K}\sum_{t=1}^{K} w(t-1,T)$$

$$= w(T+1) - [w(T) - \frac{1}{K} w(K,T)] \ . \quad (3.3)$$

Since the working set size cannot exceed n, the total number of task pages, the last term in the above relation is bounded from above by n/K. For very long reference strings this is negligible, so that:

$$f(T) \approx w(T+1) - w(T) \ , \text{ for K large.} \quad (3.4)$$

This means that the page fault rate under working set memory management is essentially the _derivative_[2] of the working set curve, for long reference strings. A plot of f(T) against T is called a _page fault (rate) curve_; an example appears in figure 3.2. Note that when T=K, where K is the length of the reference string, then f(T)=n/K, assuming that n distinct pages are referenced in the string. With this value of window size, no page ever leaves the working set, so that only the first reference to each page causes a fault.

There is another way to determine f(T). Page r(t+1) will be omitted from w(t,T) if it has never been referenced previously, or if the elapsed time since its previous reference exceeds T. Let _backward distance_ Ψ(t) be the elapsed time (number of references) since the previous reference to page r(t). Specifically, r(t-Ψ(t))=r(t), and none of the references r(t-Ψ(t)+1)...r(t-1) are the same as r(t). We define Ψ(t) to be infinity if r(t) has never been referenced prior to time t. Then:

$\nabla(t,T)=1$ if and only if $\Psi(t)>T$

for page fault characteristic function $\nabla(t,T)$. A page fault occurs under working set memory management whenever Ψ(t)>T. Clearly:

---

2) More accurately, it is the _first difference_, which is the discrete analog of the derivative.

$$f(T) = 1-G(T) \tag{3.5}$$

where $G(x)$ is the relative frequency of backward distances which do not exceed x. Function $G(x)$ is called the __backward distance empirical probability distribution__; its "derivative" is:

$$g(x) = G(x)-G(x-1), \tag{3.6}$$

so that:

$$-g(T+1) = f(T+1)-f(T) .$$

Obviously, $g(x)$ is the __empirical probability__ (or relative frequency) that a backward distance equals x. Its measurement is straightforward (see section 5.2): If a backward distance of value x is observed i times in reference string $r(1)...r(K)$, then $g(x)=i/K$. Notice that function $g(x)$, $x<\infty$, gives the frequency of distances between successive references to the same page, regardless of the page's identity. Since $\Psi(t)=\infty$ if page $r(t)$ has never before been referenced, $g(\infty)$ is the number of distinct pages in the string divided by K (every page is referenced a first time). For this reason, $g(x)$ is often called the __interreference frequency function__ of the task, and $G(x)$ the (empirical) __interreference distribution__.

In the same way that $f(T)$ is essentially the derivative of $w(T)$, it is clear from formula (3.6) that $g(T)$ is essentially the (negative of the) derivative of $f(T)$. Thus, we see that the working set curve $w(T)$ can yield much information about the task it represents. The first derivative gives the mean working set page fault rate for any window size; the second derivative gives the overall interreference frequency function of the task (this is an important statistical characterization). The concavity of the working set curve has important implications, which we shall mention in section 3.1.4. As a matter of fact, it has been observed experimentally [87] that the page fault rate curve is often approximately __convex__ (concave up). Although this is not a direct property of the working set model, it is implied by locality properties 1) and 2) of section 2.4. It means intuitively that the pages most likely to be referenced are those which were referenced in the near past.

Denning and Schwartz [36, 20] have shown that the

3.1.1 The Working Set Model

<u>working</u> <u>set</u> <u>size</u> $w(t,T) = |W(t,T)|$ is <u>normally</u> <u>distributed</u> (or <u>Gaussian</u>), provided that the references at times far apart are uncorrelated (locality property 3, section 2.4). The working set size, being the memory space demand of a task under working set memory management, is clearly of interest in system modeling. By the definition of a normal distribution:

$$\Pr[w(t,T) = w] = \frac{1}{\sigma(T)\sqrt{2\pi}} e^{-[w(t,T) - w(T)]/2\sigma^2(T)} \qquad (3.7)$$

where $\sigma^2(T)$ is the working set size variance, and where $w(T)$ is the mean size, as before.

There are some mathematical difficulties that make (3.7) only an approximation. For one thing, working set sizes are positive-integer-valued, whereas the normal distribution defines a continuous-valued random variable having negative, as well as positive, range. Thus, for the approximation to hold, a task must have both: a) a wide range of likely working set sizes, so that the discrete-valued working set size can be approximated by a continuous distribution, yet b) a small enough variance, relative to the mean, so that the predicted probability of a zero or negative working set size is negligible. Condition a) is satisfied if $\sigma(T) \gg 1$; condition b) if $w(T) \geq 3\ \sigma(T)$ [using the conventional three-standard-deviation rule for a normal process.] Both conditions often hold in practice. For instance, Rodriguez-Rosell [75] has reported measurements on an IBM 360 assembler with a page size of 1024 words. For window sizes T of practical interest (10,000-100,000 references), he found $w(T) \approx 20$ and $\sigma(T) \approx 4$. The dependence of the mean and the variance on the actual value of T in this range was quite weak. We see that condition b) is satisfied here, and a) is marginally satisfied.

Another difficulty is in attempting to extend "normally distributed random variable" to "normal random process". A <u>normal</u> (<u>Gaussian</u>) <u>process</u> is one in which any collection of observations at distinct times are jointly normal. The central limit theorem argument does predict that the working set sizes _at_ _widely_ _spaced_ _points_ _in_ _time_ will be jointly normal. However, at neighboring times there is such high correlation that these discrete-valued sizes cannot be considered jointly normal. In particular, $w(t+1,T)$ can have only one of the following values: $w(t,T)-1$, $w(t,T)$, $w(t,T)+1$. At widely spaced times, the correlation is weaker, and joint normality may be a reasonable approximation if condition a) on the spread of likely sizes holds.

As a practical matter, measurements of real tasks [16, 45, 49, 74, 75] have often shown the working set size to be non-normal. Frequently observed are _several_ _peaks_, or several preferred working set sizes. A likely interpretation is: The measurements were taken over time intervals spanning a few phase transitions. Within each phase, there is a preferred working set size, but other sizes were less common. Ghanem and Kobayashi [49 and private communication] have determined that their measured distributions were approximately _multinormal_. By this we mean that the distributions had several peaks, each of which had the shape of a normal distribution. Within each phase, there seems to be (approximately) Gaussian behavior, in spite of the fact that there are probably serial correlations of long persistence among these references. If the preferred locality set size within each phase is randomly chosen, and if enough phases fall within the measurement interval, the overall distribution will be more nearly normal. However, some tasks do not execute long enough for this to happen, so that the effects of a few phases will dominate. We conclude that the Gaussian working set size distribution, if it exists at all, is part of the _micro-behavior_ of tasks.

3.1.2 _Belady's_ _Lifetime_ _Function_

Belady and Kuehner [8] have analyzed the results of experiments to measure the mean length of an _execution_ _interval_ (virtual time between page faults), as a function of the allocated memory size. A typical, somewhat idealized, result appears in figure 3.3. The horizontal axis is the mean memory allocation m of a task, and the vertical axis is the

3.1.2 Belady's Lifetime Function 63

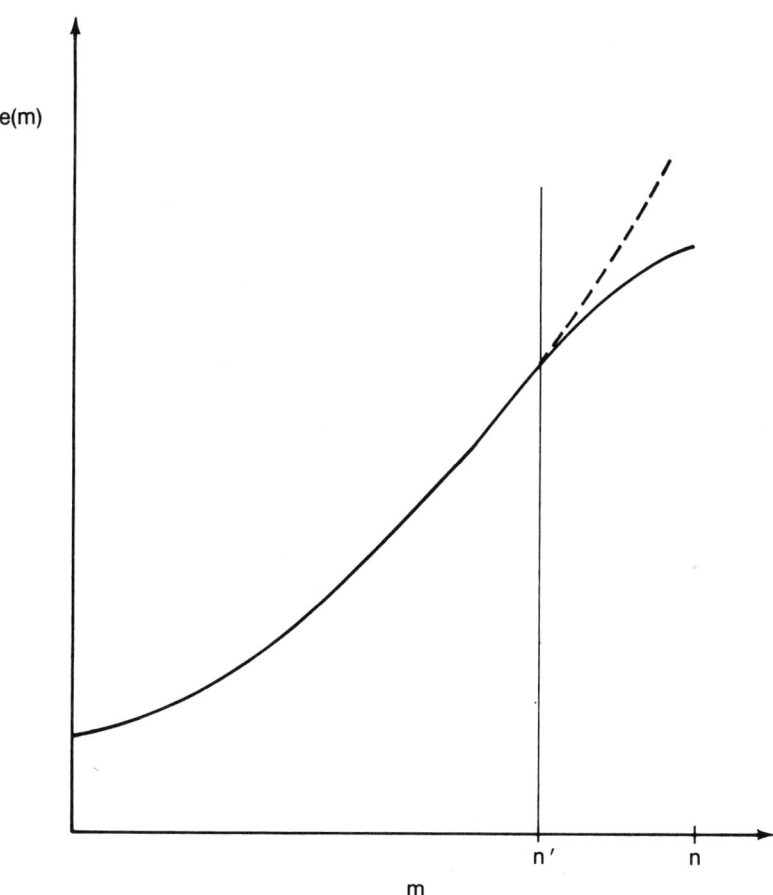

Figure 3.3 Example lifetime function. The dotted line shows the continuation of Belady's form (3.8) beyond the point of tail-off.

mean lifetime, where we use the term "lifetime" to denote the length of an execution interval. It is apparent that for much of its length, the lifetime curve is convex. In fact, Belady and Kuehner reported that such curves were reasonably well approximated by the following convex function (Belady's lifetime function):

$$e(m) = a(m^b) \tag{3.8}$$

for parameters a and b, with b on the order of 2. Similar results have appeared elsewhere [85]. It may be seen in figure 3.3 that the approximation holds only in the interval $1 \leq m \leq n'$, for some $n' < n$.

There are two likely reasons for the tail-off (or concave region) for $m > n'$:

1) First references to pages always cause page faults, no matter how large the allocation. Thus, for a reference string of length K containing n distinct pages, we have $e(n) \approx K/n$. For allocations close to n, the mean lifetime will remain strongly influenced by K. If we suppose that the lifetime function exclusive of first faults obeys (3.8) for all $m \leq n$, there will be n first faults, and about $K/(am^b)$ other faults, in a reference string of length K. Thus, we can write:

$$e(m) \approx K/[n + K/(am^b)], \quad 1 \leq m \leq n$$

where the term "n" in the denominator is negligible except for large m. The second derivative of this with respect to m is:

$$e''(m) = h(m)\left[\frac{2b}{a} m^{-b} - (b+1)\left(\frac{n}{K} + \frac{m^{-b}}{a}\right)\right] \quad 1 \leq m \leq n$$

for some $h(m) > 0$. A differentiable curve is concave (convex) if and only if its second derivative is negative (positive). It is easily seen that $e''(m)$ is positive for m sufficiently small, and negative for m sufficiently large. Thus, there is an inflection point (not necessarily in the region 1≤m≤n) at:

$$m = \left[\frac{(b-1)k}{an(b+1)} \right]^{1/b}$$

Beyond this point, the lifetime function is concave and not well-approximated by (3.8). For typical values of a, b, n and K, this point is at least on the order of the observed beginning of tail-off.

2) Another possible reason for the tail-off is the effect of locality. If the lifetime curve were to continue to be convex until m=n, this would mean that each additional allocated page frame would cause a larger and larger increase in the mean lifetime. However, once enough page frames are allocated to contain the locality set, additional allocation should have a diminished effect. We expect the locality set size of a task to vary over its running time, but there will be a largest such set. Above the size of this set, additional page frames cannot be used effectively.

Denning and Kahn [35] argue that the knee of the lifetime curve --- roughly the point at which its derivative falls to value one --- is often attributable to phase-of-execution behavior. Specifically, the set of all pages referenced within a phase can be considered to be a locality set, in which case the knee occurs at an allocation approximately equal to the average size of these phase-spanning locality sets. Any larger allocation would mean that no-longer-needed pages from preceding phases are maintained in memory, causing little improvement in the average lifetime. The key assumption here is that the locality sets on opposite sides of a phase transition are almost disjoint, so that there is little advantage in retaining pages from preceding phases.

A few measurements [37] have shown the tail-off to be much less pronounced when first faults are ignored, suggesting that reason 1) above may be the more important[3].

Suppose e(m) is the mean lifetime over a time interval spanning many page faults: then the mean virtual time _page_ _fault_ _rate_ (or _page_ _fault_ _probability_) during that interval is[4]:

$$f(m) = 1/e(m) = (1/a) m^{-b} . \qquad (3.9)$$

[By writing f(m) we are taking the fault rate to be a function of m, rather than of window size T as in section 3.1.1.] Figure 3.3 can thus be used to predict page fault rates as well. Since b is typically about 2, we can expect that doubling a task's main memory allocation will reduce its page fault rate by a factor on the order of 4, as long as we do not too closely approach n. The reader should keep in mind that although formula (3.8) gives the _mean_ lifetime for each allocation, individual lifetimes may vary far from the mean. Measurements of the standard deviation

---

3) In real systems, there is another "first fault" effect, which is not reflected in the lifetime curve. Suppose a task is temporarily deactivated, and must later be swapped back into memory. The larger its main memory set S(t), the longer the swapping will take. In terms of total pages fetched into memory, either from swapping or page faulting, the swapped-in pages have the same effect as first faults. They are independent of the paging algorithm. One could measure an "effective" lifetime function, defined as the ratio of the total number of references to the total number of pages fetched, for each mean memory size. Such a curve might exhibit a swapping-induced tail-off.

4) This is really an _asymptotic_ formula, valid only for long reference strings. For short strings, _end_ _effects_ at the beginning and end of the string cause this to be only an approximation. If we include the interval until the first page fault, and the interval after the last page fault, in our calculation of e(m), we will show in section 3.1.4 that a more exact formula is:

$$f(m) = 1/e(m) - 1/K .$$

3.1.2 Belady's Lifetime Function 67

have generally shown it to exceed the mean [47, 62].

If the paging algorithm in use is any stack algorithm A, functions e(m) and f(m) can be estimated for a real task by recording its distance string with respect to algorithm A. Suppose we measure distance string $d(1)...d(K)$. Let c_i be the observed number of occurrences of distance i. Estimates of f(m) and e(m) are:

$$\hat{f}(m) = (c_{m+1} + ... + c_n + c_\infty)/K$$

$$\hat{e}(m) = 1/\hat{f}(m) .$$

Details of the measurement procedure appear in chapter 5.

Figure 3.4a shows the beginning of the measured LRU lifetime function from 200,000 references of a long-running Fortran program, to be called reference string A. A larger portion of the curve is shown in figure 3.4b. The largest observed distance was actually 27, but we only show the curve for 1≤m≤20 because there were only one or two occurrences of each distance above 20. Even for m≤20, the larger values are of questionable statistical significance.

The curve shown in the figures represents behavior in the interval $r(5001)...r(205000)$. The first 5000 references were skipped to avoid the initialization portion of the program, with behavior atypical of most of the span of the program's execution. However, the stack was maintained starting at $r(1)$, so that the initial memory content S(5000) was non-empty. This is sometimes termed warm start measurement [37]. Since many of the page faults due to first references to pages occurred prior to the interval of measured behavior, it is not surprising that no tail-off is apparent in figure 3.4b. But it is quite possible that a tail-off would be visible if the curve were extended to higher values of m.

Also shown in figures 3.4a and 3.4b is the function of form (3.8) chosen for best fit in the interval 1≤m≤20. The figures indicate that the fit is poor for small m. The sharp jump in the curve between memory allocations 4 and 5 indicates a locality of 5 pages that strongly dominates the task's behavior in

68 PROGRAM BEHAVIOR: MODELS AND MEASUREMENTS

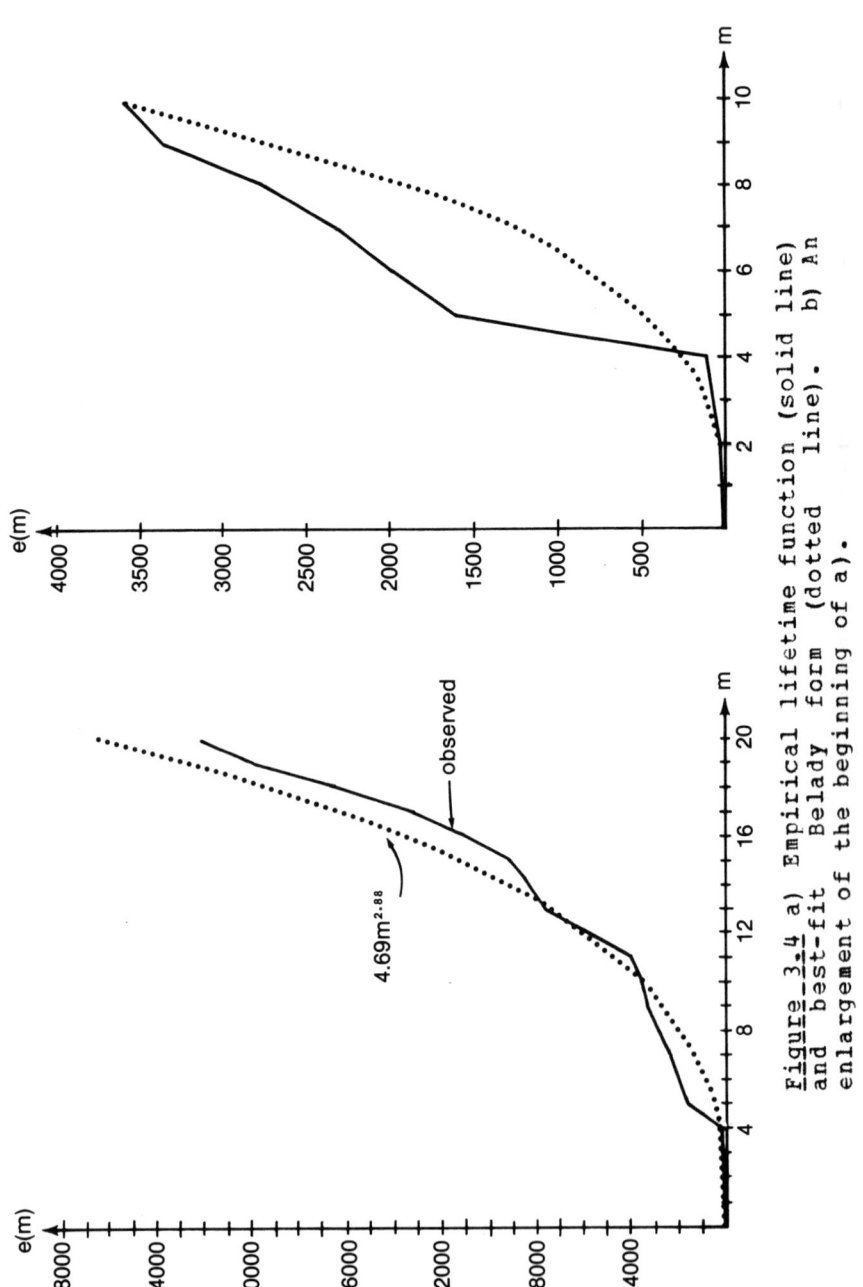

Figure 3.4 a) Empirical lifetime function (solid line) and best-fit Belady form (dotted line). b) An enlargement of the beginning of a).

3.1.2 Belady's Lifetime Function

this time interval. A conclusion is that Belady's lifetime function is most applicable to <u>very long</u> reference strings spanning many changes of locality. Nevertheless, it is useful in this example to predict e(m) for large m.

Functions of the form (3.8) and (3.9) appear as straight lines on graph paper having logarithmic scales on both axes. Figure 3.5 shows f(m) for reference string A this way. Again, the best-fit Belady lifetime function appears as a dashed straight line. If the data is graphed this way, the line may simply be estimated by eye, or it may be found formally by a <u>linear regression</u>, fitting the equation:

$$\log[f(m)] = -b \log[m] - \log[a]$$

to the data points $(1,\hat{f}(1))$, $(2,\hat{f}(2))$, ... [this was the method used here]. Since the linear regression procedure minimizes the sum of squared deviations from linearity, and since equal distances on a logarithmic scale correspond to equal <u>ratios</u>, this method can be shown asymptotically equivalent to the following procedure: Minimize the sum of squares of the <u>relative errors</u> $e_1, e_2, \ldots$, defined to be:

$$e_i = [f(i) - \hat{f}(i)]/\hat{f}(i)$$

where $\hat{f}(i)$ is the observed fault rate, and $f(i)$ is the modeled fault rate. However, the equivalence of method holds only for small relative errors. When even the best fit will be poor, a more formal minimization of the sum of squared relative errors should be employed. (Relative, rather than actual errors should be minimized, since curves e(m) and f(m) span several orders of magnitude.)

Recent measurements [78] on the Multics system have tended to confirm (3.8), except that the measured curves were nearly <u>linear</u>, with b=1. An essential difference here was that overall system performance was measured, rather than the performance of individual tasks. During an interval of real time, the productive central processor running time was divided by the total number of page faults (from all

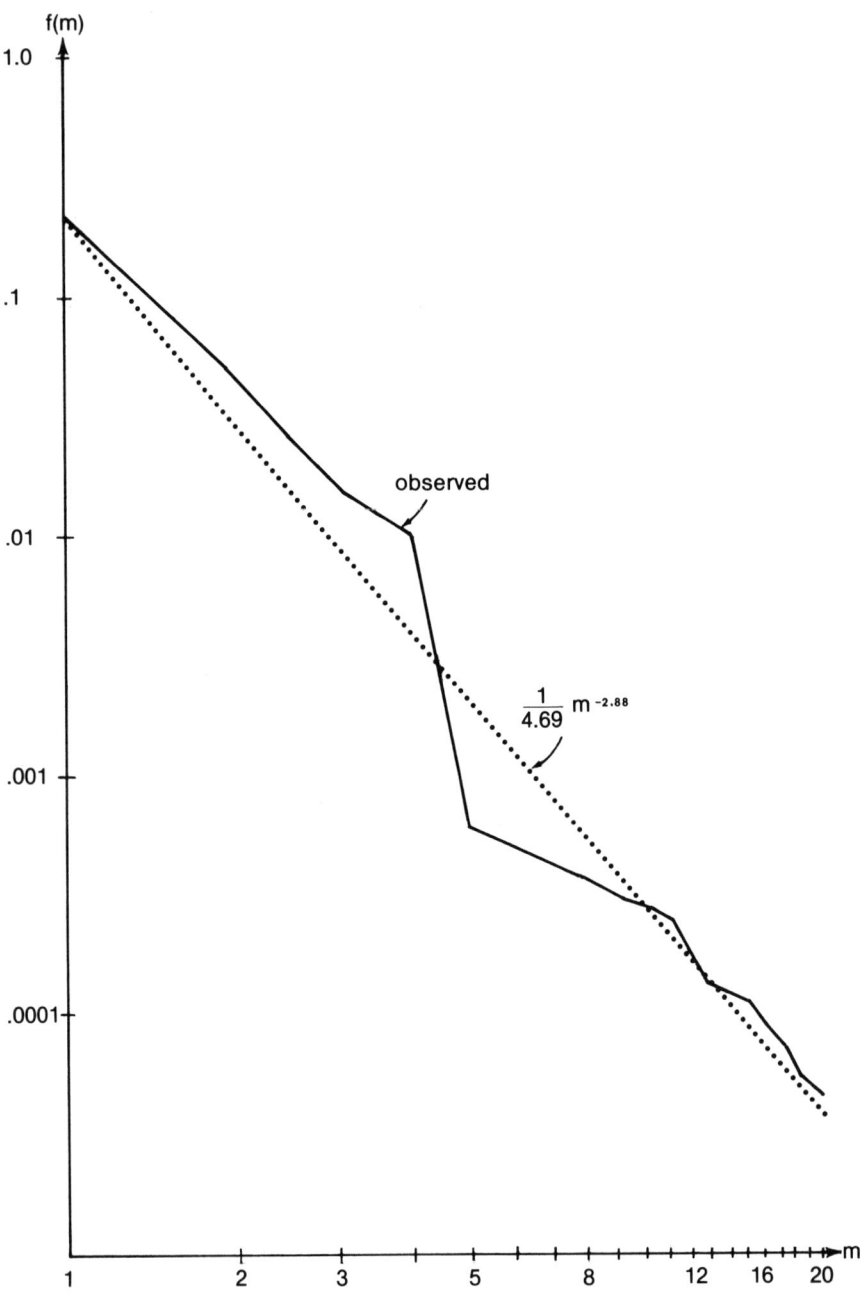

Figure 3.5 Empirical page fault rate function f(m) (solid line) and best-fit Belady lifetime function (dotted line).

3.1.2 Belady's Lifetime Function

sources) to obtain a mean system-wide execution interval. It is not clear how such a measurement relates to measurements of a single task, as we noted in section 1.5.1. The fit to expression (3.8) of a single task depends on the characteristics of the task and on the paging algorithm in use. A similar system-wide curve will be influenced by many additional system characteristics (i.e.--- central processor and external memory scheduling, the mechanism for controlling the multiprogramming level, the mechanism for allocating the total available main memory among the several active user and system tasks, etc.). Denning [32] elaborates on this. It is not known if the linear relationship discovered in the Multics system applies to any other system, or even if it in fact is the actual lifetime function of an "average" Multics task.

3.1.3 An Application to Thrashing

We can use Belady's lifetime function to model more directly the phenomenon of thrashing, as introduced in section 2.2. Thrashing is properly a type of _system_ behavior, and requires a system model. Figure 3.6 shows the simplified model we propose: a central processor and an external memory device, each with a first-come-first-served queue. A task waits for processor service, eventually is allocated the processor in its turn, and then executes until a page fault is generated. At this point, the task leaves the processor queue and enters the external memory queue to await service there. When it reaches the front of the queue, it initiates a page fetch from the device, waits for its completion, and then leaves the external memory queue and reenters the processor queue. Note that a task remains queued for a server until service is _completed_.

The number of tasks (degree of multiprogramming) is assumed to be a fixed number k. No tasks ever enter or leave the system --- this approximates a more realistic situation in which each completion of a task is immediately followed by an admission of a new task to the active set. For mathematical tractability, we assume that all service times are independent, exponentially distributed random variables with mean

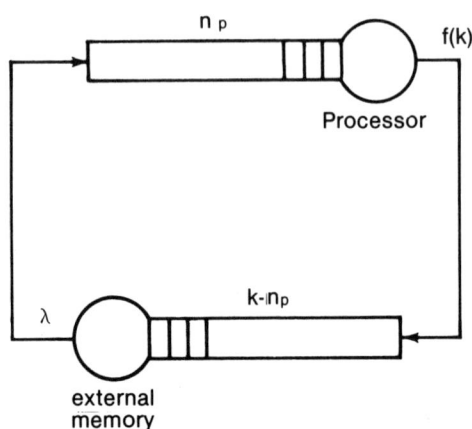

Figure 3.6 A system model which predicts thrashing

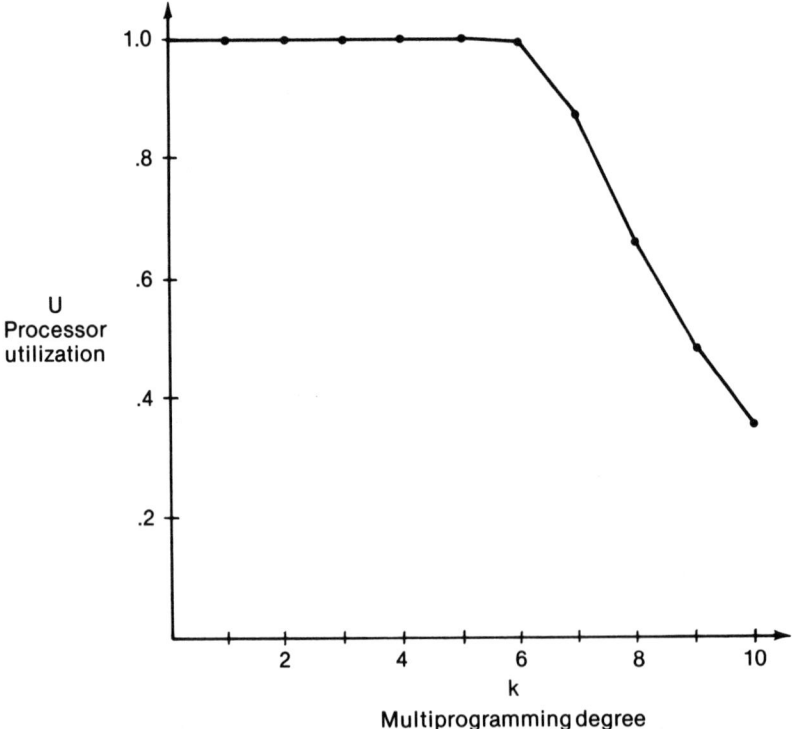

Figure 3.7 Processor utilization of the above model as a function of the degree of multiprogramming.

3.1.3 An Application to Thrashing

$1/f(k)$ in the case of the processor, and mean $1/\lambda$ in the case of the external memory device. Of course, $f(k)$ is the page fault rate, assumed identical for all tasks. The rate is a function of the degree of multiprogramming since the more tasks, the fewer page frames are available to each.

One way to analyze this model is by observing its equivalence to a single FCFS queue with Poisson arrivals and <u>finite waiting room</u>. Let n_p denote the number of tasks in the processor queue, including the one in service. Consider the output of the external memory server. As long as $n_p < k$, there is at least one task in the external memory queue; hence departures from the external memory occur at independent intervals, having a common exponential distribution with mean $1/\lambda$. This is in fact a Poisson process with rate λ, when $n_p < k$. Of course, if $n_p = k$, there is no task in external memory, and the rate of arrivals to the processor queue drops to zero. This is equivalent to the following single-queue system: Consider a queue with Poisson arrival and a limited capacity of k tasks, including the one in service. If an attempted arrival occurs when $n_p = k$, the arriving task does not enter the queue; it is simply lost. The equilibrium state-occupancy probabilities of such a queue are known to be (c.f. [77]):

$$\Pr[n_p = i] = (1-\rho)\rho^i / (1-\rho^{k+1}) \qquad (3.10)$$

where:

$$\rho = \lambda / f(k) .$$

We have the equilibrium probability that the processor queue will contain any given number of tasks. Of particular interest is the probability of <u>zero</u> tasks, which is the fraction of real time that the processor is <u>idle</u>. From (3.10) this is:

$$P(0) = \Pr[n_p = 0] = (1-\rho)/(1-\rho^{k+1}) .$$

The processor utilization is

$$U = 1-P(0).$$

To find the effect of the degree of multiprogramming on processor utilization, we must evaluate f(k). Suppose there is a total of M page frames available in the system for all tasks, and that each task receives an equal share. Each task's allocation is then M/k, so that from (3.9):

$$f(k) = \frac{1}{a} (M/k)^{-b}$$

$$\rho = \lambda/f(k) = \lambda a (M/k)^b$$

$$U = 1 - \frac{1 - \lambda a (M/k)^b}{1 - [\lambda a (M/k)^b]^{k+1}}$$

Using $\lambda = .0001$, which is typical for drums, and the values of a and b obtained for the measured task in the previous section, the functional dependence of processor utilization on multiprogramming degree k appears in figure 3.7. For k≤6, the processor is busy nearly 100 percent of the time, but above this abscissa value idleness rises sharply. In fact, increasing the multiprogramming degree from 7 to 8 causes a 24 percent drop in processor utilization. There is obviously a critical degree of multiprogramming, beyond which too few pages are available to each process and performance degrades sharply.

Processor utilization, although an indicator of

3.1.3 An Application to Thrashing

system efficiency, is not the most direct performance measure. Of more interest is the system _throughput rate_, or number of tasks completed per unit time. However, figure 3.7 has a direct interpretation in this respect. _Suppose the mean virtual time to complete a task is one time unit_ (we can ensure this by choosing the time scale). Since the central processor is busy a fraction U of real time, it will complete a total of U units of virtual time processing on all tasks, in each unit of real time. Thus, on the average, U tasks will complete per unit real time. Utilization is now interpretable as throughput.

Of course, this model is very much simplified, and ignores many important features of a real system. Input/Output, for example, is not included. See Denning and Graham [34] for a model which includes I/O. Also note that we have assumed lifetime function (3.8) to be valid for all m, ignoring the possibility of tail-off for large m. The effect of such a tail-off is to reduce the utilization which would be observed at small multiprogramming degrees. One way to model the effect of a tail-off is to assume that each task has a minimum page fault rate, below which it will not fall no matter how many page frames are allocated to it. When this effect is included in the model, there will be an _optimal_ degree of multiprogramming, since processor utilization will drop if too few (as well as too many) tasks are active.

3.1.4 _Convexity Implications_

We have seen that the working set curve w(T) is concave (down), and that the working set fault rate curve f(T) is often convex (concave up). Belady lifetime functions of the form (3.8) or (3.9) are also easily seen to be convex. Functions of this nature satisfy an inequality (c.f. Feller [38]):

Proposition 3.1 (Jensen's Inequality) Let g(x) and
h(x) be functions, fixed in time, which are concave
and convex, respectively. Let x(t) be a random
variable and let E{.} denote expectation over time.
Then:

$$E\{g(x(t))\} \leq g(E\{x(t)\})$$

$$E\{h(x(t))\} \geq h(E\{x(t)\}) .$$

An example for a convex function h(x) appears in
figure 3.8. Here, x(t) has value $\bar{x}+\delta$ half the
(virtual) time, and $\bar{x}-\delta$ the other half. The value of
$h(\bar{x})$, shown on the curve, is less than the average of
$h(\bar{x}-\delta)$ and $h(\bar{x}+\delta)$ which is on the chord above the
curve. This is a very simple example; the inequality
applies for *any* variation of x(t) with mean x.

We can apply Jensen's inequality to the working
set curve to compare fixed versus variable window
sizes, or to Belady's lifetime function to compare
fixed versus variable memory allocations. However,
this must be done with great caution. The working set
and Belady curves are *averages*, valid only over long
time intervals. With high resolution, we would
observe that the *functions themselves* are changing;
i.e. --- w(t,T) and e(m,t) are time varying even with
fixed T and m. Jensen's inequality applies only to
fixed functions g and h. Fortunately, as we will
show, we can still apply it, if the variation in T or
m is independent of the working set size or lifetime,
respectively. In that case, we can proceed as though
the function were valid at each time instant, and not
just on the average.

For instance, consider working set size w(t,T(t))
when T(t) has mean value $\bar{T}$ over the interval of
measurement t=1,2,...,K. Let NUM[.] denote the number
of occurrences of event [.] during the interval. Then
if K is large, so that the law of large numbers can be
assumed to hold, and so that end effects are
negligible:

3.1.4 Convexity Implications

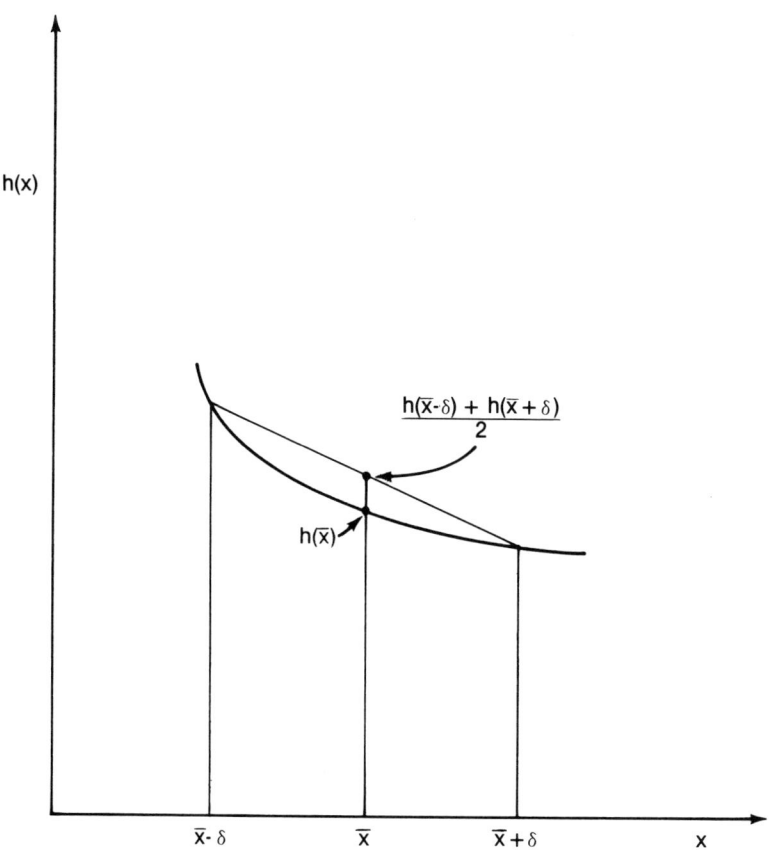

Figure 3.8 Convex function and illustration of Jensen's inequality.

$$E\{w(t,T(t))\} = \lim_{K\to\infty} \frac{1}{K} \sum_{t=1}^{K} w(t,T(t))$$

$$= \lim_{K\to\infty} \frac{1}{K} \sum_{i=1}^{n} i \cdot NUM[w(t,T(t)) = i]$$

$$= \lim_{K\to\infty} \sum_{i=1}^{n} i \sum_{\tau=1}^{\infty} \frac{NUM[w(t,T(t)) = i \text{ and } T(t) = \tau]}{K}$$

$$= \sum_{i,\tau} i \cdot \Pr[w(t,\tau) = i | T(t) = \tau] \cdot \Pr[T(t) = \tau]$$

using Bayes' theorem on conditional probability. If T(t) varies independently of the working set size, then:

$$\Pr[w(t,\tau) = i | T(t) = \tau] = \Pr[w(t,\tau) = i]$$

so that:

3.1.4 Convexity Implications

$$E\{w(t,T(t))\} = \sum_{i,\tau} i \cdot \Pr[w(t,\tau) = i] \cdot \Pr[T(t) = \tau]$$

$$= \sum_{i,\tau} i \cdot \Pr[w(t,\tau) = i \text{ and } T(t) = \tau]$$

$$= \sum_{i} i \cdot \Pr[w(t,T(t)) = i]$$

$$= E\{w(T(t))\}.$$

Thus, we can treat the time-varying working set size $w(t,T(t))$ as though it were a fixed function of a time-varying argument $T(t)$. Applying Jensen's inequality, if $T(t)$ is independent of the sequence of working set sizes:

$$E\{w(t,T(t))\} \leq w(E\{T(t)\}) . \tag{3.11}$$

Also, if fault rate function $f(T)$ is convex:

$$E\{f(t,T(t))\} \geq f(E\{T(t)\}) . \tag{3.12}$$

Varying the window size yields a larger mean fault rate and a smaller mean working set size as compared with a time-invariant window of length $E\{T(t)\}$. To show that this does not hold true for all variations of $T(t)$, consider the following periodic reference string and window size sequence:

```
r(t):  1 2 3 4 4 1 2 3 4 4 1 2 3 4 4 ...
T(t):  1 2 3 4 0 1 2 3 4 0 1 2 3 4 0 ...
```

For which $\bar{T} = E\{T(t)\} = 2$, $E\{w(t,T(t))\} = 2$, but $w(\bar{T}) = 1.8 < 2$ [note that $w(t,0) = 0$].

The corresponding results for Belady lifetime functions e(m) and f(m) are:

$$E\{e(m(t),t)\} \geq e(E\{m(t)\}) \qquad (3.13)$$

$$E\{f(m(t),t)\} \geq f(E\{m(t)\}) , \qquad (3.14)$$

again, for m(t) varying independently of e or f. Here, both the lifetime and the fault rate functions are convex. This may seem to be a contradiction: How can the mean lifetime and mean fault rate both be increased by dynamic allocation? The explanation is that the mean lifetime is **not** properly computed as an average of the lifetimes at each time instant, as is implicit in Jensen's inequality (c.f. [85])[5]. Suppose that page faults are observed at times $t_1, t_2, \ldots, t_j$ during a measurement interval of K references. Then if e(m(t)) denotes the average execution interval under allocation sequence m(t), we define:

$$e(m(t)) = \frac{1}{j+1} \sum_{1}^{j+1} [t_i - t_{i-1}]$$

where $t_0 = 0$ and $t_{j+1} = K$. Note that the interval from time zero until the first fault, and the interval from the last fault until time K, are included in the calculation. The expression is easily simplified to get:

$$e(m(t)) = K/(j+1)$$

[Compare this with f(m(t))=j/K to obtain a relation between the lifetime and fault rate functions valid even for small K.] As K (and j) become large:

---

5) By analogy, consider that average velocity is not computed by taking the average of each instantaneous velocity --- it is simply the total distance divided by the total time.

3.1.4 Convexity Implications

$$e(m(t)) \to K/j$$
$$= 1/E\{f(m(t),t)\}$$

but it can easily be shown by example that:

$$e(m(t)) \ne E\{e(m(t),t)\} \ .$$

Thus, although inequality (3.13) for $e(m,t)$ is correct as written, it does not imply that the mean lifetime is increased by dynamic allocation --- it decreases because the fault rate increases. Note that this only holds for variation of the memory size which is independent of the page fault rate. In particular, the memory size $m(t)=w(t,T)$ under the working set algorithm is correlated with the page fault probability $f(t,T)$, so the analysis is inapplicable for the working set. Even if $m(t)$ is varied at random, independent of the fault rate, the result may not hold in practice because of the phase-of-execution effect (we will see an example in theorem 4.22, section 4.2.2).

3.1.5 Bounded Locality Intervals

By using the stack algorithm concept, it is possible to specify the memory content under LRU paging for any memory size. If LRU performs well over some given reference string, we can assume that it is retaining the intrinsic locality set in memory at nearly all times, so we can simply define the extrinsic locality set to be the memory content (m most recently used pages) at each instant of time. But memory size m can have any value in the range $1 \le m \le n$. Thus, this yields n localities at each virtual time instant, where the locality of size ℓ is the set of pages in the top ℓ pages of the LRU stack. All localities are significant: the one to use is the one equal in size to the memory allocation (assuming that the allocation is externally imposed). But some locality sets will more accurately describe the task's behavior than others. A page should be currently in use to be considered truly in the task's locality.

Let $L(\ell,t)$ denote the (unordered) set of pages in positions 1 through ℓ of LRU stack $\underline{s}(t)$. If we observe the stack at times 1,2,...,t, we can determine the time t'≤t at which set L(ℓ,t) was **formed**. By this we mean that L(ℓ,t'-1)≠L(ℓ,t'), but that L(ℓ,t')=L(ℓ,t'+1)=...=L(ℓ,t). If a page at stack distance i is referenced, it changes the contents of stack positions 1,2,...,i, but the sets L(i,t), L(i+1,t), ... remain unchanged. Thus, we observe that the locality set L(ℓ,t) was formed at the time of the most recent occurrence of a distance exceeding ℓ.

When a locality set is formed, a non-locality page has replaced one which was in the locality, and it is possible that the task is in a period of rapid locality transition. Once all pages in a locality set are re-referenced after the set is formed, we are more secure in believing that a stable configuration has been reached. Madison and Batson [65] define an <u>activity set</u> to be a locality set, all of whose pages have been referenced since the set was formed. There are at most n such sets at any time, but there will usually be many fewer. There may even be none at all. For example, consider the following reference string with an empty initial LRU stack:

```
R =   1 1 2 1 2 1 3 4 5 4 5 5 6 4 5 6 6 5 5 6
D =   ∞ 1 ∞ 2 2 2 ∞ ∞ ∞ 2 2 1 ∞ 3 3 3 1 2 1 2

t =           5         10        15        20
```

At time 20, the LRU stack is:

    <u>s</u>(20) = [6,5,4,3,1,2]

The locality sets and their formation times are:

set		formation time
L(1,20)	{6}	20
L(2,20)	{5,6}	16
L(3,20)	{4,5,6}	13
L(4,20)	{3,4,5,6}	13
L(5,20)	{1,3,4,5,6}	13
L(6,20)	{1,2,3,4,5,6}	13

Of these, only L(2,20) and L(3,20) are activity sets. L(1,20) is not an activity set, since its page has not been referenced since its formation time. Page 3 is a

3.1.5 Bounded Locality Intervals

member of all localities of size exceeding 3, none of which can be an activity set since page 3 was last referenced before time 13. It is easy to confirm that if several sets are all formed at the same time, only the smallest has the possibility of being an activity set.

When a set is newly formed, we cannot know immediately that it is an activity set. We must wait until all its pages are re-referenced. But once a locality is determined to be an activity set, we consider it to have been in effect since its formation as a set. An activity set, together with its holding time, is called a bounded locality interval (BLI). The bounded locality intervals are shown below for the example reference string:

```
R = 1 1 2 1 2 1 3 4 5 4 5 5 6 4 5 6 6 5 5 6
D = ∞ 1 ∞ 2 2 2 ∞ ∞ ∞ 2 2 1 ∞ 3 3 3 1 2 1 2
    .   .           .   .   .   .
    .   .           .   .   .   .
    .   .           .   .   .   .    {4,5,6}
    .   .           .   .   .   |----------------
    .   .           .   .   .
    .       {1,2}         {4,5}           {5,6}
    .       |-------|     |-------|       |----------
    .                         .
    {1}                       {5}
    |---|                     |---|
```

Note the existence of an interval of locality transition [references r(7), r(8)] during which there is no BLI.

When more than one activity set exists at a given time, the largest such set includes the others as subsets. Madison and Batson [65] observed that these largest, or "level-one" BLI's tend to describe the major <u>phases</u> of execution[6]. This means that a task's macro-behavior can be described by its level-one BLI's. To do this, it may be necessary to ignore BLI's of less than some specified duration, as Madison and Batson observed many level-one BLI's having very short lifetimes.

It should be noted, however, that the largest activity set is not necessarily the best locality set to retain in memory. A smaller set, representing micro-behavior, may be preferable if the phase holding times are very long. Moreover, merely because a page is in a level-one BLI does not necessarily mean that the page is in use. If our sample reference string continues to reference only pages 5 and 6 after time 20, page 4 will nevertheless remain in the level-one BLI. In this case the level-two BLI, containing only pages 5 and 6, is a more accurate indicator of locality behavior. Batson and Madison [6] have investigated an alternative method which considers BLI's at all levels, and tries to find the one most appropriate at each time instant. However, the method requires extended searches and seems to be computationally expensive.

3.2 <u>Intrinsic Models of Locality</u>

In section 1.5.1, we discussed intrinsic locality models. Such a model is a probabilistic structure having states which imply locality page sets. Thus, the concepts of locality are built into the underlying structure of the model, rather than observed by the measurement of the reference string (as in the case of extrinsic models). Models we shall consider include the <u>independent reference model</u>, and a class of <u>simple</u>

---

[6] Note, however, that a BLI is terminated by referencing a page having an infinite stack distance, or even just a distance larger than the activity set associated with the BLI. But intuitively, we might consider a program to be in a single phase even if it occasionally references a new page --- say a previously unused data page. On the other hand, if <u>several</u> new pages are referenced in quick succession, then a phase transition has probably occurred.

3.2 Intrinsic Locality Models

stack models including the LRU stack model. These and others are special cases of a general locality model.

Of importance in the models we shall present are the dual concepts of a locality list and of a hierarchy of localities. These allow specification of locality sets of any given size to fit within any pre-specified memory allocation. Consider the pages of a modeled task at time t+1. Each page i has some probability of reference p(i,t+1) at that time, so we can rank the pages of the task by decreasing order of probability. This ranking will be called the locality list, and will be denoted L(t). We define the ranking L(t) on the basis of the probabilities $\{p(i,t+1)\}$, since we desire, as in other notation, to make L(t) the locality list after the occurrence of r(t). Suppose $L(t) = [x_1,\ldots,x_n]$, where the x_i are the pages of the task (all task pages are represented). Then we have:

$$p(x_1,t+1) \geq p(x_2,t+1) \geq \ldots \geq p(x_n,t+1)$$

and, of course:

$$p(x_1,t+1) + p(x_2,t+1) + \ldots + p(x_n,t+1) = 1.$$

Obviously, the pages x_i for small i are the pages most likely to be referenced at time t+1. However, they are not necessarily the lowest (long term) cost pages to retain in memory, since the locality list is subject to change at any time. But for a sufficiently short term (i.e., until the list changes), the pages x_i for small i are the lowest cost pages to retain in memory (we shall prove this).

A full hierarchy of localities consists of a single locality set of each size 1, 2,..., n. The locality at time t consisting of ℓ pages will be denoted $L(\ell,t)$. Suppose the locality list is $L(t) = [x_1,\ldots,x_n]$. Since localities are sets of highly probable pages, we define:

$$L(\ell,t) = \{x_1,\ldots,x_\ell\}.$$

In other words, the locality of size ℓ is the first ℓ members of $\underline{L}(t)$, or the ℓ most probable pages to be referenced at time t+1. The reader should note that there is a correspondence between paging algorithm stacks and memory contents on the one hand, and locality lists and locality sets on the other.

It seems reasonable (and for several models, we shall prove) that an attempt should be made to keep as large a locality set as possible in a given allocated memory space. This must be accomplished within the constraints of demand paging. For certain models (all simple stack models, section 3.2.3) it will be possible to retain L(m,t) in a memory of size m for all t with demand paging. This will be possible since for these models:

$$L(m,t+1) - L(m,t) = \begin{cases} \emptyset & \text{if } r(t+1) \in L(m,t) \\ \{r(t+1)\} & \text{if } r(t+1) \notin L(m,t) \end{cases}$$

In other words, if the locality changes, the change will be in only a single page. Moreover, the new locality page will be referenced at the time of the transition, so it can be fetched into memory on demand.

For other intrinsic locality models (such as the general locality model, section 3.2.1, and the independent reference model, section 3.2.2), it will not be possible to retain L(m,t) in memory at all times. In the case of the independent reference model, the optimal algorithm will succeed in retaining L(m-1,t) in memory at all times.

Since $\underline{L}(t)$ is an ordering of all pages of a task, it can be used as the priority list of a priority paging algorithm (section 2.3.2). This priority algorithm will always replace the least probable page in memory, and will thus tend to keep mostly high probability pages in memory. This algorithm will be proved optimal for several intrinsic locality models. Thus, for the independent reference model, all simple stack models, and certain other models, an optimal paging algorithm will be a priority algorithm having $\underline{PL}(t) = \underline{L}(t)$ for all t. We shall call this algorithm the _locality priority algorithm_ (LPA). As noted in section 2.3.2, this algorithm will be a stack algorithm (as will any priority algorithm).

3.2 Intrinsic Locality Models

With fixed memory allocation, the LPA replaces the lowest priority page in $\underline{L}(t)$ at each page fault time t. Replacements for fixed allocation paging algorithms occur only at page fault times. If variable allocation is desired, the LPA will still be optimal in the following sense: Memory expansion in a demand algorithm can occur in increments of only one page, at page fault times. Thus, no replacement decision is involved for memory expansion. Suppose memory contraction at time t is desired (whether or not at the time of a page fault), and suppose k pages are to be removed from memory. Then the k lowest probability pages in $\underline{L}(t)$ should be removed.

However, it should be noted that replacements other than that of a single page at each page fault time may destroy the stack property of the LPA. For example, let $\underline{L}(t)$ be fixed, as follows:

$\underline{L}(t) = [1,2,3]$, for all t.

Consider two memory allocation sequences. The first is:

$[m_1(t)] = 1,2,3,2,2$, $1 \leq t \leq 5$

and the second is:

$[m_2(t)] = 1,2,2,2,2$, $1 \leq t \leq 5$.

Let $S_1(t)$ denote the contents of memory under LPA paging using sequence $[m_1(t)]$; similarly for $S_2(t)$ and $[m_2(t)]$. Both memories are assumed to be initially empty. Below are shown the consequences of a possible reference string (asterisks denote the occurrence of page faults):

```
t    =  1  2  3  4  5

r(t) =  1  2  3  1  3

        *  *  *     *
S₁(t) = 1  1  1  1  1
           2  2  2  3
              3

        *  *  *
S₂(t) = 1  1  1  1  1
           2  3  3  3
```

Page 3 has been removed from $S_1(3)$ to get $S_1(4)$. Although $m_2(t) \leq m_1(t)$ for all t, $S_2(4) \not\subseteq S_1(4)$, and the stack property is destroyed. Once this occurs, it is possible for the larger memory to experience a higher page fault rate, as can be seen at time 5.

We have mentioned the use of extrinsic models to estimate intrinsic localities. The most useful extrinsic measurement seems to be the working set; this will be the extrinsic model of prime concern to us. We shall discuss the ability of the working set to estimate intrinsic localities. Intrinsic models whose locality can be estimated accurately by the working set are of special interest, since the LPA and all optimal paging algorithms we shall discuss require locality information.

Finally, as we have noted, it is essential that any proposed model be validated to compare its behavior with real tasks. In chapters 5 and 6, we shall discuss the results of such validation experiments.

3.2.1 A General Locality Model (GLM)

We now propose a quite general intrinsic model [85] which is motivated by the ideas of locality. Associated with a task during an interval of execution will be a locality list sequence $L(1), L(2), \ldots$, with $L(t)$ the locality list in effect at time t. Any

3.2.1 A General Locality Model

permutation of the task page set $N=\{0,1,\ldots,n-1\}$ may appear as a locality list. Thus, there are n! states in this intrinsic model, corresponding to the range of possible locality lists.

It is possible to be more specific about the nature of the locality list sequence. Let us number the possible locality lists of a task: $\underline{L}_1, \underline{L}_2, \ldots, \underline{L}_k$. Since we assume that localities usually change slowly, we expect that there exist time intervals $t, \ldots, t+i$ during which $\underline{L}(t) = \underline{L}(t+1) = \ldots = \underline{L}(t+i)$. Thus, we postulate a holding time for each locality list, and we can write the locality list sequence in shortened form as a sequence of pairs $(\underline{L}_{i_1}, T_1)(\underline{L}_{i_2}, T_2)\ldots$, where $\underline{L}_{i_j}$ is a locality list and T_j is the holding time of that locality list. For example, the sequence $(\underline{L}_2, 3)(\underline{L}_1, 4)\ldots$ means that the locality list sequence is $\underline{L}_2 \underline{L}_2 \underline{L}_2 \underline{L}_1 \underline{L}_1 \underline{L}_1 \underline{L}_1 \ldots$ In this example, a locality list transition occurs at times 4 and 8.

During the holding time of a given locality list, the page reference probabilities of a GLM task are free to vary in any manner, provided the ranking implied by the locality list is obeyed. The probabilities will in general be time-varying and dependent on the current state and history of the task. During the holding time of a given locality list, the GLM is equivalent to the "almost stationary" independent reference model (section 3.2.2), which assumes a single fixed locality list. However, locality list transitions build the dynamic, or time-varying, aspects of locality into an intrinsic model. These transitions, which can occur as often as every reference, make the GLM very different from the independent reference model.

Figure 3.9 shows the general locality model pictorially. The locus of task execution proceeds from locality list to locality list. The hierarchy of localities is shown within each list. Looking at the figure, it seems intuitively clear that the GLM is sufficiently robust to approximate closely the behavior of almost any real task. The locality lists change arbitrarily often; any possible permutation on N may be a locality list; and reference probabilities

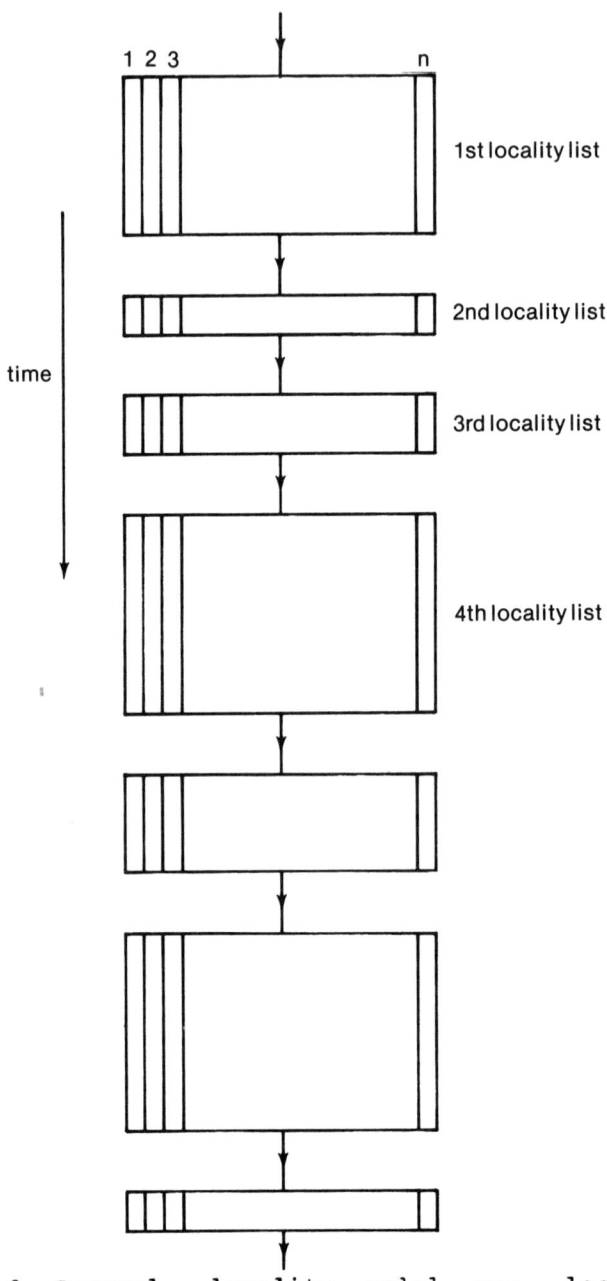

Figure 3.9 General locality model --- locus of locality lists.

3.2.1 A General Locality Model

are non-stationary and task-state-dependent.

We can now define a (time-varying) <u>semi-Markov process</u> in which the states are the locality lists. To do this, we assume a holding time probability function $h(x,\underline{L},t)$, defined to be the probability that the holding time of $\underline{L}$ is x, given that a locality list transition to $\underline{L}$ occurs at time t. We also define a set of transition probabilities $\{p(i,j,t)\}$ for $1 \leq i, j \leq k$, where $p(i,j,t)$ is the probability that $\underline{L}(t)=\underline{L}_j$, given that $\underline{L}(t-1)=\underline{L}_i$ and that $\underline{L}(t) \neq \underline{L}(t-1)$. A <u>configuration</u> of this model at time t is a pair $c(t)=(\underline{L},y)$, where $\underline{L}$ is the locality list in effect at time t and y is the <u>residual</u> holding time for $\underline{L}$. The next configuration $c(t+1)=(\underline{L}',y')$ is determined as follows:

a) If $y=0$, a new locality list $\underline{L}'$ is selected according to the transition probabilities of the semi-Markov process. A holding time T is chosen according to the probability function $h(T,\underline{L}',t+1)$; set $y'=T$.

b) If $y>0$, $\underline{L}'=\underline{L}$ and $y'=y-1$.

The GLM has many appealing qualities. It allows either a slow drift among neighboring localities (micro-behavior), or a sudden change to a disjoint locality (macro-behavior, change of phase). Indeed, since the reference probabilities and list holding times are non-stationary, almost any type of program behavior imaginable can be described by this model. Unfortunately, the model is descriptive, rather than generative, and its structure is too general to yield to validation or to much analysis. Thus we shall consider some special cases, both descriptive (for use in analysis) and generative (for both analysis and simulation).

3.2.2 The Independent Reference Model (IRM): Static Locality

This intrinsic, generative model was studied by Aho, Denning, and Ullman [1]. It assigns to each page x∈N a fixed stationary probability p(x) of being referenced. Thus, there are n-1 independent parameters, p(1),p(2),...,p(n-1), or any other choice of n-1 out of n. References at any given time are selected by an independent trials process, without regard to the state or the history of the task. Though it is a crude model for real tasks, it can be used as a benchmark against which to compare the validity of more complex models[7]. As the first non-trivial model for which an optimal paging strategy was proved, it has historical interest as well.

The model examined by Aho, Denning, and Ullman was actually more general than that described above. They required for their analysis only that the page reference probabilities be "almost stationary" --- the probabilities could change slightly provided that the ranking by probability remained fixed. We call this generalization the _almost stationary independent reference model_. Clearly, this is a special case of the GLM with only a single locality list.

Suppose an IRM task has n pages: then there is a hierarchy of n localities. The ith locality L(i) consists of the i most probable pages. Since reference probablities are fixed (or almost stationary) in this model, the localities remain fixed throughout the lifetime of the IRM task. This is an example of _static locality_. In particular, since phase-type behavior cannot be exhibited by this model, the IRM must be considered a _micro-model_.

Aho, Denning, and Ullman have shown that the optimal paging strategy for stationary, or almost stationary, IRM tasks is to replace the lowest probability page in memory. Thus, the LPA is optimal for this model. It can be easily seen that such a replaced page will never be in L(m-1) for memory allocation m. The optimal algorithm retains L(m-1) in memory; the mth page frame is taken up by the most recently referenced page not in L(m-1). In terms of the demand paging definition of section 2.3, the replaced page z(t) is the only page in memory not in L(m-1). It can be easily shown that this algorithm implements the expected forward distance criterion

---

7) That is to say, one could question whether a more complicated model is sufficiently more accurate than the IRM to justify its complexity.

3.2.2 The Independent Reference Model

(section 2.3.1), which is truly optimal for the IRM.

Although the independent reference model does define a hierarchy of localities, it is undesirable as an intrinsic locality model for several reasons. The primary one is that the localities in this model are of static content. This conflicts with our intuitive notions of how a non-trivial task executes. We expect that the locality list should be slowly changing for most of the time span of the task, with occasional rapid changes. The experiments we describe in chapter 5 support the inadequacy of the IRM as a model of realistic task behavior.

3.2.3 Simple Stack Models

This class of program behavior models is based on the concept of a stack algorithm. Let A be a non-lookahead stack algorithm[8]. For the simple A stack model (which we shall often refer to in shortened form as the A stack model), a distance string $d(1)d(2)...d(K)$ is generated as a sequence of independent trials, where:

$$Pr[d(t)=i] = a_i, \text{ for all } t, 1 \leq i \leq n. \quad (3.15)$$

The set $\{a_i\}$ is called the set of distance probabilities. The a_i are assumed to be stationary, so that this model is the distance string analog of the independent reference model. If the initial stack $\underline{s}(0)$ containing all n pages is specified, we have seen (section 2.3.2) that the distance string $d(1)...d(K)$ uniquely defines the stack at each of the times $1,...,K$. Even if $\underline{s}(0)$ is unknown, the stack sequence can be reconstructed to within a renaming of the pages. Thus, we assume that the stack is known in

---

[8] The model of primary interest is based on the LRU paging algorithm, which is, of course, a stack algorithm. We choose to develop a class of models for an arbitrary stack algorithm because some of the analytical results will apply to any such model.

this model. The reference string r(1)...r(K) is also uniquely determined, since for all t, $r(t) = s_1(t)$. We refer to this as the "simple" A stack model, because methods of generating a distance string more sophisticated than (3.15) have been proposed, as we shall see in section 4.3.

It will be convenient to define a set of cumulative distance probabilities. We define:

$$A_i = a_1 + a_2 + \ldots + a_i . \qquad (3.16)$$

Note that if locality $L(m,t)$ is in memory, $1-A_m$ is the probability of a page fault at time t+1.

By proper selection of the a_i, we can cause the simple A stack model to exhibit locality. The pages referenced most recently tend to be those near the top of the stack, so to cause the clustering of references associated with locality we would expect the a_i to be biased toward the top of the stack. We define the locality set of size ℓ for the simple A stack model to be the top ℓ pages of the stack $\underline{s}(t)$:

$$L(\ell, t) = \{s_1(t), \ldots, s_\ell(t)\} .$$

Clearly, in the simple A stack model, $L(\ell,t)$ and $L(\ell,t+1)$ are either identical, or differ by one page. This is a <u>micro-model</u>, since only slow changes in the locality set are possible. In keeping with the idea of a locality set, we should require that all pages within the locality be favored (have a not-lower probability) over all those outside the locality. For a specific value of ℓ, this requirement is equivalent to:

$$\min\{a_1, \ldots, a_\ell\} \geq \max\{a_{\ell+1}, \ldots, a_n\} . \qquad (3.17)$$

We shall refer to this as the <u>weak locality condition</u> (with respect to ℓ) on the a_i. A necessary and sufficient condition for every locality in the <u>full hierarchy</u> to have its members favored is that the a_i

3.2.3 Simple Stack Models

be monotonically non-increasing:

$$a_1 \geq a_2 \geq \ldots \geq a_n \; . \tag{3.18}$$

Inequality (3.18) will usually be assumed for all simple A stack models. We shall refer to this as the **strong locality condition** on the a_i.

It is clear that the A stack model is a special case of the GLM. If the strong locality condition holds, the locality list and stack are identical. Thus, we define $\underline{L}(t) = \underline{s}(t)$ for all t, and if the stack is known, so is the locality list. A full hierarchy of localities can be defined under the condition of strong locality.

If only the weak locality condition holds for some given locality size ℓ, the stack and locality list are not the same. In this case, $\underline{L}(t)$ will consist of the pages in $\underline{s}(t)$ reordered by decreasing a_i. For locality size ℓ, the top ℓ pages of $\underline{L}(t)$ and the top ℓ pages of $\underline{s}(t)$ are the same set. However, if we try to define a locality set of some other size $\ell' \neq \ell$, we find that the top ℓ' pages of the stack and of the locality list do not agree in general. In this case, our definition of $L(\ell',t)$ as the top ℓ' pages of the stack is inconsistent with the requirement that the pages in the locality set have highest probability of reference. For this reason, we shall only speak of the locality of size under the weak locality condition.

3.3 On the Optimal Paging Algorithm for the GLM

One of our objectives is to show that the LPA is optimal for various intrinsic locality model tasks. However, this statement is not true for the general locality model, because locality lists can change rapidly and arbitrarily. For example, suppose m=2. Consider a locality list $\underline{L}=[1,2,3]$ at time t, with a residual holding time of h time units. Clearly, $L(m,t)=\{1,2\}$. After these h time units, the new locality list will be $\underline{L}'=[1,3,2]$ with probability 1.

Suppose the probability structure within $\underline{L}$ is such that $p(2,t')=p(3,t')=0$ for all times t' in the range $t<t'\leq t+h$. Let the memory content be $S(t)=\{2,3\}$ and suppose $r(t+1)$ is page 1 (this is not surprising). This causes a page fault, and either page 2 or page 3 must be replaced. Since page 2 is in $L(m,t+1)$ and page 3 is not, the LPA would choose page 3 for replacement. But in this case, page 2 is probably the better replacement, since neither 2 nor 3 will be referenced during the remainder of the holding time of list $\underline{L}$; but 3 will be in the new locality $L(m,t+h+1)$, whereas 2 will not.

Nevertheless, while the current locality list is in effect, the LPA is an optimal paging algorithm. Thus, the LPA minimizes the <u>short</u> term expected cost. This follows immediately from the proof by Aho, Denning, and Ullman [1] of the optimality of the LPA for the independent reference model --- we have noted that the almost stationary IRM is a GLM having only a single locality list. Thus, using the notation of section 2.3.1, we have:

<u>Proposition 3.2</u> Let $\underline{L}(t)=[x_1,\ldots,x_n]$ have a residual holding time of at least h time units with probability 1, for an instance of the GLM. Then for $0\leq k\leq h$ and for $i<j$,

$$C_k(S-x_i,t) \geq C_k(S-x_j,t)$$

for any set of pages $S \subseteq N$ containing both x_i and x_j.

This means that if x_i and x_j are possible page replacements, the one having lower priority in $\underline{L}(t)$ will be the better short-term choice. We conjecture that if locality list holding times are sufficiently

3.3 On GLM Optimal Paging

long, the effects of future lists will be negligible, so that barring certain pathological cases[9], the LPA will be optimal, even in the long term.

---

9) Which might occur if the pages in two successive locality list positions continue to have the same probability. Then either page is an equally good candidate for replacement, but the LPA will always choose the lower priority page, which might be sub-optimal when the list changes.

Chapter 4
The LRU and Related Stack Models

4.1 Paging in Simple Stack Models

The simple stack model of primary interest to us is the simple LRU (Least Recently Used) stack model. LRU is the best-known fixed allocation, non-lookahead, demand paging algorithm. Of course, the OPT algorithm (also a stack algorithm) is superior. However, it makes little sense to define a "simple OPT stack model", since the OPT algorithm implies exact knowledge of future references; whereas future references generated by simple stack models are by definition stochastic. Models corresponding to other stack algorithms, although well-defined, are probably less accurate approximators of realistic program behavior than the LRU model. Suppose this were false for some stack algorithm A≠LRU. Then the A stack model would be as valid as the LRU stack model; as a result, we would expect that paging algorithm A would be as good as the LRU paging algorithm (we shall prove this in proposition 4.6). No such stack algorithm A is known. Moreover, the stack updating procedure for LRU is the least complex of all stack algorithms; hence the LRU model is easier to understand than other stack models.

Nevertheless, it is convenient to discuss optimal paging in terms of the simple A stack model for arbitrary stack algorithm A. The fact that optimality of the LPA (section 3.2) does not depend on the particular properties of the LRU algorithm indicates the strength of the result, and the proof is essentially the same.

Recall from section 3.2.3 that for the simple A stack model, a distance string (with respect to algorithm A's stack) is generated as a series of independent trials. The probability of distance i is given by a_i, $1 \leq i \leq n$. We shall use the following notation. Let:

4.1 Paging in Simple Stack Models

$d(x,\underline{s})$ denote the distance of page x in stack $\underline{s}$.

$\underline{s}.x$ denote the updated stack after page x is referenced in stack $\underline{s}$. (In particular, the page at the top of $\underline{s}.x$ is x.)

We will use dynamic programming formulation (2.5) to prove the LPA optimal for simple A stack model tasks. If the distance probabilities a_i satisfy the strong locality condition (3.18), we will show that it is optimal to replace the page farthest down in the stack. This page cannot be in locality set L(m,t) for a memory of size m. Later, we shall prove a somewhat weaker result under the weak locality condition (3.17).

Let w be the page *in memory* which is farthest down in a stack model's stack at some time instant (there may be pages not in memory which are below w in the stack). In order to apply an induction argument, we shall need to know something about the page farthest down at the succeeding instant. If the next reference is higher than w in the stack, then w will remain farthest down. If the next reference is below w, then w may no longer be lowest; however, at most one page can move below w. These statements are proved in the following lemma:

Lemma 4.1 Suppose w∈S, and $d(w,\underline{s})>d(x,\underline{s})$ for all x∈S-w, for the simple A stack model with stack $\underline{s}$. Suppose page y∈N is referenced. Then:

a) If $d(y,\underline{s})<d(w,\underline{s})$, then $d(w,\underline{s}.y)>d(x,\underline{s}.y)$ for all x∈S-w.

b) If $d(y,\underline{s})>d(w,\underline{s})$, then there is at most one page x∈S such that $d(x,\underline{s}.y)>d(w,\underline{s}.y)$.

Proof Part a) is immediate, since only those pages in positions 1,2,...,$d(y,\underline{s})$ in $\underline{s}$ can have different positions in $\underline{s}.y$.

Suppose part b) is false. Since w is not referenced, w cannot move up the stack, so $d(w,\underline{s}.y) \geq d(w,\underline{s})$. Consider stack algorithm A operating with a memory allocation of size $m = d(w,\underline{s}.y)$, as shown in figure 4.1. All pages in the set S are in memory before y is referenced. Assuming b) false, there are distinct pages $u,v \in S$ such that $d(u,\underline{s}.y) > d(v,\underline{s}.y) > d(w,\underline{s}.y)$, so that pages u and v are both removed from memory when y is referenced. But this is impossible for a fixed allocation demand paging algorithm.

□

We define the minimal-expected-cost function for the simple A stack model by adapting the dynamic programming formulation in (2.5). Here we shall write $C_k(S,\underline{s},t)$, since the cost depends on the initial stack $\underline{s}$. Recall that this is the **minimal** expected cost over the next k references, starting with memory content S and stack $\underline{s}$ at time t. We have:

$$C_0(S,\underline{s},t) = 0$$

$$C_{k+1}(S,\underline{s},t) = \sum_{x \in S} p(x,t+1) C_k(S,\underline{s}.x,t+1)$$

(4.1)

$$+ \sum_{x \in \bar{S}} p(x,t+1) [1 + \min_{z \in S} C_k(S+x-z,\underline{s}.x,t+1)]$$

Note a possible point of confusion: we shall use the notations $\underline{s}$ or $\underline{s}(t)$ to mean the **stack model's stack**, not the stack of the paging algorithm processing references from the model[1]. We are now ready to prove the optimal non-lookahead, demand paging algorithm for the simple A stack model. In the following several theorems, we shall not require the stack distance probabilities to be strictly stationary --- it will

---

1) The two stacks can be very different. For example, one might use the OPT **paging algorithm** to process references from a simple LRU stack **model** task. The OPT and LRU stacks will obviously differ.

4.1 Paging in Simple Stack Models   101

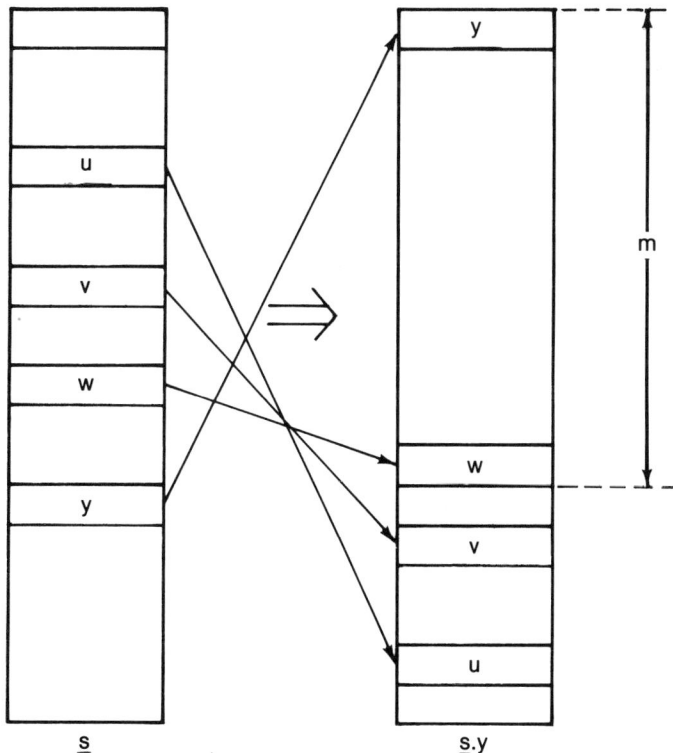

Figure 4.1 Proof of lemma 4.1, part b

only be necessary that their _ranking be preserved_.
Thus, an _almost stationary_ simple A stack model is
said to satisfy the strong locality condition if:

$$a_1(t) \geq a_2(t) \geq \ldots \geq a_n(t)$$

for all t, but $a_i(t)$ need not equal $a_i(t+1)$. The weak
locality condition for an almost stationary model is
similarly defined.

Theorem 4.2 Suppose an almost stationary simple A
stack model satisfies the strong locality
condition. Let w'∈S be the page in memory lowest
in the stack, so that $d(w', \underline{s}) > d(x, \underline{s})$ for all
x∈S-w'. Let w∈S be any other page in S. Then for
all k≥0:

$$C_k(S-w, \underline{s}, t) \geq C_k(S-w', \underline{s}, t) .$$

Proof The theorem is clearly true for k=0, since in
that case both costs are zero.

Now, suppose the theorem is true for all k≤K, for
some number K. We shall prove it true for k=K+1.
Using (4.1), let:

$$C_{K+1}(S-w, \underline{s}, t) - C_{K+1}(S-w', \underline{s}, t) = \nabla_1 + \nabla_2 + \nabla_3 + \nabla_4 + \nabla_5$$

where:

4.1 Paging in Simple Stack Models 103

$$\nabla_1 = \sum_{\substack{x \in \\ S-w-w'}} p(x,t+1)[C_K(S-w,\underline{s}.x,t+1) - C_K(S-w',\underline{s}.x,t+1)]$$

$$\nabla_2 = p(w,t+1) - p(w',t+1)$$

$$\nabla_3 = p(w,t+1)[\min_{z \in S-w} C_K(S-z,\underline{s}.w,t+1) - C_K(S-w',\underline{s}.w,t+1)]$$

$$\nabla_4 = p(w',t+1)[C_K(S-w,\underline{s}.w',t+1)$$
$$- \min_{z' \in S-w'} C_K(S-z',\underline{s}.w',t+1)]$$

$$\nabla_5 = \sum_{x \in \overline{S}} p(x,t+1)[\min_{z \in S-w} C_K(S-w+x-z,\underline{s}.x,t+1)$$
$$- \min_{z' \in S-w'} C_K(S-w'+x-z',\underline{s}.x,t+1)]$$

We shall consider the ∇_i individually:

∇_1: By lemma 4.1 part a), $d(w',\underline{s}.x)$ is still the largest distance of pages in S. Therefore, $\nabla_1 \geq 0$ by the inductive hypothesis.

∇_2: By the strong locality condition, $\nabla_2 \geq 0$, since $d(w',\underline{s}) > d(w,\underline{s})$.

∇_3: By lemma 4.1 part a), $d(w',\underline{s}.w)$ is still the largest distance. Therefore $z=w'$ is an optimal replacement by the inductive hypothesis. Therefore $\nabla_3 = 0$.

V_4: Choosing z'=w (perhaps non-optimal) makes V_4=0. Therefore, choosing an optimal replacement z' must make $V_4 \geq 0$.

V_5: There are three cases, depending on which page in S has greatest distance in s.x :

> **w' is greatest** By the inductive hypothesis, z=w' is an optimal replacement choice. Choosing z'=w (perhaps non-optimal) makes V_5=0. Therefore, choosing an optimal replacement z' must make $V_5 \geq 0$.
>
> **w is greatest** By lemma 4.1 part b), w' has the greatest distance in s.x among pages in S-w. Thus, z=w' is optimal by the inductive hypothesis. Also by the inductive hypothesis, z'=w is optimal. Thus V_5=0.
>
> **y∈S-w-w' is greatest** By the inductive hypothesis, z=y and z'=y are optimal. By lemma 4.1 part b), w' has the greatest distance among pages in S+x-y. Therefore, by the inductive hypothesis, $V_5 \geq 0$.

Since we have shown that $V_i \geq 0$ for all i, their sum is non-negative and the theorem is proved.
□

Corollary 4.3 Consider a reference string generated by an almost stationary simple A stack model with strong locality. Suppose r(t)∉S(t-1), a page fault. Then the lowest cost page z(t) to replace is the page farthest down in the model's stack s(t).

Proof In theorem 4.2, use S=S(t-1)+r(t) and s=s(t).
□

4.1 Paging in Simple Stack Models

Theorem 4.2 shows that the least cost page to replace is the page farthest down in the stack <u>after</u> the stack is updated to reflect the reference which caused the fault. This is exactly the LPA when $\underline{L}(t)=\underline{s}(t)$ for all t, which is our definition of $\underline{L}(t)$ under the strong locality condition.

Now, consider the memory content for simple A stack model tasks under LPA paging. From corollary 2.4, we know that the LPA [the priority algorithm with priority list $\underline{L}(t)$] is equivalent to a priority algorithm whose priority list equals the LPA's stack. However, even though $\underline{L}(t)=\underline{s}(t)$ for all t, this does not necessarily imply that the LPA's stack is identical to the model's stack $\underline{s}(t)$. In particular, if locality $L(m,0)$ is not loaded initially into memory at time 0, the initial stack of the LPA will not equal the initial stack of the model. The top m pages of the LPA's stack will be $S(m,0)$ initially, but the top m pages of the model's stack $\underline{s}(0)$ will by definition be $L(m,0)$.

On the other hand, once the locality of size m is acquired into memory, it is easily seen that the LPA will retain the locality in memory thereafter. This is true even in the case of the weak locality condition (3.17), for which $\underline{L}(t) \neq \underline{s}(t)$ in general. We shall now prove it assuming the weak locality condition. Note that strong locality is an instance of weak locality, so the proof applies in the strong locality case as well:

<u>Proposition</u> 4.4 Consider an almost stationary simple A stack model satisfying at all times the weak locality condition for locality size $\ell = m$. Suppose $S(t')=L(m,t')$ for some t'. Then for all $t \geq t'$, the LPA will keep $S(t)=L(m,t)$.

Proof   By   assumption, $S(t')=L(m,t')$.   Suppose
$S(t)=L(m,t)$ for some $t \geq t'$. If $r(t+1) \in S(t)$, then
there is no page fault and $S(t+1)=S(t)$. But
$L(m,t+1)=L(m,t)$ in this case, since $d(t+1) \leq m$ and
only the pages in stack positions $1,2,..,d(t+1)$ can
have different positions in the updated stack. If
$r(t+1) \notin S(t)$, a page fault occurs, then
$L(m,t+1)=L(m,t)+r(t+1)-y$, where y is the page
removed from the locality by the stack updating
procedure. Page y is at some distance $d > \ell$ in
stack $\underline{s}(t+1)$. But because of the weak locality
condition, page y will have lowest probability in
$\underline{L}(t+1)$ of all pages in $S(t)=L(m,t)$, so the LPA will
choose page y for replacement. Thus,
$L(m,t+1)=S(t+1)$ in this case, too.

□

Proposition 4.4 implies the optimal paging
algorithm for simple A stack models satisfying only
the weak locality condition, provided the locality is
initially in memory:

Proposition 4.5 Suppose an almost stationary simple A
stack model satisfies at all times the weak
locality condition for locality size $\ell = m$, and
suppose that $S(t')=L(m,t')$ for some time t'. Then
the LPA is optimal for all $t \geq t'$.

Proof By proposition 4.4, we have $S(t)=L(m,t)$ for all
$t \geq t'$. Thus, the m most probable pages at time t
will be in memory at time t, for all $t \geq t'$. This
clearly has at least as low an expected cost as
another paging algorithm for which $S(t) \neq L(m,t)$ for
some $t \geq t'$.

□

Note that under the weak locality condition with
$\ell = m$ and the locality initially in memory, the LPA
reduces to the following algorithm: replace the page
which leaves the locality. This is identical to using
algorithm A as the paging algorithm. If $S(t) \neq L(m,t)$
for some time t, the LPA is still optimal starting at
t if the strong locality condition holds. However,
since $\underline{L}(t)=\underline{s}(t)$ (where $\underline{s}(t)$ is the model's stack) for

4.1 Paging in Simple Stack Models

all t in this case, it is clear from proposition 2.3 that the LPA implements stack algorithm A. Thus we have:

Proposition 4.6 Algorithm A is optimal for the almost stationary simple A stack model starting at time t, if either of the following two conditions holds:

a) the strong locality condition,

or

b) the weak locality condition with $\ell = m$, and $S(t) = L(m,t)$.

□

If the locality is in memory at some time, we have seen that the LPA will retain it there. We shall now demonstrate that even if $S(t) \neq L(m,t)$, the LPA will eventually cause $S(t') = L(m,t')$ for some $t' > t$:

Proposition 4.7 Suppose for an almost stationary simple A stack model that $|L(m,t) - S(t)| = \nabla(t) > 0$. Then under the LPA paging algorithm, $\nabla(t+1) \leq \nabla(t)$.

Proof There are four cases:

$\underline{r(t+1) \in S(t) \cap L(m,t)}$ Then $S(t+1) = S(t)$ and $L(m,t+1) = L(m,t)$. Therefore $\nabla(t+1) = \nabla(t)$.

$\underline{r(t+1) \in S(t) \cap \overline{L}(m,t)}$ Then $S(t+1) = S(t)$. Also, $L(m,t+1) = L(m,t) + r(t+1) - y$, for some page y. If $y \in S(t)$ then $\nabla(t+1) = \nabla(t)$; otherwise $\nabla(t+1) = \nabla(t) - 1$.

$\underline{r(t+1) \in \overline{S}(t) \cap L(m,t)}$ Then $S(t+1) = S(t) + r(t+1) - z$, for some page z. Since the paging algorithm is the LPA, we must have $z \notin L(m,t+1)$, since the lowest priority page in memory can never be one of the m most probable pages when $\nabla(t) > 0$. We also have $L(t+1) = L(t)$. Thus $\nabla(t+1) = \nabla(t) - 1$.

$r(t+1) \in \bar{S}(t) \cap \bar{L}(m,t)$. Then $S(t+1) = S(t) + r(t+1) - z$, for some replaced page $z \notin L(m,t+1)$. But $L(m,t+1) = L(m,t) + r(t+1) - y$, for some page y. If $y \in S(t+1)$ then $\nabla(t+1) = \nabla(t)$; otherwise $\nabla(t+1) = \nabla(t) - 1$. □

Corollary 4.8 Under LPA paging, there exists time t', such that $S(t) = L(m,t)$ for all $t \geq t'$.

Proof The third case above, $r(t+1) \in \bar{S}(t) \cap L(m,t)$, will periodically occur. □

Once the locality set is acquired into memory by the LPA, it is easy to evaluate the cost of paging, since exactly the locality will be retained thereafter in memory. The expected cost of any reference $r(t)$ is simply the probability of a non-locality reference, which is

$$a_{m+1}(t) + a_{m+2}(t) + \ldots + a_n(t).$$

We have proved:

Proposition 4.9 Suppose for an almost stationary simple A stack model that $S = L(m,t)$ for stack $\underline{s}$ at time t. Suppose the distance probabilities $\{a_i(t')\}$ satisfy either the weak locality condition for locality size $\ell = m$, or the strong locality condition, for all $t' > t$. Then for all $k \geq 0$:

$$C_k(S, \underline{s}, t) = \sum_{i=1}^{k} [1 - A_m(t+i)]$$

where $A_m(t') = a_1(t') + \ldots + a_m(t')$. □

4.1 Paging in Simple Stack Models

If the distance probabilities $\{a_i(t)\}$ are <u>stationary</u> (constant in time), then once the locality is acquired into memory, the page fault probability is also constant:

$$f(m,t) = f(m) = a_{m+1} + \ldots + a_n \qquad (4.2)$$

$$= 1 - A_m .$$

For the (stationary) simple A stack model, the page fault times are independent of one another, so that the lifetimes are independent, geometrically distributed random variables having the probability distribution:

$$\Pr[e(m) \leq x] = 1 - A_m^x . \qquad (4.3)$$

When an active interval for a task is about to begin, it is often desirable to preload an initial set of pages into memory, to prevent an initial cluster of page faults. For simple stack models, it is fairly obvious that the optimal set to preload is the locality set equal in size to the memory allocation. This can be proven as follows: if the locality is initially in memory, it will remain in memory under control of the optimal LPA. Since the locality is the set of most probable pages at every time instant, this set must have minimal cost. No other policy can yield a lower page fault probability at any time. Therefore, we have:

<u>Proposition</u> 4.10 Consider an almost stationary simple A stack model satisfying at every time instant either the weak locality condition for locality size $\ell = m$, or the strong locality condition. Then $S(t) = L(m,t)$ is an optimal initial memory content at time t; i.e., for any $S'(t) \subseteq N$ with $|S'(t)| = m$:

$$C_k(S'(t),\underline{s},t) \geq C_k(S(t),\underline{s},t) \quad \text{for all } k \geq 0.$$

□

An obvious question is: What is the added cost of

starting with a non-optimal memory content? We can use proposition 2.1 on prepaging algorithms to put an upper bound (albeit weak) on this added cost:

<u>Proposition</u> <u>4.11</u> Consider sets $S, S' \subseteq N$, with $|S|=|S'|=m$ and $S=L(m,t)$. Let $\nabla = |L(m,t)-S'|$. Then for all $k \geq 0$:

$$C_k(S', \underline{s}, t) \leq C_k(S, \underline{s}, t) + \nabla .$$

<u>Proof</u> Immediately prepage all ∇ members of $L(m,t)-S'$ into memory set S', removing ∇ non-locality pages. This costs ∇ pages fetched. Now $S=S'$ and thus the cost of the remaining processing is the same for both. By proposition 2.1, there is a demand algorithm at least as good as the above prepaging algorithm; hence the result.

□

Combining propositions 4.10 and 4.11, we have an upper and a lower bound on the cost starting with any memory content S'. Defining ∇ as in proposition 4.11, and assuming stationary distance probabilities:

$$C_k(L(m,t), \underline{s}, t) = k(1-A_m) \leq C_k(S', \underline{s}, t)$$

$$\leq C_k(L(m,t), \underline{s}, t) + \nabla$$

$$= k(1-A_m) + \nabla .$$

Dividing by k and taking limits:

$$\lim_{k \to \infty} C_k(S', \underline{s}, t)/k = 1-A_m , \qquad (4.4)$$

regardless of S' and $\underline{s}$. For the almost stationary

4.1 Paging in Simple Stack Models   111

model, the corresponding result is:

$$\lim_{k\to\infty} C_k(S',\underline{s},t)/k = \lim_{k\to\infty} \frac{1}{k} \sum_{i=1}^{k} (1-A_m(t+i)) \qquad (4.5)$$

provided, of course, that the limiting average value of $1-A_m(t)$ exists. The long-run cost per reference of using the optimal paging algorithm A is independent of the initial memory content or stack. Since the LPA eventually acquires the locality set into memory, and retains it once acquired, this result is expected.

By comparing theorem 4.2 and proposition 4.5, we see that most of the complication in the proof of the former comes from assuming an arbitrary initial memory content. Thus, if a poor estimate of the initial locality set is pre-loaded into memory at the start of an active interval, the LPA will still be optimal, if the strong locality condition applies. If only the weak locality condition holds, then the LPA will become optimal once the locality set is acquired into memory. In either case, the initial memory content has no effect on the long-run cost per reference when using the LPA (or algorithm A).

4.2 The LRU Stack Model (SLRUM)

Although we have presented and analyzed a class of many stack models, we are primarily interested in the simple LRU stack model (SLRUM). This is the model that we intuitively expect to resemble real programs, and is (to our knowledge) the only simple stack model that has been experimentally validated (section 5.2.1). These experiments have shown the simple LRU stack model to approximate well some aspects of the working set behavior of real programs. We shall now consider some of the properties of SLRUM tasks operating under a fixed memory allocation. In section 4.2.2 we shall consider variable allocation.

4.2.1 Properties of the Simple LRU Stack Model

The SLRUM has been applied in several models [70, 71, 72, 85] of multiprocessing systems. Its popularity was based originally on the fact that LRU seems to perform well as a paging algorithm. It is also the most understandable member of the class of simple stack models, because of the relative simplicity of the LRU stack updating procedure.

We shall follow common terminology and refer informally to the SLRUM as the LRU stack model. Figure 4.2 illustrates the stack updating procedure in the model. A referenced page is moved to the top of the stack, while all pages which were formerly above it are pushed down one position. Of course, pages below the point of reference remain fixed.

Since the LRU stack model is an intrinsic locality model, an important issue is the accuracy with which the locality of a given size can be measured extrinsically[2]. Without locality information, the optimal LPA paging algorithm cannot be implemented. In the case of the LRU stack model, the working set exactly measures an intrinsic locality. In fact, $W(t,T)=L(\ell,t)$, where ℓ is the number of distinct pages among $r(t-T+1)...r(t)$. This is apparent when one considers that the working set consists of the $w(t,T)$ most recently used pages. Thus, to determine $L(\ell,t)$ for a given ℓ for the LRU stack model, choose any window size T such that $w(t,T) = \ell$[3]. The working set $W(t,T)$ is then the desired locality. The ease and accuracy of locality measurement in this model enhances its usefulness.

We shall now prove several results about LRU stack model tasks. These results apply specifically to the LRU stack model, and not to simple A stack models in general. The first result shows that a page

---

2) For some useful, generative program models (c.f. [85]), the locality set can only be estimated, not exactly measured, because of the difficulty of identifying pages which leave the locality set.

3) The value of T will be time-varying in general. Another approach is to maintain an LRU stack for the given task --- this makes the entire locality list known.

4.2.1 LRU Stack Model Properties

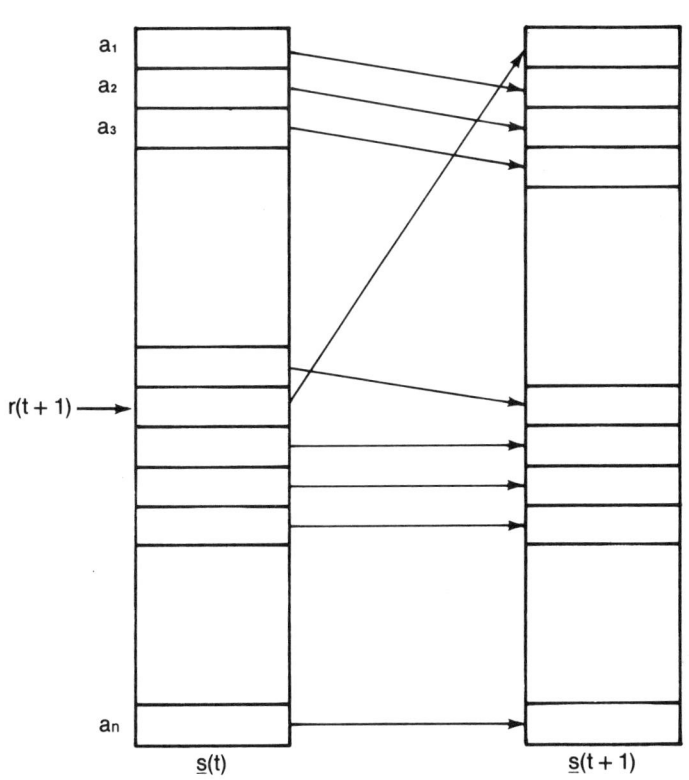

Figure 4.2 SLRUM stack updating procedure

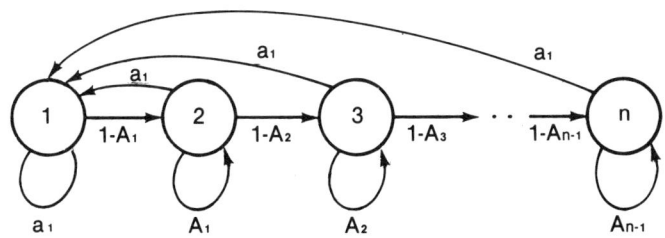

Figure 4.3 Tagged page in an LRU stack model

anywhere in the LRU stack at time t "forgets" its time t position at time t+k, for large k. In fact, no matter where a page is located in an initial stack, the page is equally likely to be in any stack position after a sufficiently long time interval.

We will make one additional assumption in the following analysis: we will assume that a_n, the probability of referencing the page at the bottom of the stack, is non-zero. If we had $a_n=0$, the page at the bottom could never be referenced, and might as well be removed from the model. Requiring $a_n>0$ is necessary and sufficient to guarantee that all n pages will be referenced eventually.

Let us construct a Markov chain whose states are the positions of some given page x in the stack. Thus, state 1 corresponds to x appearing at the top of the stack, etc. See figure 4.3. It is easily seen that the transition probabilities for the Markov chain are as follows:

$p(i,1) = a_i$ $1 \leq i \leq n$

$p(i,i) = A_{i-1}$ $2 \leq i \leq n$

$p(i,i+1) = 1-A_i$ $1 \leq i \leq n-1$

$p(i,j) = 0$ otherwise.

Since $a_n>0$, page x can be cycled through all states ...1,2,...,n,1,... by successive references to stack position n. Thus, the Markov chain is ergodic (Kemeny and Snell [59]), and non-decomposable.

Now, as must be the case for a Markov chain:

$$\sum_j p(i,j) = 1 \quad \text{for all } i.$$

4.2.1 LRU Stack Model Properties

But we shall now show, additionally, that:

$$\sum_i p(i,j) = 1 \quad \text{for all } j.$$

There are two cases. If $j=1$ then:

$$\sum_i p(i,1) = a_1 + \ldots + a_n = 1.$$

If $j \neq 1$ then:

$$p(j-1,j) + p(j,j) = 1 - A_{j-1} + A_{j-1} = 1.$$

Thus, we have a so-called <u>doubly stochastic</u> transition probability matrix. It is well known (c.f. Feller [38]) that the equilibrium state-occupancy probabilities of such a Markov chain are all equal, provided the chain is ergodic. We have just proved:

<u>Proposition</u> <u>4.12</u> Let x∈N be a page of an LRU stack model task with $a_n > 0$. Then

$$\lim_{t \to \infty} \Pr[d(x,\underline{s}(t)) = i] = 1/n, \quad 1 \leq i \leq n$$

independent of the position of page x in initial stack $\underline{s}(0)$.
□

By comparison, consider the simple LIFO stack model (see section 2.3.3 for a definition of the LIFO, or Last-In-First-Out, paging algorithm). Pages in the LIFO stack appear in increasing order of <u>first</u> occurrence in the reference string, except for the page in position 1, which is the current reference. Thus, a given page x in the LIFO stack can occupy only one of three possible stack positions, 1, k(x), or k(x)+1, at any time, for some k(x)≥1.

<u>Corollary 4.13</u> Consider an LRU stack model with $a_n > 0$.

Then the expected number of references to any page x∈N in the reference string r(1)...r(t) is t/n, for t large.

<u>Proof</u> By the above proposition, $\Pr[d(x,\underline{s}(t))=1] = 1/n$ for t large. Thus, page x is at the top of the stack (hence referenced) an expected fraction 1/n of the references.
□

Corollary 4.13 points out an apparently undesirable feature of the LRU stack model; namely, that all pages are referenced an expected equal number of times in a long time interval. In a real task, some pages are referenced more frequently than others in the long run. However, values of a_i for i>6 or so are usually very small (on the order of .0001) when the LRU stack model is fit experimentally to real tasks. Thus it will require a long time interval, indeed, actually to observe an equal distribution of references. Although the model is stationary, for typical $\{a_i\}$ distributions it generates (in effect) non-stationary reference strings, as pages far down in the stack are slowly referenced and brought to the top. Recall that the SLRUM is a <u>micro-model</u>, applying only within a single phase of program behavior. Phases will generally be much too short to achieve statistical equilibrium of the model.

If all stack distance probabilities are non-zero, it is possible to prove a stronger result than proposition 4.12; namely, that all possible <u>permutations of pages</u> in the stack are asymptotically equally likely:

4.2.1 LRU Stack Model Properties

Proposition 4.14 Let $\underline{s}$ be any permutation of the page set $N=\{0,1,\ldots,n-1\}$ of an LRU stack model task with $a_i > 0$ for $1 \le i \le n$. Then

$$\lim_{t \to \infty} \Pr[\underline{s}(t) = \underline{s}] = 1/n!$$

independent of the initial stack $\underline{s}(0)$.

Proof Consider a Markov chain having n! states corresponding to all possible LRU stack orderings. Each state can be entered in n ways, by referencing any of stack positions $1,\ldots,n$. Thus the sum of transition probabilities into any state is $a_1 + \ldots + a_n = 1$, and the matrix is doubly stochastic.

Since the a_i are all non-zero, it is clear that any state can be reached from any other in a finite number of steps, so the chain is ergodic[4]. Hence, all states are equally probable in equilibrium. □

Not only are all stacks equally likely, but the stacks at times far apart are asymptotically **independent**:

---

[4] In order to guarantee ergodicity, it is clearly not necessary, only sufficient, that all a_i be non-zero.

Since most realistic LRU stack models have all non-zero distance probabilities (see chapter 5), we shall not investigate this further.

Proposition 4.15 In an LRU stack model task with $a_i > 0$, $1 \le i \le n$ and $n \ge 2$, the stacks $\underline{s}(t)$ and $\underline{s}(t+k)$ are asymptotically independent for large k.

Proof It is only necessary to show that the Markov chain of proposition 4.14 is regular [59]; i.e. --- that there exists j such that given $\underline{s}(t)$, any of the n! states are possible at time t+j. The proof is by induction on n. For n=2, there are only two states and j=1. Suppose the proposition is true for all n<n'. For n=n', it is possible for any page in the stack to move into position n in precisely n-1 references. If only stack positions 1,...,n-1 are referenced thereafter, the result is proved by the inductive hypothesis.
□

The following two corollaries relate to the discussion of locality property 3 (section 2.4) on the asymptotic uncorrelation of references, and to the discussion of normally distributed working set sizes (section 3.1.1).

Corollary 4.16 In an LRU stack model task with $a_i > 0$, $1 \le i \le n$, the references $r(t)$ and $r(t+k)$ are asymptotically independent for large k.

Proof Immediate from proposition 4.15, since $r(t)$ is at the top of the stack for all t.
□

Corollary 4.17 Working set sizes of an LRU stack model task, with all distance probabilities non-zero, are approximately normally distributed.

Proof This is the Denning-Schwartz [36] result for asymptotically uncorrelated reference strings.
□

4.2.1 LRU Stack Model Properties

Thus, to the extent that the LRU stack model reflects realistic program behavior, we expect that working set sizes within a single phase of execution will be approximately normal. This is only meaningful if the variance of the working set size is reasonably large, which will often fail to occur within a single phase. In appendix A we derive the exact distribution of working set sizes of an LRU stack model task. The result does not appear to resemble a normal distribution; however, simulations by Coffman and Ryan [21] have shown it to be very nearly normal, as we have demonstrated in corollary 4.17.

Note that proposition 4.12 is not enough to guarantee asymptotic independence (even non-correlation) of references. For instance, if

$$a_i = \begin{cases} 0 & \text{if } i \neq n \\ 1 & \text{if } i = n \end{cases}$$

then the pages cycle around in the stack position by position, so that $r(t) = r(t+k)$ if and only if k is divisible by n.

We will now show that the optimal paging algorithm for LRU stack model tasks implements the <u>expected</u> <u>forward</u> <u>distance</u> <u>criterion</u> (section 2.3.1). That is to say, the page with the expected longest time until next reference is replaced. First we shall prove a lemma which is interesting in its own right, since it gives a simple expression for the expected time until the next reference to a page currently in any given stack position.

<u>Lemma</u> <u>4.18</u> Let g(i) denote the expected time until the next reference to a page currently in stack position i, in an LRU stack model with $a_n > 0$. Then:

$$g(i) = (n-i+1)/(1-A_{i-1}), \quad 1 \leq i \leq n,$$

where we define $A_0 = 0$.

Proof Using the Markov chain introduced in proposition 4.12, we note that a page in stack position i, 1<i<n, can move in three ways when a reference is processed. It can remain in the same position, it can move to position i+1, or it can be referenced and move to position 1. If it moves to position i+1, its expected time until next reference _from that time on_ is g(i+1), since the Markov chain has no memory. Likewise, if it remains in position i, its expected time until next reference from that time on is g(i). Thus, for 1<i<n we can write:

$$g(i) = p(i,1)[1] + p(i,i)[1+g(i)]$$
$$+ p(i,i+1)[1+g(i+1)].$$

Substituting the forms for the transition probabilities as given in the proof of proposition 4.12, we have for 1<i<n:

$$g(i) = a_i + A_{i-1}[1+g(i)] + (1-A_i)[1+g(i+1)],$$

so that:

$$g(i) = [g(i+1)(1-A_i) + 1]/[1 - A_{i-1}] \qquad (4.6)$$

For the case i=1, we have:

$$g(1) = p(1,1) + p(1,2)[1+g(2)] = g(2)[1-A_1] + 1,$$

confirming (4.6) for i=1 as well.

4.2.1 LRU Stack Model Properties

Now we use backwards induction to prove the statement of the lemma. For i=n, the page cannot move farther down the stack. It is referenced with probability a_n and remains in position n with probability $1-a_n$. This is a simple independent trials process, so that $g(n)=1/a_n$, which proves the lemma for i=n.

Now, suppose the lemma is true for all i>i', for some i'≥1. We shall prove it true for i=i'. By (4.6) and the inductive hypothesis, we have:

$$g(i') = \frac{1}{1-A_{i'-1}} \left[\frac{n-i'}{1-A_{i'}} (1-A_{i'}) + 1 \right]$$

$$= \frac{n-i'+1}{1-A_{i'-1}}$$

□

Note that lemma 4.18 gives $g(1)=n$, which is consistent with corollary 4.13. We now prove that the expected forward distance criterion is in fact optimal for LRU stack model tasks, under the conditions of proposition 4.5. That is, the weak locality condition will be assumed, and the locality will be assumed to be initially in memory. A corresponding result can be proved given the strong locality condition without requiring that the locality be initially in memory; however, the proof is similar so we shall omit it.

<u>Proposition 4.19</u> Consider an LRU stack model task having $a_n>0$. Suppose $S(0)=L(m,0)$ initially, and suppose the weak locality condition holds for locality size m. Then:

$g(m+1) \geq g(i)$, for all i≤m .

Proof By the weak locality condition, there exists a positive real number c such that $\min\{a_1,\ldots,a_m\} \geq c \geq \max\{a_{m+1},\ldots,a_n\}$. Let $\lambda = 1-A_m$.

By lemma 4.18 we have:

$$g(m+1) = (n-m)/\lambda.$$

For $i \leq m$, we have:

$$g(i) = \frac{n-i+1}{a_i+\ldots+a_m+\lambda}$$

$$\leq \frac{n-i+1}{(m-i+1)c+\lambda}$$

$$= \frac{(m-i+1)+(n-m)}{(m-i+1)c+\lambda}$$

Suppose the proposition is false. Then there exists $j \leq m$ such that $g(j) > g(m+1)$, or:

$$\frac{(m-j+1)+(n-m)}{(m-j+1)c+\lambda} > \frac{n-m}{\lambda}$$

which can be easily manipulated to $\lambda > c(n-m)$. But $c(n-m) \geq a_{m+1}+\ldots+a_n = \lambda$, which is a contradiction.

□

In the LRU stack model, a page leaving $L(m,t)$ must enter stack position $m+1$. Thus proposition 4.19 shows that the page leaving the locality at a page fault time has at least as long an expected time until next reference as any page in the locality. Removing the non-locality page implements the expected forward

4.2.1 LRU Stack Model Properties

distance criterion.

In the strong locality case, it can be similarly shown that $g(i+1) \geq g(i)$ for all i: the expected time until next reference is monotonically non-decreasing down the stack.

4.2.2 The LRU Stack Model Under Dynamic Allocation

We have stressed the fact that any simple stack model defines a full hierarchy of localities at every time instant. Thus, regardless of the memory allocation, there is always a locality that will exactly fit into memory. But suppose the memory allocation is allowed to vary, so that m(t) denotes the allocation at time t. We would like to show that it is optimal to retain in memory the locality of size m(t), for all t. We let the locality size grow and shrink to fit the changing memory allocation. Of course, the LPA still applies; whenever one or more pages must be removed from memory, those of lowest priority in the locality list should be chosen. If $S(0) = L(m(0),0)$ initially, then the priority list $\underline{L}(t)$ and the LPA stack will be identical, so that the lowest stacked pages will always be replaced, keeping $L(m(t),t)$ in $S(t)$ for all t. We shall prove this. Compare with the example in section 3.2, in which it was shown that for another kind of model (fixed locality list), that $L(m(t),t)$ might not remain in memory.

There is no difficulty with this procedure if the allocation shrinks at some point, since pages can be removed from memory to adjust the locality size. But if the allocation suddenly expands, additional pages must be added to enlarge the locality. These pages are not, by our assumption, loaded immediately; they are fetched on demand when they are next referenced. The expanded memory will be partially empty for a while until the enlarged locality can be acquired. This is undesirable and unrealistic. The only circumstance in which this will not occur is when the allocation is increased by exactly one page frame at the time of a page fault. In that case, the missing page is loaded, but no pages are replaced, so that the added space is used immediately. Note that this is the only means by which the dynamic allocation paging algorithms of section 2.3.3, working set, VMIN, and PFF, expand their allocations.

We assume that the sequence of memory allocations $m(0), m(1), \ldots$ is imposed by an external mechanism. This allows us to compare different paging algorithms knowing that their allocations at each time instant will be the same. Moreover, we require that for all t, $m(t) \leq m(t-1)+1$, and if $m(t) = m(t-1)+1$ then $r(t) \notin S(t-1)$, a page fault. We allow the allocation to be reduced at any time by any amount, under the definition of loose demand paging (2.3). A memory allocation sequence satisfying these constraints will be called a <u>demand allocation sequence</u>.

We shall now prove that if memory initially contains the locality of an LRU stack model task satisfying the strong locality condition, then the LPA is optimal under an arbitrary demand allocation sequence.

<u>Theorem 4.20</u> Consider an almost stationary LRU stack model task satisfying the strong locality condition at every time instant. Suppose $m(0), m(1), \ldots$ is a demand allocation sequence, and suppose $S(0) = L(m(0), 0)$. Then the LPA minimizes the expected frequency of page faults over all non-lookahead, demand paging algorithms operating under this allocation sequence.

<u>Proof</u> The proof consists in showing that under LPA control, $S(t) = L(m(t), t)$ for all t. Thus, at every time t, the $m(t)$ pages most probable of reference are in memory. The expected cost of such an algorithm is clearly minimal.

For $t=0$, $S(0) = L(m(0), 0)$ by assumption. Suppose $S(t-1) = L(m(t-1), t-1)$; we shall prove that $S(t) = L(m(t), t)$. There are three cases:

4.2.2 SLRUM Under Dynamic Allocation

__m(t)≤m(t-1)__
Since the stack of the LRU stack model and the LPA priority list are identical, those pages removed from memory by the LPA will be those at the bottom of the updated LRU stack.

__m(t)=m(t-1)__
$S(t)=L(m(t),t)$ by proposition 4.4.

__m(t)=m(t-1)+1__
In this case, $r(t) \notin S(t-1)$ and $S(t)=S(t-1)+r(t)$. We also have $r(t) \notin L(m(t-1),t-1)$. By the particular properties of the LRU stack, if $r(t) \notin L(m(t-1),t-1)$ then $L(m(t-1)+1,t)=L(m(t-1),t-1)+r(t)$ [as can be easily seen since the page leaving $L(m(t-1),t-1)$ enters stack position $m(t-1)+1$]. Thus $S(t)=L(m(t),t)$.

□

In particular, we can show:

__Corollary 4.21__ Let $w(1,T), w(2,T), \ldots$ be the sequence of working set sizes of an LRU stack model task satisfying the strong locality condition. Let the memory allocation sequence be $m(t)=w(t,T)$ for all t. Then if $S(0)=W(0,T)=\emptyset$, the working set algorithm is optimal (minimal expected page fault rate) with respect to the given memory allocation sequence.

__Proof__ As we have noted, $W(t,T)=L(w(t,T),t)$ for the LRU stack model. The working set is a perfect estimator of the locality. The result follows from the above theorem.

□

Thus, we see that the working set algorithm is optimal for LRU stack model tasks (satisfying the strong locality condition) with respect to the sequence of working set sizes. In like manner, the LRU algorithm is optimal with respect to a fixed memory allocation. If the working set is used to measure an SLRUM locality, we may either vary the window size to achieve an optimal fixed allocation algorithm, or we may simply fix the window size and achieve a dynamic allocation algorithm which is optimal for the generated memory size sequence.

In theorem 4.20, we have assumed a demand allocation sequence to prevent the occurrence of empty page frames. But since the allocation can expand at page fault times and no other times, the allocation sequence is dependent in part on the paging algorithm. This weakens the result, which shows, in effect, that the LPA is optimal with respect to an allocation sequence whose expansion times are determined by the LPA.

Another way to compare two dynamic allocation algorithms, without introducing empty page frames, is by means of the VMIN cost function [73] of section 2.3.1. In particular, if two such algorithms have equal mean allocations in virtual time, we may simply compare their page fault rates. Using Jensen's inequality (section 3.1.4), we can easily show that <u>static allocation</u> is superior to dynamic for LRU stack model tasks with stationary distance probabilities and strong locality:

<u>Theorem 4.22</u> Let $m(0),m(1),...,m(K-1)$ be a demand allocation sequence with virtual-time-average value $\bar{m}$ (assumed to be an integer). Let $r(1)...r(K)$ be generated by a stationary LRU stack model satisfying the strong locality condition. Consider two paging algorithms: one generating the memory set sequence $S(0),S(1),...,S(K-1)$, and the other generating $S'(0),S'(1),...,S'(K-1)$, with $S(t)=L(\bar{m},t)$ and $S'(t)=L(m(t),t)$, for all t. Then the expected number of page faults generated under fixed allocation $\bar{m}$ does not exceed that generated under the time-varying allocation.

4.2.2 SLRUM Under Dynamic Allocation

Proof The page fault probability function $f(m,t)$ versus m is:

$$f(m,t) = 1-A_m = a_{m+1} + \ldots + a_n .$$

Comparing the slopes (derivatives) of successive line segments in the graph of this function [since the derivative of piecewise-linear function $f(m,t)$ does not exist for integer m, we will consider points on the curve at $i\pm.5$, for integer i]:

$$f'(i+.5,t)-f'(i-.5,t) = (-a_{i+1})-(-a_i)$$

$$\geq 0$$

by the strong locality condition. Thus, the page fault probability function is convex. Moreover, it is time-invariant since by assumption the distance probabilities are constants. Thus, we can apply Jensen's inequality to show:

$$E\{f(m(t),t)\} \geq f(m) .$$

□

This result is not intended to show that LRU is better than working set, nor that the LRU stack model is a failure. Since the model simulates only intra-phase task behavior, this result applies only within a single phase of execution. Even then, it is not known whether the effect is observable in real tasks. The working set algorithm is responsive to changes in locality set size at phase transitions, but LRU is not. Since working set is known to improve over LRU empirically for real tasks, we see that some model of macro-behavior is necessary to study dynamic allocation.

4.2.3 A Model with an Explicit Locality Set

Many reference strings, particularly short ones, exhibit a preferred locality set size. Reference string A of section 3.1.2 is an example. The **Very Simple Locality Model (VSLM)** has been proposed [87] as a model of such strings. In this model, the (sole) locality set has a fixed size of   pages. All pages within the set are equally probable of reference. All non-locality pages are likewise equally probable. If a non-locality page is referenced, it enters the locality set, replacing the least-recently-used locality page[5].

We can choose LRU stack model distance probabilities to duplicate the VSLM. Let λ be the probability of reference to any non-locality page at time t. Let the locality set size be $\ell = |L(t)|$, fixed for all t (see figure 4.4). Then:

$$p(x,t) = \begin{cases} (1-\lambda)/\ell & \text{if } x \in L(t-1) \\ \lambda/(n-\ell) & \text{if } x \notin L(t-1) \end{cases}$$

so that:

$$a_i = \begin{cases} (1-\lambda)/\ell & 1 \leq i \leq \ell \\ \lambda/(n-\ell) & \ell < i \leq n \end{cases} \qquad (4.7)$$

to obtain the VSLM. This model is characterized completely by only three parameters: ℓ, λ, and n.

In order that the strong (or weak) locality condition be satisfied for this model, we must have $a_\ell \geq a_{\ell+1}$, or after manipulation:

$$\lambda \leq (n-\ell)/n \ . \qquad (4.8)$$

Under this condition, LRU is the optimal paging algorithm for VSLM-generated reference strings, by proposition 4.6.

---

5) The model as originally proposed is not quite as specified here; however, the essential details are the same.

4.2.4 Choosing the Distance Probabilities

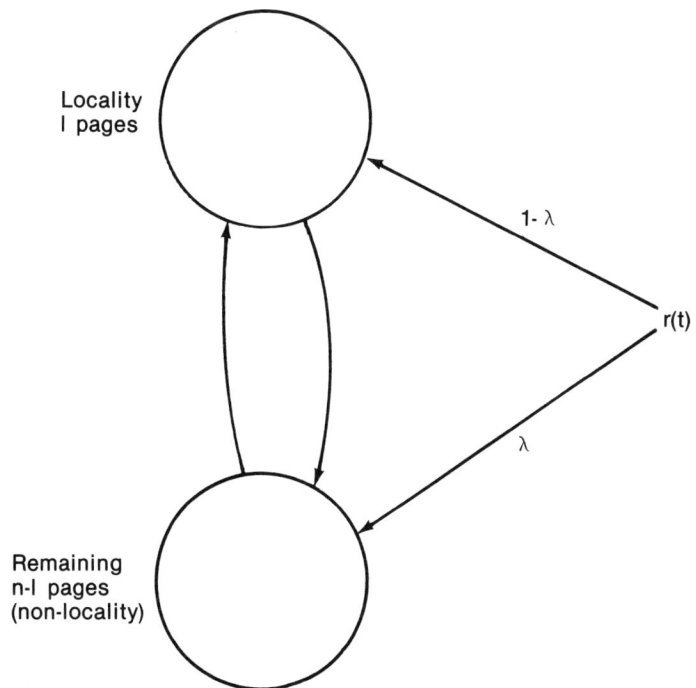

Figure 4.4 The very simple locality model

4.2.4 Choosing the Distance Probabilities for the SLRUM

By maintaining an LRU stack, one can count the occurrences of each distance in some measured reference string. These counts, divided by the total length of the string, can be used as the distance probabilities of an LRU stack model which approximates the measured task. We shall discuss particulars of this method in chapter 5.

However, the above procedure requires measurement of n-1 parameters (the nth distance probability is determined by normalization). The measurement procedure is not difficult, but models more parsimonious are often desirable. If all distance probabilities are specified by only a few parameters, the parameters can be perturbed to model various forms of behavior. This is especially useful if the parameters have an intuitive meaning, for example the locality set size.

Belady's lifetime function (section 3.1.2) gives the page fault rate as a function of the memory allocation. Since the page fault rate for a single reference is just the fault probability, we can equate them in the model. Thus we have:

$$f(m,t) = 1-A_m = m^{-b}/a$$

for parameters a and b, so that:

$$a_1 = 1-1/a$$

$$a_i = [(i-1)^{-b} - i^{-b}]/a , \quad i>1 .$$

(4.9)

For many applications, it will be necessary to normalize this form for a_i, since the program has only n pages altogether. This is accomplished by dividing each a_i by $1-n^{-b}/a$. If a simple but rough formulation is desired, one might use the binomial theorem to get:

4.2.4 Choosing the Distance Probabilities

$$a_i = [(i-1)^{-b} - i^{-b}]/a$$

$$\approx (b/a)i^{-b} \qquad i \leq i \leq n \qquad (4.10)$$

which has the same form as Belady's lifetime function. However, the error introduced by this approximation is quite large for small and moderate i, exceeding ten percent for i as high as 10. Nevertheless, it is often a usable approximation since Belady's lifetime function is itself imprecise. As before, this form for a_i may have to be normalized.

Thus, we can create a reasonable program model by choosing a, $b \approx 2$, and n. The value of b is a measure of the <u>degree of locality</u> of the program: the greater b is, the steeper will be the decline in page fault rate as page frames are added. One advantage of approximation (4.10) is that it is not necessary to estimate parameter a; one need only choose values for b and n, then normalize. Subsequently, n and b can be varied to model programs of differing size and degree of locality, respectively.

We have thus far assumed that Belady's lifetime function applies for $1 \leq m \leq n$. This is often reasonable in a model of <u>steady state</u> performance, in which faults due to first references to each of the n pages are to be ignored. We can easily model the effect of first faults into the set $\{a_i\}$ by adding the term n/K, K the length of the reference string, to the fault probability $1 - A_m$ at each memory size m. Let the set $\{A_1, A_2, \ldots, A_n\}$ be normalized so that $A_n = 1$. Then to include the effect of first faults, we choose

$$A'_i = A_i - n/K$$

which is equivalent to

$$a'_i = A'_i - A'_{i-1} = \begin{cases} a_1 - n/K & \text{if } i=1 \\ a_i & 1 < i \le n \end{cases}$$

$$a'_\infty = n/K .$$

Note that we now have probability a'_∞ of generating a distance infinity, presumably by referencing a page for the first time. But since all pages are initially in the stack, the first reference to any given page might actually occur by generation of a finite distance. It is therefore unclear how to update the LRU stack when an infinite distance does occur. However, in many applications, only the distance string --- not the reference string --- is required of the model. Then, if the distance probabilities are chosen in this way, a tail-off will often be observed in the lifetime curve at some n'<n (see section 3.1.2).

4.3 Extensions to the LRU Stack Model

One of the most striking statistical features of the SLRUM is that the page fault probability

$$f(m,t) = 1 - A_m$$

is constant for all t. Page faults in fact occur independently of each other, as a Bernoulli process (the discrete-time analog of a Poisson process). Intuitively, we expect that page faults will often occur in bursts, during transitions between disjoint localities. Program macro-behavior is not simulated by the model. In any application in which statistics more detailed than the mean fault rate are required, this may not be an adequate functional model.

Lewis and Shedler [62] have pointed out that there exists a certain theoretical basis to justify a Bernoulli page fault sequence. So-called *rare event theory* allows characterization of processes, such as page faults, which hardly ever occur. A result of

4.3 Extensions to the LRU Stack Model

this theory is that (under suitable conditions) if the event is rare enough, it will be Poisson [26]. However, it is not clear that page faults are rare enough for this effect to be realized. In addition, the available theory is really not very general --- its mathematical basis is the deletion (or "thinning") of independently chosen events of some process until the remaining events resemble a Poisson process. Thinning of events in a page fault process corresponds to increasing the memory allocation, so that fewer and fewer faults occur. In LRU stack model tasks, independently selected faults are deleted at each increase of allocation, since an increase from m-1 to m eliminates the page faults caused by references to distance m. But in real tasks, there seem to be sufficient dependencies among successive distances to render the theory inapplicable for moderate allocations. For very large allocations there is, however, evidence [62] that the rare event theory may begin to take effect.

Some proposed extensions to the LRU stack model have involved more sophisticated methods of distance string generation than independent trials. The direct motivations have been to predict the un-Poisson-like clustering of page faults [83], and to predict working set page fault rate and memory demand behavior more accurately [3] (see section 5.2). The tendency for page faults to cluster has been demonstrated in experiments [62, 63]; we have noted its explanation as a phase transition effect. Even for transitions between overlapping localities, some poorly designed paging algorithms can choose high cost replacements, causing a temporarily high fault rate.

Markov distance string models of various types are capable of predicting bursts in the page fault rate. In one type of model, the Markov states are chosen to be the stack distances themselves. Markov state transition probability p_{ij} then denotes the probability that a distance i is immediately followed by a distance j. If the matrix $[p_{ij}]$ is strongly diagonalized, small distances will tend to be followed by small distances and large by large. However, since only the most recently generated distance is remembered, any tendency to cluster will take the form of _uninterrupted runs_ of large distances, which is not especially realistic. Consider a transition between disjoint localities: after a page in the new locality is initially referenced, it will often be re-referenced several times before the next new page is accessed. Thus, small distances will be interspersed among large. For example, if $L_1 = \{0,1,2\}$ and $L_2 = \{3,4,5\}$ are two localities, the reference sub-string just before and after a transition might be:

$$R = \ldots\ 1\ 2\ 1\ |\ 4\ 4\ 4\ 3\ 3\ 4\ 3\ 4\ 5 \ldots$$
$$L_1L_2$$

If pages 3, 4, and 5 have not been referenced recently, the corresponding distance string D might be:

$$R = \ldots\ 1\ 2\ 1\ 4\ 4\ 4\ 3\ 3\ 4\ 3\ 4\ 5 \ldots$$
$$D = \ldots\ 1\ 2\ 2\ 20\ 1\ 1\ 22\ 1\ 2\ 2\ 2\ 23 \ldots$$

We may define a "large distance" to be anything exceeding a task's preferred locality size. Tests on the distance strings of a few real tasks on an IBM 360 showed the fraction of large distances in a large distance "cluster" to be small, about .01-.05. (The lengths of successive intervals between large distances were printed out, then subjectively grouped into clusters.) A model capable of predicting this behavior would have long dependencies --- each distance depending on the previous 20 or so. We shall present such a model momentarily, but first we shall discuss a special case of the above Markov model devised by Shedler and Tung [83].

4.3.1 Shedler and Tung's Model

The transition probability matrix for a Markov distance string model has n^2 entries, which is hardly parsimonious, even though the probabilities can be

4.3.1 Shedler and Tung's Model

easily estimated from a measured distance string[6]. Reducing the number of parameters has a purpose other than simplicity: it more precisely specifies the type of behavior we want, since obviously not all Markov models exhibit a large distance clustering tendency. One way to coalesce parameters is to specify the transition probabilities as functions of i and j. For example, one might try (c.f. Lewis and Yue [63]):

$$p_{ij} = a_i e^{b_i |i-j|}$$

which has only n freely chosen parameters $b_1, \ldots, b_n$ (the values of $a_1, \ldots, a_n$ are determined by normalization). Another approach, used by Shedler and Tung, is simply to assume some of the transition probabilities to be zero. Their model is expressed as an (n, ℓ) graph --- examples for (5,2) and (7,3) are shown in figure 4.5. The vertices are states (stack distances), and the edges are the allowable state transitions (those with non-zero probability). Distances 1,...,ℓ correspond to references from within the locality of size ℓ. Any two such distances can appear consecutively. Distances exceeding ℓ can occur only in the pattern:

... 1 d d+1 ... d+i 1 ...

for any d>ℓ and any i such that d+i≤n. The assumption is that pages of a new locality will tend to appear in consecutive order somewhere down in the stack. Loosely speaking, stack distances in this model can be thought of as a two "state" phenomenon, although it is not actually possible to lump the states of the model into a small distance state and a large distance state.

Shedler and Tung have used this model in a queueing analysis of multiprogramming, but there are undoubtedly other Markov distance string models which come closer to reproducing observed reference

---

[6] The maximum likelihood estimate of p_{ij} is the fraction of occurrences of the sequence i,j in the distance string.

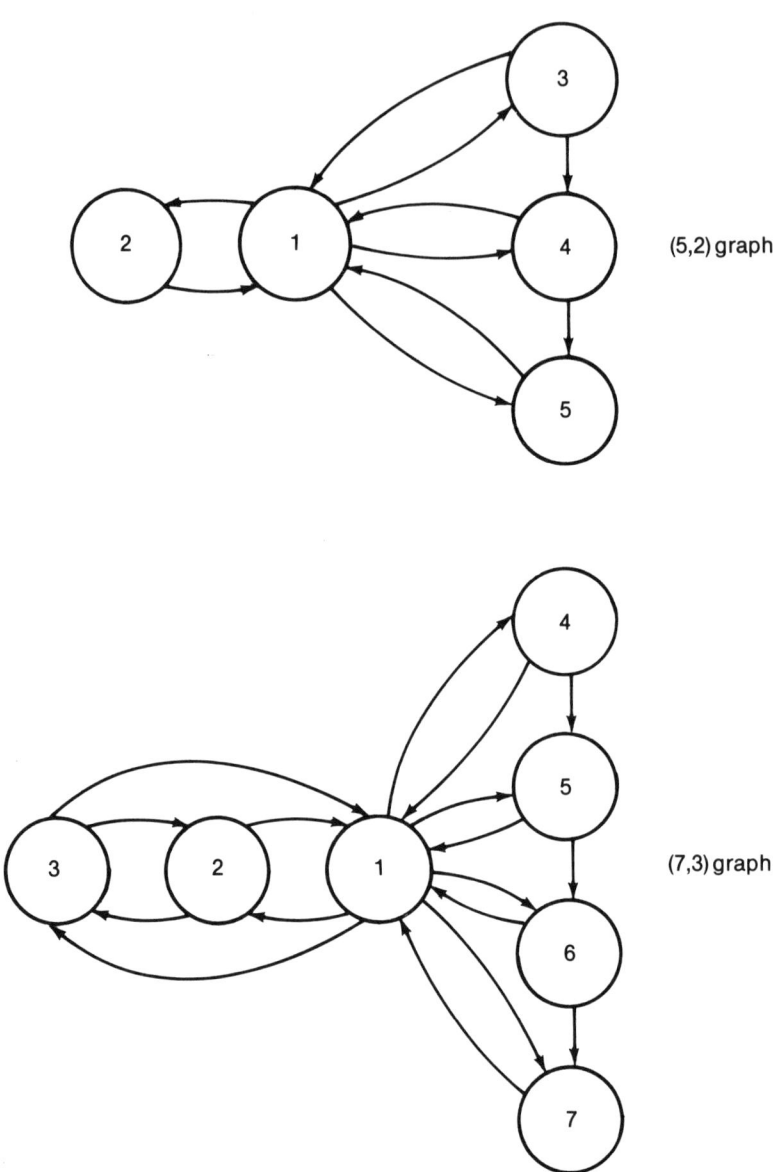

Figure 4.5 Two example Shedler-Tung models

4.3.1 Shedler and Tung's Model

patterns. Figure 4.6, from Lewis and Shedler [62][7], is the matrix of transition counts from a measured distance string of nearly nine million references[8]. The (i,j)th entry is the number of times distance i was immediately followed by distance j. There is no particular tendency towards transitions between distances i and i+1 for large i. In fact, it can be seen that many of the large distances are followed more often by distance 2, than by distance 1 as in the (n, ℓ) model. This peculiar looking behavior can be most plausibily explained as follows: many large distances represent data references to pages not in the locality. The succeeding reference is an instruction fetch from the same page as the previous instruction; this page is now at distance 2. In chapter 6, we shall examine this particular distance string more closely.

The matrix in figure 4.6 need not imply that the (n, ℓ) graph is a poor model --- it may be functionally adequate. The model does not predict clusters of large distances interspersed with small, but this may be of little consequence. If a cluster of five page faults is generated, it will make little difference in many applications whether the cluster spans five references or five hundred. In either case, the time between page faults is negligible.

4.3.2 Multiple Stack Distance Distributions

There does exist a reasonable method of modeling the observed form of large distance clustering with small distances interspersed. Suppose stack distances are chosen independently according to the probabilities $\{a_1,...,a_n\}$ as in the LRU stack model. Suppose, however, that there is a second set of distance probabilities $\{b_1,...,b_n\}$ which is

---

[7] Figure 4.6 is copyright 1973 by International Business Machines Corporation. Reprinted courtesy IBM.

[8] This data was unavailable when the Shedler-Tung model was formulated.

i/j	1	2	3	4	5	6	7
1	2,943,817	840,912	210,914	78,002	41,500	24,281	16,792
2	1,048,310	2,151,371	146,163	35,192	26,012	13,591	7,931
3	130,957	271,850	176,386	16,570	5,693	2,804	2,318
4	22,878	70,630	35,013	10,338	3,721	1,516	1,643
5	18,512	36,744	16,366	5,258	4,017	393	235
6	10,685	20,180	7,959	1,650	812	1,914	223
7	11,549	11,324	3,596	846	280	233	271
8	7,957	9,934	4,405	1,261	182	128	61
9	9,451	8,248	3,457	834	184	145	56
10	7,274	8,657	2,641	769	639	268	76

Figure 4.6 Empirical LRU distance string transition counts [62]

4.3.2 Multiple Distance Distributions

occasionally in effect. A two-state Markov (or perhaps semi-Markov) process can be used to choose between the distributions. Thus, while the Markov process in in state 1, distances are chosen according to the probabilities $\{a_i\}$, which are highly biased toward the top of the stack (intra-phase behavior). In state 2, the distances are chosen according to the less highly biased probabilities $\{b_i\}$, generating clusters of large distances interspersed with small (phase transition behavior). Although the distances are selected by independent trials at each time instant, successive distances are correlated in this model, since successive distance probabilities are correlated.

This method can clearly be extended to more than two distributions [3]. Unfortunately, validation experiments [3, 87] have shown no significant improvement in the two-distribution model over the single-distribution SLRUM, nor in the multi-distribution model over the two-distribution. The validation criteria were ability to predict the working set and page fault rate curves (section 5.2). One problem has been in choosing the number and form of the distributions --- it seems to be difficult to find intrinsically meaningful parameter values by measurement. It should be noted that each additional distance distribution adds n-1 parameters for the distribution itself, plus several additional parameters for the Markov model to choose among the distributions.

We shall describe in chapter 6 a Markovian method of distance string generation having only four parameters, based on autoregressive sequences. The rationale of the model is difficult to describe without prior discussion of measurement techniques, so we shall postpone its discussion.

4.3.3 Quasi-Stationary Stack Distance Distribution

We have shown (section 4.2.2) for LRU stack models that fixed memory allocation is better than variable allocation in terms of page fault rate.

Although this does not actually imply that dynamic allocation is inferior (a more realistic comparison would be of algorithms with equal real-time-average allocations, not virtual time [85]), experiments by B. Prieve (as reported in [50]) have shown this relation to be incorrect in practice. Prieve observed that even the virtual-time-average fault rate of real tasks was lower under working set management than under the corresponding fixed allocation algorithm (LRU with allocation equal to the virtual-time-average working set size). An example is shown in the graph in figure 4.7. The simple LRU stack model cannot account for this effect.

Since the failure is in prediction of a dynamic allocation phenomenon, Graham and Denning [50] have concluded that the LRU stack model (with constant distance probabilities) fails to predict a form of locality size variation. Irrespective of the locality list in effect, the size of the set of "likely" page references is fixed. But in real tasks, the set of in-use pages varies in size (locality property 4, section 2.4). To model this effect, we should make the distance probabilities time-varying by some mechanism. The multiple stack distance distribution idea of the previous section is a possible solution --- we might have a different distribution for each locality (or for each phase). In general, locality and phase holding times tend to be long, implying that the distance probabilities will be quasi-stationary; i.e. --- that their variation will be slow, with long intervals of little or no change. Many analyses which assume fixed probabilities will still hold, at least approximately. If locality holding times are long enough, the variation in distance probabilities will be so slow as to be ignorable for purposes of analysis (see for example proposition 3.2).

4.3.4 Micro/Macro Modeling

It is possible to create a model separating micro and macro behavior, in which each phase is modeled by a distinct LRU stack model. A semi-Markov macro-model can be used to choose among several SLRUM micro-models. Aside from the plethora of parameters, a problem here is in modeling the overlap of the

4.3.4 Micro/Macro Modeling

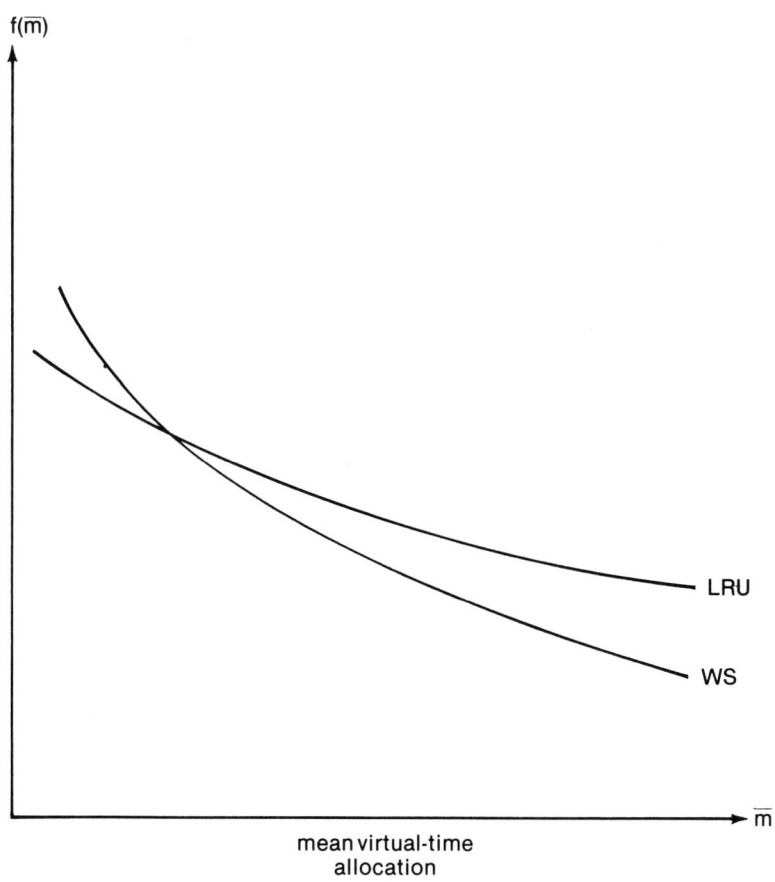

Figure 4.7 LRU and working set page fault curves

locality sets on either side of phase transitions (they will be largely, but perhaps not entirely, disjoint). A random variable might be used to specify how many of the pages in the old phase are retained in the new.

Denning and Kahn [35, 57] have tried this approach; however, for economy, they mostly used simple, rather ad hoc, micro-models instead of the SLRUM. A few experiments were tried with the LRU stack model, which indicated that the choice of micro-model affected primarily the convex, small-allocation region of simulated lifetime functions (section 3.1.2). The concave, or tail-off region of the curve was affected primarily by the choice of macro-model. Behavior other than that of lifetime functions was not investigated.

For simplicity, Denning and Kahn assumed completely disjoint changes of locality at phase transitions. This is not unreasonable, since changes in locality set of only a page or two are likely to be within a single phase of execution. The true overlap of localities at phase transitions is difficult to measure in real programs; moreover, its introduction into the model would result in additional complexity and parameters.

Chapter 5
Tools for Measurement and Validation

At the risk of triteness, the saying, "If you can't solve the problem, find a problem you can solve," applies more often than we would like to admit. In program behavior studies, this often means careful tailoring of the model to let the analysis proceed. Such a method may be a useful initial step in a new area of investigation, but eventually one must question whether the model (and hence the analysis) is applicable to the real world. Currently available program behavior models are susceptible in this regard because the best of them are quite inexact --- by comparison, Newton's laws of motion (an approximate model of the physical world) have unmeasurable error at ordinary velocities. To establish their practical utility, program models should be validated, or compared against example real tasks.

In this chapter we shall discuss methods for measuring and describing existing reference strings. Such measurements can be used to test the validity of a proposed model. They can also imply improvements to an existing model, or indicate entirely new models.

5.1 What Should We Validate?

. When validating a model, it may not be obvious which behavioral characteristics of the model and real task to compare. Generally speaking, for maximum success we must omit from the validation those criteria which are irrelevant to the intended uses of the model. We term this functional validation, corresponding to functional modeling. For example, memory reference detail at finer than the page level is usually of no consequence; we should not try to compare reference patterns to individual words. Less obvious is the fact that we need only model page fault behavior in many cases. Sequences of references among pages in memory need not be modeled exactly, so that we are primarily interested in references to non-locality pages. Lewis and Shedler [62] (section 6.2) used this point of view to model page faults only; they ignored all reference detail other than page fault occurrences. However, in studies of memory space demand (especially under dynamic allocation, as in the working set) such a model may not provide enough detail. Most modeling activity has centered on reference strings (or equivalently, on distance strings) which can be used to study both page fault incidence and memory space demand. Such reference string models can also be used to drive computer simulations of paging systems.

The most obvious way to validate a generative model is to compare statistically a generated and an actual measured reference string. An immediate problem is that real tasks need not use all of their pages; i.e. --- only the four pages 1, 3, 6, and 8 might be referenced. As a matter of convenience, we can usually rename these pages 0, 1, 2, and 3 with no change in system performance. We thus validate to within a renaming of pages. A reference string is a sequence of nominal data, or data whose values are names having no numerical significance. Such data can be analyzed by using non-parametric statistical techniques (c.f. Conover [24]), or by point process analysis (cf. [25]), or by classical time series analysis (c.f. [13, 51, 55, 60]). Of particular interest is the interreference distribution --- the distribution of times between references to the same page --- since it yields directly the program's working set behavior (section 3.1.1).

But there is a serious difficulty with statistical analysis of reference strings. The principle of locality works against us. As the locality changes, the page names vary in the reference string, indicating non-stationary behavior. A stationary model (such as the independent reference model) will not be a good statistical approximation. Techniques for statistical analysis and modeling of non-stationary data are less well-developed, and harder to use, than those for stationary data. Much of our effort in previous chapters has been to model non-stationary behavior with models that are actually stationary (the LRU stack model and its variations). Nevertheless, it is doubtful that good results can be obtained when attempting to validate such models by direct comparison of reference strings.

5.1 What Should We Validate?

A premise of the LRU stack model indicates one way to proceed. Although the reference string is non-stationary, the stack distances in that model are chosen independently according to a stationary probability distribution. In section 2.3.2, we noted that reference strings and distance strings were equivalent characterizations of memory reference behavior, so it is usually a better validation procedure to compare _distance strings_ generated by a real task and its model. In the case of the LRU stack model, we simply test a measured distance string of the real task for independence and stationarity. In more complicated distance string models (section 4.3) we apply statistical tests to the measured string to test the validity of the model assumptions. In general, we expect the distance string to be much more nearly stationary than the reference string. Moreover, since stack distances do have numerical significance, there is a larger selection of applicable statistical methods. Distance string techniques work even for models not based explicitly on stack distances; we must calculate the distance string properties or else measure references emitted by the model, converting to distances.

Validation by use of distance strings has another advantage: it simplifies functional validation for models in which only the page fault behavior must approximate reality. Suppose, for example, that the paging algorithm is LRU with memory allocation m. To validate functionally such a model, we need not distinguish among distances greater than m (all of which cause page faults), or among those less than or equal to m (none of which cause page faults). If the model is subsequently to be used to predict memory references or stack distances, we can re-validate using the original measured and modeled distances, but the fit will usually be worse.

5.2 Measurement of Working Set Behavior

There are several choices of functional criteria by which a real task and its model may be compared. The working set curve is one possible selection, since it is easily measured and it concisely indicates many aspects of the behavior of a task in a paging system (even, as an approximation, where working set memory management is not used). In section 3.1.1, we reviewed the working set curve w(T) and its derivatives, the page fault rate curve f(T) and the overall interreference frequency function g(T). Following is a one-pass algorithm (from [33]) for measuring these curves:

Algorithm 5.1
begin;

    declare g(1:Tmax), f(0:Tmax), w(0:Tmax),
        time(0:n-1), adj(1:Tmax), r(1:K);

    comment r(1)...r(K) is an observed reference string over the page set {0,1,...,n-1}. time(i) is an internal array which holds the time of the most recent reference to page i. Array adj and scalar f1 are temporaries used to correct w(T) for end-effects (see formula 3.3). Specifically, after the *i*th pass through the final loop, f1 will have value f(i)-w(K,i)/K.

    At the conclusion of this algorithm:

- g(i), $1 \leq i < T_{max}$, holds the probability of an execution interval of length i.

- g(Tmax) holds the probability of an execution interval of length $\geq$ Tmax. The execution interval until the *first* reference to a page is assumed infinite; thus g(Tmax) includes the probability of referencing a page for the first time.

- f(T), $0 \leq T < T_{max}$, holds the page fault probability with window size T.

- w(T), $0 \leq T \leq T_{max}$, holds the mean working set size with window size T.

    If memory space is scarce, array adj can be combined with array g by (for example) letting the sign of g(i) indicate the value of adj(i).

5.2 Working Set Measurement

```
do i=0 to n-1;
   time(i) = -Tmax;
end;

do i=1 to Tmax;
   g(i)=0; adj(i)=0;
end;

do i=1 to K;
   delta = i-time(r(i));
   if delta<Tmax then g(delta) = g(delta)+1;
                 else g(Tmax) = g(Tmax)+1;
   time(r(i)) = i;
end;

do i=0 to n-1;
   delta = K+1-time(i);
   if delta<Tmax then adj(delta)=1/K;
end;

w(0)=0; f(0)=1; f1=1;
do i=1 to Tmax;
   g(i) = g(i)/K;
   f(i) = f(i-1)-g(i);
   w(i) = w(i-1)+f1;
   f1 = f1-g(i)-adj(i);
end;
end;
```

The above algorithm makes a single pass through the reference string, followed by a single pass through the arrays. Since the reference string is scanned only once, it need not be stored; the algorithm can process references as they are produced. Alternatively, the reference string can be conveniently written to peripheral storage in conjunction with processing by the algorithm. To estimate w(Tmax) accurately for a task, we must examine many non-overlapping intervals of length Tmax, so we can assume that K, the reference string length, is much greater than Tmax. In that case, the algorithm executes in O(K) time and uses O(Tmax) storage (assuming the reference string is not stored).

In practice, however, this algorithm may be too expensive to use. If the observed reference string is sufficiently long, we may want to compute the working set and related curves for very large window sizes T.

Values of T on the order of 10,000 to 100,000 references are commonly found in implementations of the working set algorithm. When measuring the curves for T this large, it is hardly necessary to know all of $w(0), w(1), w(2), \ldots$; points at <u>selected</u> window sizes $T_1, T_2, \ldots, T_{J-1}$ would be sufficient. (The value of J would typically be chosen in the range 100-1000.) We can modify algorithm 5.1 to compute functions $w(T)$, $f(T)$, and $g(T)$ only at these J-1 points, plus at the point $T_0=0$. The cost of this is some extra processing

per reference in the pass through the reference string. The following algorithm takes $O(K)$ time and uses $O(J)$ storage (again, assuming the reference string is not stored):

<u>Algorithm 5.2</u>
<u>begin</u>;

<u>declare</u> $g(1:J)$, $f(0:J)$, $w(0:J)$, $g1(1:J)$, $adj(1:J)$, $time(0:n-1)$, $r(1:K)$, $T(0:J-1)$;

<u>comment</u> At the conclusion of this algorithm:

$g(i)$, $1 \leq i \leq J-1$ holds the probability that a lifetime e is in the range $T_{i-1} < e \leq T_i$.

$g(J)$ holds the probability that a lifetime exceeds T_{J-1}.

$f(i)$, $0 \leq i \leq J-1$, holds the page fault probability with window size T_i.

$w(i)$, $0 \leq i \leq J-1$, holds the mean working set size with window size T_i.

Arrays g1 and adj are temporaries, as is scalar w1. As in the previous algorithm, arrays adj and g or g1 can be combined if storage space is scarce. This algorithm is adapted from Denning [33].

5.2 Working Set Measurement   149

```
    do i=0 to n-1;
       time(i) = -T(J-1);
    end;

    do i=1 to J;
       g(i)=0; g1(i)=0; adj(i)=0;
    end;

    do i=1 to K;
       delta = i-time(r(i));
       if delta≤T(J-1) then find j such
                              that T(j-1)<delta≤T(j);
                       else j=J;
       g(j)=g(j)+1; g1(j)=g1(j)+delta;
       time(r(i)) = i;
    end;

    do i=0 to n-1;
       delta = K+1-time(i);
       if delta≤T(J-1) then begin;
          find j such that T(j-1)<delta≤T(j);
          adj(j)=adj(j)+1/K; g1(j)=g1(j)-T(j)+delta;
       end;
    end;

    w(0)=0; f(0)=1; w1=0;
    do i=1 to J;
       g(i) = g(i)/K;
       f(i) = f(i-1)-g(i);
       w(i) = w(i-1) + g1(i)/K - T(i-1)*g(i)
                    + (T(i)-T(i-1))*(f(i)-w1);
       w1 = w1+adj(i);
    end;
end;
```

The commands to "find j" in the above algorithm can be very fast if there is a functional relationship from delta to j. For example, if we choose <u>equally spaced</u> window sizes $T=h*i$, $0 \leq i < J$, for some constant h, then we can replace the "find j" commands by:

$$j = \lfloor (delta+h-1)/h \rfloor;$$

where the notation $\lfloor x \rfloor$ denotes the largest integer not greater than x (this is the usual truncating integer division).

As in algorithm 5.1, the above algorithm computes functions $w(T)$, $f(T)$, and $g(T)$ exactly for finite length strings.

At times $1 \le t < T$, the working set $W(t,T)$ of a task spans only the t references $r(1)...r(t)$, rather than a full T references. The working set behavior thus exhibits a start-up effect, tending to have atypically small working set sizes and atypically high page fault rates during the first T references. It is often possible to derive the working set and page fault rate curves of a given model without need for simulation. But such curves may be more easily derived for steady-state behavior, in which the first T-1 working sets are not averaged into the working set size, and in which the first T references are not considered in calculating the page fault rate, for each value of T. For comparison with such calculations, we should measure steady-state curves as well. Such steady-state curves are also likely to be more accurate indicators of a program's behavior. Letting $w_s(T)$ and $f_s(T)$ denote, respectively, the steady-state average working set size and page fault rate over reference string $r(1)...r(K)$, we have:

$$w_s(T) = \frac{1}{K-T+1} \sum_{t=T}^{K} w(t,T) \tag{5.1}$$

$$f_s(T) = \frac{1}{K-T} \sum_{t=T+1}^{K} V(t,T) \tag{5.2}$$

where $V(t,T)$ is the page fault characteristic function defined in expression (3.1). Following the derivation in (3.3) we obtain:

$$f_s(T) = w_s(T+1) - [(1+\frac{1}{K-T})w_s(T) - \frac{1}{K-T} w(K,T)] \tag{5.3}$$

which can be used to calculate curve $w_s(T)$ from curve

5.2 Working Set Measurement

$f_s(T)$. To calculate $f_s(T)$, we proceed, as in section 3.1.1, by measuring the backward distance function $\psi(t)$, whence:

$$\nabla(t,T)=1 \text{ if and only if } \psi(t)>T. \quad (5.4)$$

Were we interested in only one particular window size T, we could measure only $\psi(T+1)$, $\psi(T+2)$, ... to determine the empirical steady-state interreference distribution. But we are interested in many values of T. Define a new function $\psi'(t)$ as follows:

$$\psi'(t) = \begin{cases} \psi(t) & \text{if } r(t) \in W(t-1,t-1) \\ t & \text{otherwise.} \end{cases} \quad (5.5)$$

It is apparent that $\psi'(t)$ differs from $\psi(t)$ only when page $r(t)$ is referenced for the first time, in which case $\psi(t)=\infty$ but $\psi'(t)=t$. The following relationship is easily shown to hold for every T:

$$\psi'(t)>T \text{ if and only if } \psi(t)>T, \quad T<t\leq K. \quad (5.6)$$

Expressions (5.1)-(5.6) are the basis of the following modification to algorithm 5.2 (algorithm 5.1 can be similarly modified):

Algorithm 5.3

begin;

  declare g(1:J), fs(0:J), ws(0:J), g1(1:J), r(1:K), adj1(1:J), adj2(1:J), time(0:n-1), T(0:J-1);

  comment This is a modified version of algorithm 5.2, to compute the steady-state page fault rate fs(T) and the steady-state working set size ws(T) at the points $T = T_0, T_1, T_2, \ldots, T_{J-1}$, with $T_0=0$. If the interreference frequency function g(i) is not desired, arrays g and adj1 can be combined into a single array giving the empirical frequency function of $\psi'(t)$, $1\leq t\leq K$.

```
do i=0 to n-1;
    time(i) = 0;
end;

do i=1 to J;
    g(i)=0; g1(i)=0; adj1(i)=0; adj2(i)=0;
end;

do i=1 to K;
    delta = i-time(r(i));
    if delta≤T(J-1) then find j such that
                        T(j-1)<delta≤T(j);
                    else j=J;

    if time(r(i))=0 then begin;
        adj1(j)=adj1(j)+1; g(J)=g(J)+1;
            end;
    else g(j)=g(j)+1;

    g1(j) = g1(j)+delta;
    time(r(i)) = i;
end;

do i=0 to n-1;
    delta = K+1-time(i);
    if delta≤T(J-1) then begin;
        find j such that T(j-1)<delta≤T(j);
        adj2(j)=adj2(j)+1; g1(j)=g1(j)-T(j)+delta;
    end;
end;

ws(0)=0; fs(0)=K; ws1=0;
do i=1 to J;
    fs(i)   = fs(i-1) - g(i) - adj1(i);
    fs(i-1) = fs(i-1)/(K-T(i-1));
    ws(i)   = ws(i-1) + g1(i) - T(i-1)*(g(i)+adj1(i))
              + (T(i)-T(i-1))*(fs(i)-ws1);
    ws(i-1) = ws(i-1)/(K-T(i-1)+1);
    g(i)    = g(i)/K;
    ws1     = ws1 + adj2(i);
end;
end;
```

Our experience has shown that it is very difficult to fit a model to a typical measured interreference frequency function. Measured function g(T) is usually highly discontinuous; it often has the appearance of random noise. The cumulative of this function, the interreference distribution G(T), is

5.2 Working Set Measurement

generally much easier to fit since it is monotonic and relatively smooth. As noted in section 3.1.1, $G(T)=1-f(T)$, so we may fit a model to a measured interreference distribution by fitting instead to the page fault rate curve.

An effective functional validation of a proposed program model is thus a test of its ability to predict observed working set and page fault rate curves. Such a procedure tests the model's ability to predict memory space demand (the working set curve), page fault rate (the fault rate curve), and a statistic of the interreference pattern (also the fault rate curve). It is possible for some models to express the working set curve as a function of the model parameters. An example for the LRU stack model appears in appendix A. The measured curves $w(T)$ and $f(T)$ [or $w_s(T)$ and $f_s(T)$] of a real task and those of its model are then compared, either by eye, or by a formal test, such as by the mean-squared difference between the two curves.

In some models, such as the independent reference and LRU stack models, the model parameters can be estimated directly from the measured string (section 5.2.1). Where the parameter values are not observable, it may be necessary to choose the values to be those providing a best fit to (say) the working set curve. Such a procedure is reasonable only for parsimonious models, since the more parameters, the greater the likelihood that the best fit procedure will find values which are intrinsically not meaningful, but which artificially improve the apparent model performance. (For example, it is likely that coefficients of a degree 50 polynomial can be found to demonstrate that the "polynomial model" is an excellent predictor of mean working set size. But other aspects of the given program's behavior will in all likelihood be predicted poorly.) Finally, it may be possible to estimate model parameters from statistical measurements, such as the correlogram (sections 5.5.2, 5.5.3), not directly related to working set curve functional validation.

5.2.1 An Example Working Set Validation

We will now describe a use of the working set and page fault curves to validate three models [87]. The very simple locality model (VSLM), the simple LRU stack model (SLRUM), and the independent reference model (IRM) were compared for their abilities to predict the curves of several real tasks. The VSLM (section 4.2.3) is a special case of the LRU stack model having a single, explicit locality set. Also included for comparison was an attempt to fit the working set curve to the following exponential function:

$$w(T) = n(1-e^{-BT})$$

where B>0 is a parameter. We call this the exponential model (EXP).

The measured reference strings were quite short, in most cases 20,000 references. This corresponds to 20-40 milliseconds of virtual execution time in a typical system, and is thus a very small portion of any non-trivial task. Our budget precluded measurement of longer strings. An argument in favor of strings of this length is that the working set and page fault curves are averages, so that in a long measurement interval spanning several phase transitions, any dynamic behavior might be masked by the averaging process. A serious drawback is that few references causing page faults tend to be observed in such a short string. Moreover, only small window sizes T can be used (in this case T≤1000). For comparison with the short strings, two strings of length 300,000 were also measured.

For each measured reference string, the working set and page fault rate curves were computed using algorithm 5.1. Estimated stack distance probabilities $\{\hat{a}_i\}$ and independent reference probabilities were determined by counting references to each stack distance and to each page, respectively. VSLM parameters ℓ and λ were chosen to give the best mean-squared-relative-error fit to the measured working set curve over the set of window sizes T=10,20,...,990,1000. The same procedure was used to estimate parameter B of the exponential model.

5.2.1 Example WS Validation

Tasks on two machines, the IBM 360/91 and the Digital Equipment PDP-8, were measured. Figure 5.1 summarizes the measured tasks. A total of ten different reference string segments r(k+1)...r(k+K) were measured from four tasks. Note that the first k references of each task were skipped, and the following K references were measured. Figure 5.2 gives the values of the measured parameter n and the best-fit parameters ℓ, λ, and B, for each reference string. Note that the VSLM locality size ℓ is typically less than one-fifth of the total page set size n, and that the expected time between locality transitions $1/\lambda$ is typically 30-100 references for tasks on the IBM 360. This latter figure is disappointingly low, indicating that the locality size ℓ has probably been chosen too small.

Figure 5.3 summarizes model fits to the observed working set curve, and figure 5.4 to the observed page fault rate curve. Two error measures are listed: "average relative error" over window sizes 10,20,30,...,1000, and "worst-case relative error" over window sizes 1,2,3,...,1000. (The average relative error is more precisely the root-mean-squared relative error, defined to be the square root of the average squared relative error.) By "relative error" we mean that the error is given as a per cent of the value on the measured curve. Except for the IRM, the worst-case errors occurred at very small T (less than 10); for the IRM they occurred at large T (greater than 500).

Examples of the measured and modeled curves appear in figures 5.5-5.7; the corresponding page fault rate curves appear in figures 5.8-5.10. The observed (real task) curves are labeled "OBS". The exponential model is omitted for readability. Note the logarithmic vertical scale on the fault rate curves. Three measured stack distance frequency functions appear in figures 5.11-5.13.

It is apparent from the analysis that the SLRUM exhibits the best overall ability to approximate the two curves, with the VSLM a close second. The fits of these models are usually quite good for the working set curve, but for the fault rate curve they are often only fair. We can conclude that the models are better predictors of memory demand than of page fault rate. A more highly refined model would be necessary to predict the fault rate.

156 PROGRAM BEHAVIOR: MODELS AND MEASUREMENTS

Ref. Str. No.	Machine	Page Size (words)	Description	Refs. Skipped	Refs. Measured
0	PDP-8	128	Assembler, Pass 1	0	20K
1	PDP-8	128	Assembler, Pass 1	100K	20K
2	360	256	FORTRAN (G) COMPILER	1K	20K
3	360	256	FORTRAN (G) COMPILER	200K	20K
4	360	256	Small FORTRAN job One main loop.	1K	20K
5	360	256	Small FORTRAN job. One main loop.	100K	20K
6	360	256	Small FORTRAN job. One main loop.	1K	300K
7	360	256	Medium FORTRAN job. Several Subroutines	1K	20K
8	360	256	Medium FORTRAN job. Several Subroutines	100K	20K
9	360	256	Medium FORTRAN job Several Subroutines	1K	300K

Figure 5.1 Summary of measured tasks

5.2.1 Example WS Validation

Ref. Str. No.	Total pages refd.	VSLM ℓ	λ	EXP B
0	11	4	.0025	.0013
1	12	4	.0027	.0015
2	35	5	.014	.00080
3	38	7	.022	.0012
4	20	3	.030	.0025
5	20	4	.020	.0020
6	20	4	.021	.0021
7	22	4	.024	.0020
8	20	3	.029	.0024
9	31	4	.014	.00085

Figure 5.2 Measured and best-fit parameter values

Ref. Str. No.	avg. VSLM error	VSLM worst error	avg. EXP error	EXP worst error	avg. IRM error	IRM worst error	avg. SLRUM error	SLRUM worst error
0	7.5%	56%	37%	99%	84%	97%	28%	33%
1	6.2	49	38	99	97	106	19	24
2	6.0	49	32	97	161	208	20	29
3	11	58	32	96	109	146	6.5	8.2
4	5.3	30	20	95	95	246	2.6	7.7
5	10	53	26	96	77	200	2.3	7.9
6	9.9	54	25	96	86	210	2.6	8.1
7	8.0	51	24	96	98	225	2.8	7.9
8	6.5	29	22	95	85	207	2.9	8.9
9	10	56	31	97	162	291	8.3	9.4

Figure 5.3 Model fits to working set curve

5.2.1 Example WS Validation

Ref. Str. No.	VSLM avg. error	VSLM worst error	EXP avg. error	EXP worst error	IRM avg. error	IRM worst error	SLRUM avg. error	SLRUM worst error
0	30%	228%	266%	407%	77%	376%	84%	197%
1	36	190	301	413	167	419	85	181
2	29	132	93	127	133	426	27	118
3	82	131	157	207	70	210	5.1	26
4	32	94	40	90	103	479	16	48
5	85	157	119	224	74	417	19	43
6	72	153	100	192	81	435	18	38
7	37	158	62	110	93	450	9.5	37
8	30	92	48	91	89	420	10	37
9	57	190	117	195	102	609	14	40

Figure 5.4 Model fits to page fault rate curve

160 PROGRAM BEHAVIOR: MODELS AND MEASUREMENTS

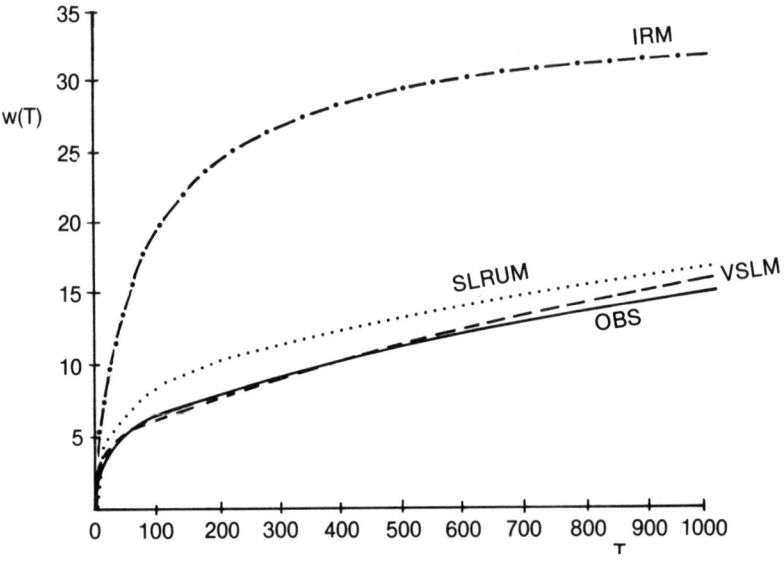

Figure 5.5 Working set curves, reference string 2

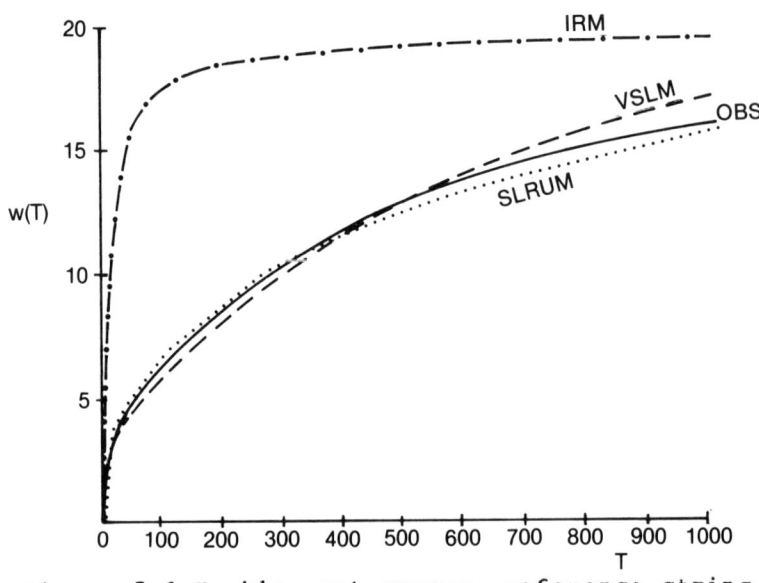

Figure 5.6 Working set curves, reference string 4

5.2.1 Example WS Validation

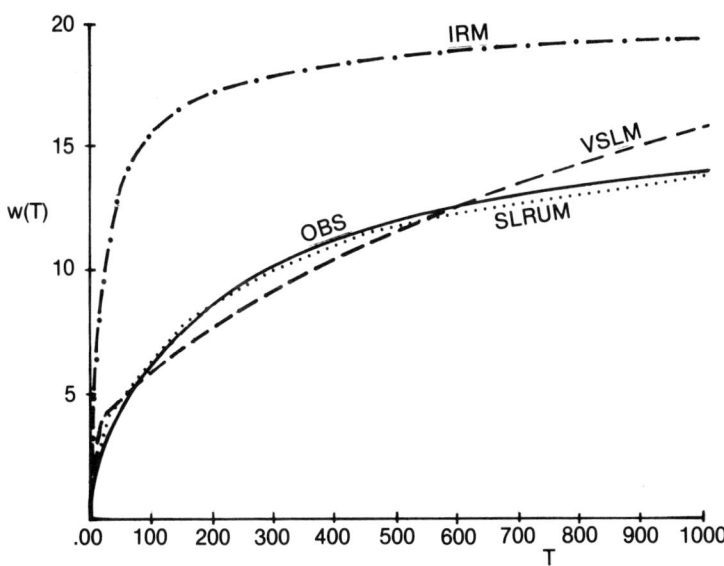

Figure 5.7 Working set curves, reference string 6

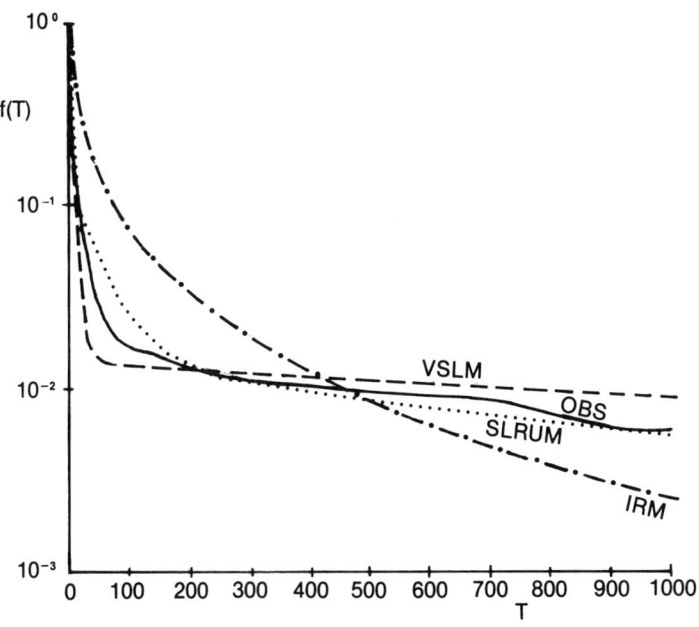

Figure 5.8 Page fault rate curves, reference string 2

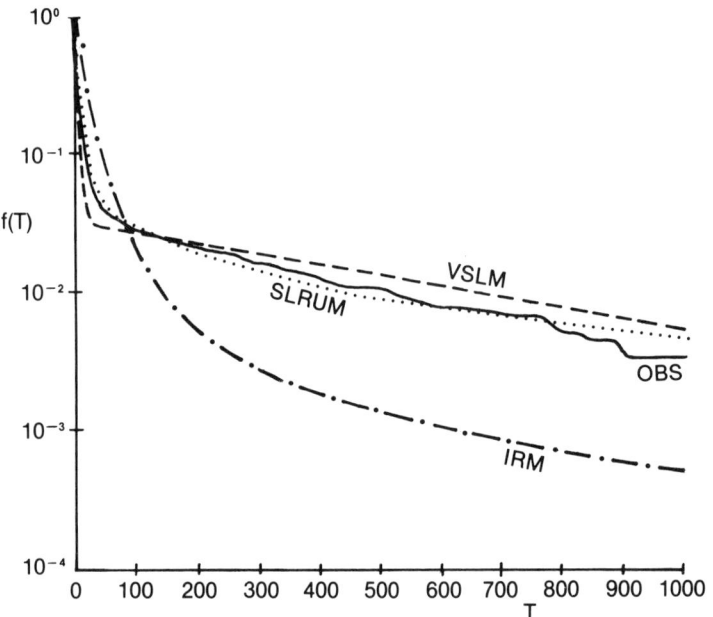

Figure 5.9 Page fault rate curves, reference string 4

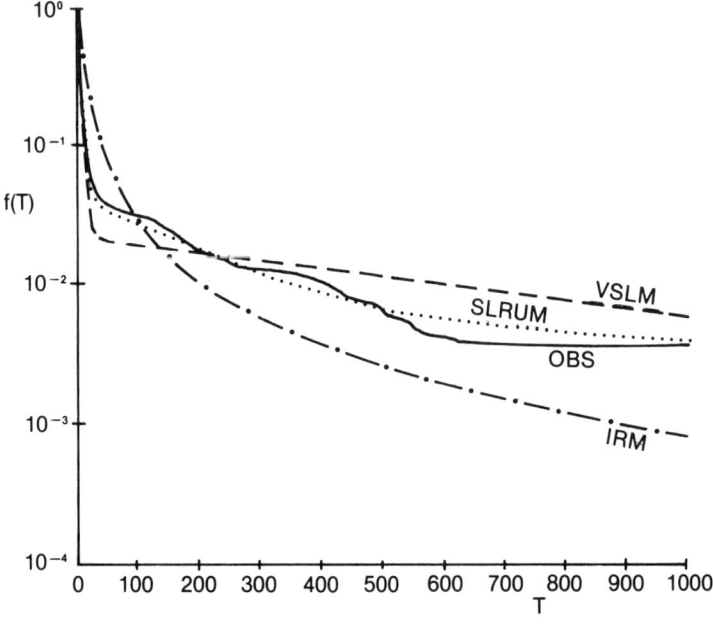

Figure 5.10 Page fault rate curves, reference string 6

5.2.1 Example WS Validation

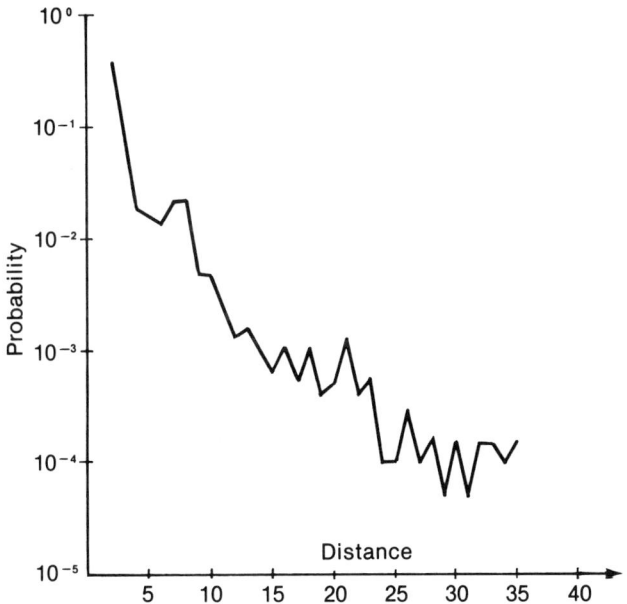

Figure 5.11 Empirical distance probabilities, reference string 2

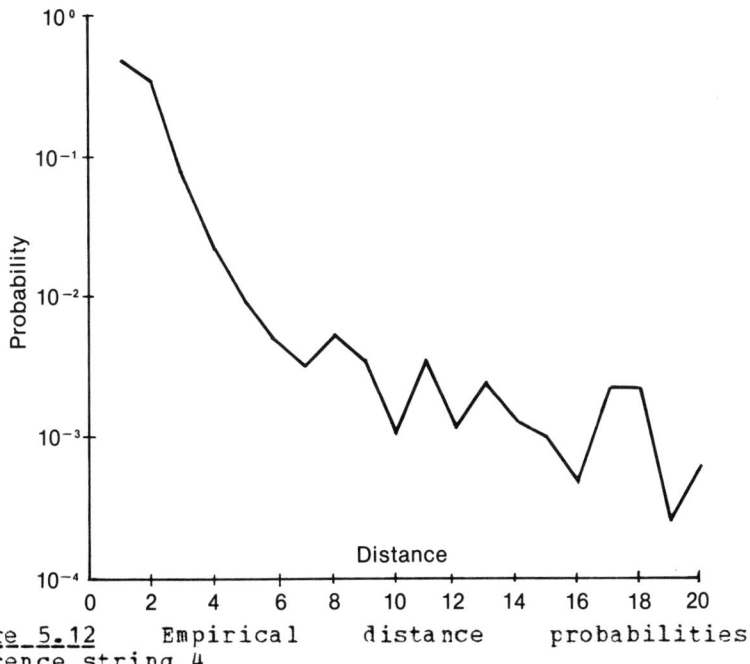

Figure 5.12 Empirical distance probabilities, reference string 4

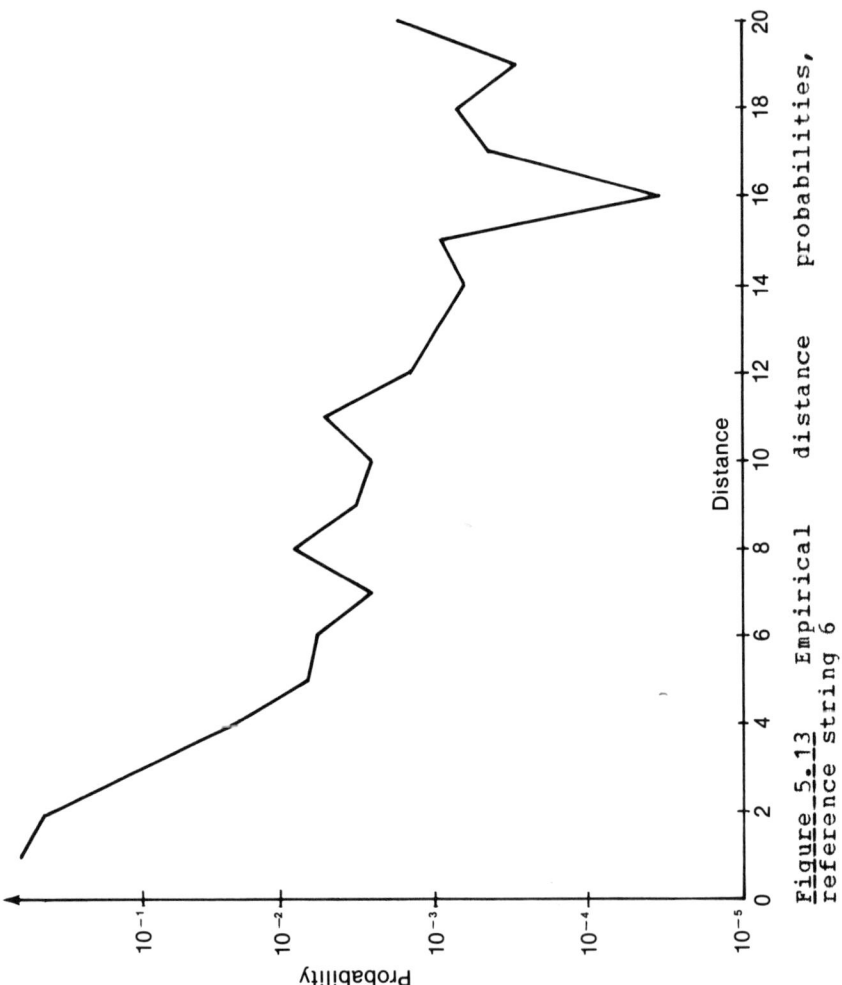

Figure 5.13 Empirical distance probabilities, reference string 6

5.2.1 Example WS Validation

Another consideration is the number of parameters, informally the "degrees of freedom" of each model. The LRU stack model has many such parameters --- the stack distance probabilities --- but these have all been given intrinsically meaningful estimates from the data. Thus, in spite of essentially no free parameter variation, the LRU stack model performs well in the validations. The two parameters ℓ and λ of the VSLM were chosen for best working set curve fit, however, and are not necessarily "true" intrinsic values. It can been seen in figures 5.5-5.10 that the curves for the VSLM have a much sharper knee than the measured curves. For instance, the working set of the VSLM corresponding to reference string 2 tends to acquire the entire locality in a window of about about 40 references. Thereafter, the working set size and page fault rate change much more slowly. For T close to 1000, the slope of the VSLM working set curve exceeds that of the observed curve --- the two are growing farther apart. In contrast, the SLRUM more closely follows the shape of the observed curves. The conclusion is that the VSLM locality is too sharply defined; the more gradual locality structure of the SLRUM is more appropriate.

5.3 Other Criteria for Validation

Comparison of working set and page fault rate curves has a drawback: only the average values of working set size or fault rate appear at each point on the curve. Moments other than the first, to say nothing of the entire probability distribution, are not considered. Characterization of the lifetime variance might be required if (for example) one wished to predict the mean time to satisfy queued external memory page requests using the model of figure 1.1. Similarly, characterization of the working set size variance would be required for a detailed analysis of system-wide dynamic allocation. Denning and Schwartz [36] have shown that this cannot be obtained from the working set curve alone.

Thus, an alternate validation procedure might be to choose a typical window size T, comparing the entire distribution of working set sizes and lifetimes of a measured task and its model. (Lifetimes are more easily measured than page fault probabilities.) In appendix A, we derive the working set size and page fault probability distributions of LRU stack model tasks. Since successive working set sizes (hence fault probabilities) are highly correlated, the exact lifetime distribution is difficult to determine, perhaps requiring simulation.

Since successive working set sizes and page fault probabilities are highly correlated in real tasks, it may be functionally useful to try to fit correlational aspects of a model to a measured task. For example, real tasks often generate clusters of page faults, as we have noted, and system performance can be sensitive to this tendency. We will presently show how to use the autocovariance function or power spectrum of a distance string to test for correlational effects.

5.4 Practical Issues of Reference String Measurement

To measure the reference string of an actual task, one must have a _virtual central processor_ (usually a program), which causes tasks to execute while recording their memory references. Such a virtual processor may run slowly, of course, largely because it must compute complex effective addresses. Ferrari [39] suggests that it is quicker to record only _instruction fetches_ and ignore operand references; however, even in that case branch addresses must be decoded. Such a measurement would allow only characterization of instruction fetch sequences. We shall here assume measurement of the entire reference string, instructions and data.

There is an additional major problem, that of retaining large amounts of measured data. There are two approaches: a) "analysis on the fly", or statistical summarization without recording individual references (for example, algorithms 5.1-5.3), or b) permanent storage of the entire reference or distance string for later use. Approach b) is recommended, because the data can be retained compactly (as we shall see), and because this method allows additional analyses to be performed later without the expensive necessity of re-measuring the

5.4 Reference String Measurement

program.

For storage space efficiency, when the data is stored in an on-line medium such as a disk, the referenced page names may be converted to stack distances before storage. The reference string can later be recovered, if desired. Alternatively, a hash table can be used to rename the measured page numbers into the set $\{0,1,\ldots,n-1\}$. Either technique requires significantly fewer storage bits per reference than the original reference string.

An efficient algorithm for computing and recording a distance string $d(1)\ldots d(K)$ is as follows:

Algorithm 5.4
begin;

   declare stack(1:n), record(1:R), r(1:K);

   comment stack(i), $1 \leq i \leq n$, holds the number of the page in stack position i. The stack is initially empty --- pages are added as they are first referenced. "record" holds R successive distances for output to peripheral storage. "infinity" is some chosen representation for $d = \infty$; zero is a possible choice.

```
measure r(1);
stack(1) = r(1);
record(1) = infinity;
stack_length = 1;

do i=2 to K;
   measure r(i);
   distance = 1;

   do while r(i)≠stack(1);
      distance = distance+1;
      if distance≤stack_length then begin;
         temp=stack(distance);
         stack(distance)=stack(1);
         stack(1)=temp;
      end;
      else begin;
         stack(distance)=stack(1); stack(1)=r(i);
         stack_length=distance;
         distance=infinity;
      end;
   end;

   insert distance into record;
   if record is full then write record;
end;
end;
```

The inner loop to search the stack in the above algorithm is less costly than it appears. The loop will nearly always terminate quickly, since reference r(i) will almost always be near the top of the stack. In practice, the virtual central processor program (including algorithm 5.4) should be written in assembly language or in a highly optimized systems programming language. Using this algorithm on an IBM370/155, a virtual central processor has been written which runs at about 1/60 the rate of the hardware central processor. Undoubtedly, for other machines having simpler addressing mechanisms, branch instructions, etc., it would be much quicker.

5.5 Stack Distance Validation

In the remainder of this chapter we shall concentrate on validation of distance models. Many of the techniques apply to other types of models as well. The LRU stack model is inappropriate as a non-trivial example of these techniques, since successive distances are independent. To exhibit the various methods more clearly, we shall introduce a new model, based on autoregressive sequences, in chapter 6.

There is a well-defined statistical methodology for finding an appropriate model for an observed distance string (see, for example, Box and Jenkins [13] or Cox and Lewis [25]). The first step is to check for (and perhaps remove) trends in the observed string. Removal of trends, when feasible, is important because most statistical tools are sensitive to non-stationarities (for example, any trend will inflate low-frequency spectrum values). An informal test for a linear trend is to plot a graph of the distance sum $D(t) = d(1) + ... + d(t)$ versus t, checking for straight line fit. More formally (c.f. Hannan [51], chapter 5), one can attempt to fit a straight line (or polynomial) to the original measured distance string by linear (polynomial) regression. If no monotonic trend exists, then the slope of the linear regression line will be zero. If a non-zero slope is found, a monotone trend is present, which can be removed by subtracting the line from the data. However, this will yield non-integer, even negative stack distances; so it is often infeasible to remove the trend.

The next step in creating a valid model is to eliminate candidate models one by one, in a simplest-first order, until an adequate model is found. If the sequence of candidates forms a hierarchy, with the ith model a special case of the (i+1)th, a common method is to overfit a proposed model with the one next in sequence. If the ith model is valid, the (i+1)th model should reduce to it, or nearly so.

An important such model hierarchy is the sequence of Markov models of various orders. A distance string is generated by a k-th order (Markov) model, k≥0, if $d(t)$ depends directly only on the k previous distances $d(t-k)...d(t-1)$. Thus, for example, the distances are serially independent in a zero-th order model, and in a first order model $d(t)$ depends on $d(t-2), d(t-3),...$

only to the extent it depends on d(t-1). A proposed k<u>th</u> order Markov model can be tested by overfitting the observed string to a model of order k+1.

5.5.1 <u>Distributional Fitting</u>

Two basic goodness tests of a distance string model are its ability to fit the distributional and the correlational aspects, respectively, of an observed string. We shall discuss correlation --- the relationship among successive distances --- in the following sections. But it is at least as important for a model to approximate some (if not all) aspects of the observed distance distribution.

For functional purposes, it may not be necessary to duplicate an entire observed distribution. If a task is to be run under a single, fixed memory allocation with LRU paging, then only the fraction of distances exceeding the memory size need be accurately modeled. But a general purpose model, particularly one to be used under dynamic allocation, should approximate the entire tail of the distribution of the measured string. We can tolerate errors in the frequency of very small distances, which will normally cause neither page faults nor changes in the memory allocation (i.e., the working set size).

It is not obvious which statistic to use to test for distributional fit. As with interreference frequencies, generally better fits will be obtained with cumulative distribution functions than with frequency functions. But the distance distribution, the fraction of distances less than or equal to a given value, becomes extremely close to one for values of interest. Its complementary distribution, the fraction <u>exceeding</u> a given value, is more appropriate. Define the <u>survivor function</u> $S_x(x)$ of random process x(t) as follows:

$$S_x(x) = Pr[x(t) > x] \qquad (5.7)$$

for arbitrary t. If a task executes with a fixed m page frames of main memory, then its page fault rate

5.5.1 Distributional Fitting

is simply the distance string survivor function $S_d(m)$. Note that the survivor function concentrates attention on the crucial tail of the distribution.

Since a typical survivor function spans several orders of magnitude, it is usually plotted on a logarithmic scale. Figure 5.14 shows a semi-log plot (linear-scaled absicca) of an example survivor function. Such a plot can be very useful as an aid to fitting a model distribution to a measured string. Data which is well-modeled by a (continuous) exponential distribution or a (discrete) geometric distribution will plot as a straight line. These distributions are defined as follows:

0) **Exponential Distribution**

$$S_x(x) = e^{-x/\mu} \quad , \quad \mu > 0, \; x \geq 0$$

0') **Geometric Distribution**

$$S_x(k) = (1-p)^k \quad , \quad 0 < p < 1, \; k = 0, 1, 2, \ldots$$

If the plotted function is non-linear, its tail will often be either concave (down), indicating a decay faster than exponential, or convex (concave up), indicating a decay slower than exponential. The curve in figure 5.14 has a convex tail. Suppose we are attempting to fit an empirical **continuous** distribution (or a discrete distribution to be approximated as continuous). The slope of $\log[S_x(x)]$ is related to the **hazard function** $z_x(x)$:

$$z_x(x) = f_x(x) / S_x(x)$$

where $f_x(x)$ is the probability density function for the given continuous-valued process $x(t)$. Hazard $z_x(x)$ is roughly the probability that $x(t)$ will have

172

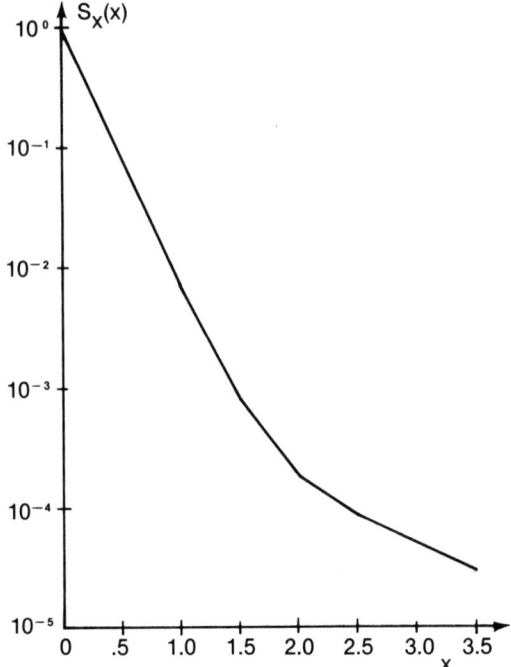

Figure 5.14 Example survivor function (semi-log scale)

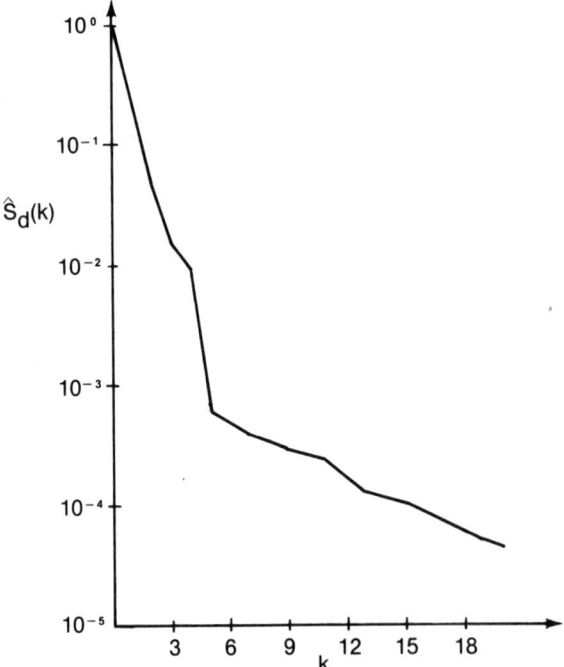

Figure 5.15 Survivor curve of distance string A

5.5.1 Distributional Fitting

value x, given that its value is at least x. (For example, when measuring the lifespans of people, the hazard is the probability that you are about to die, given your age.) The exponential and geometric distributions have a constant hazard. Other distributions have either a decreasing hazard (example --- newborn infants) or an increasing hazard (example --- elderly people) at any given value of x. It can be shown [25] that:

$$\frac{d}{dx} \ln S_x(x) = -z_x(x)$$

$$\frac{d^2}{dx^2} \ln S_x(x) = -\frac{d}{dx} z_x(x)$$

so that the slope of the survivor function, when plotted on semi-log graph paper, gives the hazard[1]. A convex (concave up) log-survivor curve indicates a decreasing hazard; conversely a concave (down) curve indicates an increasing hazard.

The hazard can be used to restrict the class of distributions of lifetimes under consideration. As we have noted, a linear log-survivor function indicates an exponential or geometric distribution. Consider the following other useful continuous-time distributions:

1) **Gamma Distribution**

$$S_x(x) = \left(\frac{a}{\mu}\right)^a \frac{1}{\Gamma(a)} \int_x^\infty x^{a-1} e^{-xa/\mu} dx \qquad a,\mu > 0; \; x \geq 0$$

---

[1] This is strictly true only for continuous distributions. It is approximately true for some discrete distributions, but only if the survivor function rate of decay is very slow. The theory can be reformulated for discrete-valued distributions, but we will work with continuous distributions, and subsequently give their discrete analogs.

2) **Weibull Distribution**

$$S_x(x) = e^{-(bx)^a} \quad , \quad a, b > 0; \; x \geq 0$$

3) **Mixed Exponential Distribution**

$$S_x(x) = \sum_{i=1}^{n} \pi_i e^{-\lambda_i x} \quad , \quad 0 < \pi_i < 1, \; \lambda_i > 0, \; 1 \leq i \leq n$$

$$\pi_1 + \pi_2 + \ldots + \pi_n = 1$$

$$x \geq 0$$

4) **Pareto Distribution**[2]

$$S_x(x) = c x^{-a} \quad , \quad a, c > 0; \; x \geq c^{1/a}$$

All of the above distributions have monotonically decreasing density functions. For the **gamma distribution**, a and μ are positive parameters with $\mu = E\{x\}$; $\Gamma(a)$ is the gamma function. The **mixed exponential distribution**[3] is a weighted average of n exponential functions, for some $n \geq 2$.

Our intention in introducing these distributions is not to describe fully how to choose among them, but merely to show how the log-survivor curve can aid in the procedure. Other considerations, especially intuition into the physical nature of the observed process, are important. The following table indicates the log-survivor shape of the various distributions:

---

[2] V. Pareto (1848-1923) *Cours d'economie politique*. This distribution was originally proposed to describe the distribution of income among people. We are concerned with it because of its relation to Belady's lifetime function.

[3] This is often called the **hyper-exponential** distribution, but its discrete analog is the **mixed geometric**, and not the so-called "hyper-geometric" distribution [38] which is something else entirely.

5.5.1 Distributional Fitting

Log-Survivor Curve
and Possible Continuous Distributions

Convex (decreasing hazard)	Concave (increasing hazard)
Gamma $(0<a<1)$	Gamma $(a>1)$
Weibull $(0<a<1)$	Weibull $(a>1)$
Mixed Exponential	
Pareto	

Any of the distributions in the left-hand column are candidates to fit the example survivor curve in figure 5.14. In fact, the curve is exactly a mixed exponential:

$$S(x) = .999e^{-5x} + .001e^{-x} .$$

In general, a distribution having a decreasing hazard has a tail which decays less quickly than that of the exponential distribution; the opposite for an increasing hazard. However, some non-exponential distributions have exponential tails. For the gamma distribution:

$$f_x(x) \sim x^{a-1} e^{-xa/\mu} = e^{(a-1)\ln x - xa/\mu}$$

$$\approx e^{-xa/\mu} \quad \text{for large } x.$$

Similarly, the term in the mixed exponential distribution with the smallest λ_i dominates for large x, also giving an exponential tail. Thus, the log-survivor curves of these two distributions approach linearity for large x.

Of course, a Pareto survivor function will plot as a straight line on log-log graph paper. This can be used to detect distributions which, although non-Pareto, have Pareto tails. Similarly, if $x(t)$ obeys a Weibull distribution, then $-\ln[S_x(x)]$ will be linear on log-log paper.

The discrete-valued distributions analogous to

distributions 1) - 4) above are shown below:

1') **Negative Binomial Distribution**

$$S_x(k) = \sum_{i=k+1}^{\infty} \binom{r+k-1}{k} p^r (1-p)^k \quad , \quad \begin{array}{l} r>0, \; 0<p<1 \\ k=0,1,2,\ldots \end{array}$$

2') **Discrete Weibull Distribution**

$$S_x(k) = e^{-(bk)^a} \quad , \quad a,b>0, \; k=0,1,2,\ldots$$

3') **Mixed Geometric Distribution**

$$S_x(k) = \sum_{i=1}^{n} \pi_i (1-p_i)^k \quad , \quad \begin{array}{l} 0<\pi_i, p_i<1, \quad 1\leq i \leq n \\ \pi_1 + \pi_2 + \ldots + \pi_n = 1 \\ k=0,1,2,\ldots \end{array}$$

4') **Discrete Pareto Distribution**

$$S_x(k) = ck^{-a} \quad , \quad a,c>0,$$

$$k=j, j+1,\ldots, \text{ for integer } j$$
$$\text{such that } j-1 < c^{1/a} \leq j.$$

The log-survivor curve shape of these discrete distributions is as follows:

5.5.1 Distributional Fitting

Log-Survivor Curve
and Possible Discrete Distributions

Convex	Concave
Negative Binomial (0<r<1)	Negative Binomial (r>1)
Discrete Weibull (0<a<1)	Discrete Weibull (a>1)
Mixed Geometric	
Discrete Pareto	

In section 3.1.2, we discussed some features of a measured distance string which we called reference string A. Its derived distance string, henceforth to be called distance string A, has the log-survivor function shown in figure 5.15. The tail of the curve is essentially convex, which is consistent with Pareto fit. See figure 3.5 for a log-log plot of the same curve.

5.5.2 The Autocovariance and Its Estimation

The LRU stack model assumes successive stack distances to be independent. More realistically, there will be serial correlation among the distances, which can be described by means of the autocovariance function. The autocovariance of lag k of a random process x(t) is defined to be:

$$c_{xx}(k) = E\{[x(t+k)-\bar{x}][x(t)-\bar{x}]\} \qquad (5.8)$$

where $E\{.\}$ denotes expectation, and where $\bar{x}=E\{x(t)\}$ is the mean of process x(t). Note that $c_{xx}(0)$ is the variance σ_x^2 of the process. Instead of the autocovariance, some sources prefer to use the autocorrelation:

$$r_{xx}(k) = c_{xx}(k)/c_{xx}(0) \ . \qquad (5.9)$$

This is a normalized and dimensionless version of the autocovariance; Feller [38] calls it "a fancy way of writing the autocovariance."

For an observed process of K samples, we can estimate the autocovariance function from the data as follows [55]:

$$\hat{c}_{xx}(k) = \frac{1}{K} \sum_{t=1}^{K-k} [x(t+k)-\hat{\bar{x}}][x(t)-\hat{\bar{x}}] \qquad (5.10)$$

where $\hat{\bar{x}}$, the estimated mean, is

$$\hat{\bar{x}} = \frac{1}{K} \sum_{1}^{K} x(t) . \qquad (5.11)$$

The autocovariance estimate (5.10) is intuitive except for the factor $1/K$ --- since $K-k$ terms are summed, it may seem that $1/(K-k)$ would be more exact. In fact, using the multiplier $1/K$ causes the estimate to be biased by a factor $(K-k)/K$, although it is clearly __asymptotically__ unbiased (unbiased for large K). Briefly, in spite of its bias, estimator (5.10) appears to have smaller expected error for most processes than the unbiased version. Use of the unbiased estimator for k close to K can lead to strange anomalies such as negative values of power spectra (see Jenkins and Watts [55] or Koopmans [60] for details).

A graph of $\hat{c}_{xx}(k)$ as a function of k is called a __correlogram__ (Hannan [51]). Since $c_{xx}(-k) = c_{xx}(k)$, only the estimated function for $k \geq 0$ need be shown.

Since K, the number of data points, is often very large in program behavior studies, it is important to calculate estimate (5.10) quickly. The computation of $\hat{\bar{x}}$ requires a pass through the data; moreover, it must be subtracted from each data point for a total of K subtractions. The following identity is easily

5.5.2 Autocovariance and Its Estimation

proved:

$$c_{xx}(k) = E\{x(t+k)x(t)\} - \bar{x}^2, \qquad (5.12)$$

so that it is tempting to write:

$$\hat{c}_{xx}(k) \stackrel{?}{=} \frac{1}{K}\sum_{t=1}^{K-k} x(t+k)x(t) - \hat{\bar{x}}^2$$

which allows $\hat{\bar{x}}$ to be computed in the same pass as the sum of lag products, and which saves $O(K)$ subtractions. However, a straightforward exercise will confirm that this expression is <u>not algebraically identical</u> to (5.10) if $k \neq 0$. We can correct it as follows:

$$\hat{c}_{xx}(k) = \frac{1}{K}\sum_{t=1}^{K-k} x(t+k)x(t) + \frac{\hat{\bar{x}}}{K}\sum_{1}^{k} x(t)$$

$$+ \frac{\hat{\bar{x}}}{K}\sum_{K-k+1}^{K} x(t) - [(K+k)/K]\hat{\bar{x}}^2 . \qquad (5.13)$$

It is easy to confirm that (5.10) and (5.13) are algebraically identical.

Formulation (5.13) can be used as the basis of a fast algorithm for computing estimated autocovariance coefficients. Suppose we wish to compute $\hat{c}_{xx}(k)$ for all k in the range $0 \leq k \leq J$, for some $J<K$. The following algorithm makes only a single pass through the data, and avoids subtracting the mean from each datum. It is a "practical" algorithm, in the sense that it assumes that K is too large for all values of $x(t)$ to be in memory. The values are assumed to appear in external memory in blocks, or "records", of r values each, $r>J$, where we stipulate for convenience that r evenly divide K. (Of course, the algorithm can be modified to remove this restriction.) If we are

computing the autocovariance function of the distance
string, then the records produced by algorithm 5.4 can
be used as input here.

Algorithm 5.5
begin;

    declare c(0:J), wa(0:1,1:r+J), adj(0:J);

    comment The autocovariances of lags 0 through J of
       random process x(t), $1 \leq t \leq K$, are stored in
       c(0),...,c(J). Values of x(t) are assumed to be
       stored externally in records of length r>J, so
       that the first record contains x(1),...,x(r);
       the second contains x(r+1),...,x(2r); and the
       last contains x(K-r+1),...,x(K). Arrays wa
       (2-dimensional) and adj (1-dimensional) are
       temporaries.

    xmean=0;
    read a record into wa(0,1)...wa(0,r);
    eof='no'; p=0;

    do k=0 to J;
       c(k)=0;
       if k=0 then adj(0)=0;
            else adj(k)=wa(0,k);
    end;

5.5.2 Autocovariance and Its Estimation

```
    do while eof='no';
      read a record into wa(1-p,1)...wa(1-p,r);
         if end-of-file encountered then begin;
            eof='yes';
            do k=1 to J;
               wa(p,r+k)=0;
               adj(k)=adj(k-1)+adj(k)+wa(p,r+1-k);
            end;
         end;
         else do k=1 to J;
            wa(p,r+k)=wa(1-p,k);
         end;

         comment The main loops begin here.
         do t=1 to r;
            xmean = xmean+wa(p,t);
            do k=0 to J;
               c(k) = c(k)+wa(p,t)*wa(p,t+k);
            end;
         end;

         p=1-p;
    end;

    xmean = xmean/K;

    do k=0 to J;
       c(k) = [c(k) - (K+k)*xmean**2 + adj(k)*xmean]/K;
    end;
end;
```

For large values of K, it is probably worth the effort of coding the above algorithm (or at least the two main nested loops) in assembly language. Work area wa is really two distinct areas; the first subscript chooses one or the other. Using a pointer in place of the first subscript, one can avoid the need to multiply subscripts at each reference to wa.

Algorithm 5.5 has computation time $O(KJ)$. If J is constant, this is linear time, but if we desire *all* lags, then $J \sim K$ and the algorithm takes $O(K^2)$ time. If $K=10^6$, which is not unreasonable, the algorithm would then take about ten days to complete on a conventional computer executing each iteration of the main innermost loop in one microsecond. Using the *fast Fourier transform* algorithm, it is possible to do the same thing in $O(K \log[K])$ time (c.f. [60]), but it will rarely be necessary to compute the autocovariance function for very large lags, as we shall see.

5.5.3 Implications of the Correlogram

A zero-th order distance string model (successive distances are independent) is indicated when the autocovariance coefficients $c_{dd}(k)$ for $k>0$ are zero [in practice, when they are small compared to the variance $c_{dd}(0)$]. Figure 5.16 shows the estimated distance string autocovariance coefficients at lags 0 through 60 for reference string A (section 3.1.2). Algorithm 5.5 was used. The lag one autocovariance, $\hat{c}_{dd}(1)$, is about 30 per cent of the variance $\hat{c}_{dd}(0)$, and the correlogram tails off slowly thereafter. Thus, the zero-th order simple LRU stack model cannot account for the correlational behavior of distance string A. This does not disqualify the LRU stack model as a functionally valid model for many purposes, but we are interested here in a model to account for the autocovariance effect. Page faults are often clustered, which is a phenomenon not predicted by the LRU stack model.

The vertical axis of figure 5.16 is logarithmic, and the straight line fit to the coefficients indicates exponential decay. Such autocovariance behavior is characteristic of a first order Markov process, as we will show in section 5.5.6. It would be straightforward in principle to fit such a process to the data: State k would denote distance k, and the state transition probabilities $\{p_{ij}\}$, $1 \leq i, j \leq n$, would be estimated by counting the number of times distance j followed distance i in the observed string. (Recall that n is the page set size as well as the maximum stack distance.) This gives a model with $n(n-1)$ independent parameters, however easily estimated. We shall attempt in chapter 6 to find a much more parsimonious model that can account for the stack distance distribution and autocovariance function.

5.5.3 Implications of the Correlogram

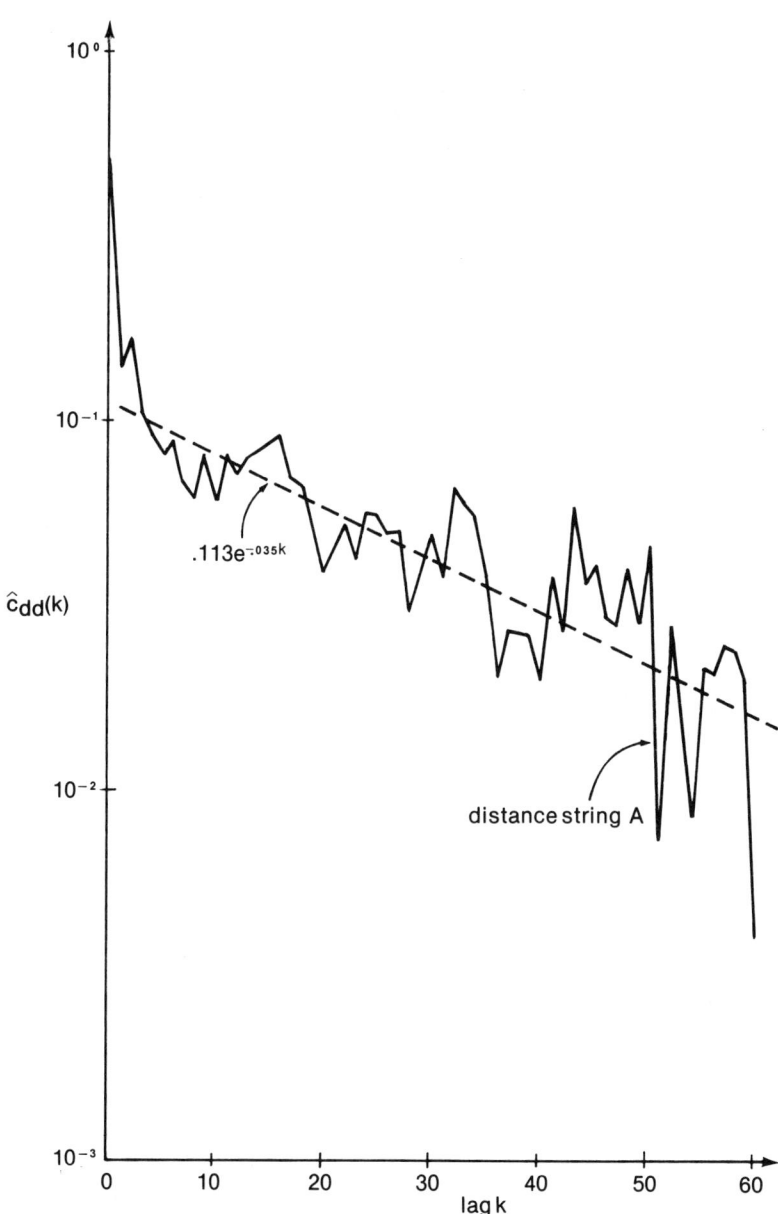

Figure 5.16 Correlogram of distance string A

A warning must be made: Experiments by Lewis and Yue [63] showed distance string serial dependencies to fall off so slowly as to be inconsistent with a Markov model of any finite order. We have only computed the autocovariance through lag 60; it is possible that the tail decays slower than exponentially for higher lags. Our attempts to validate based on the exponential assumption may thus fail to account for very long dependencies, when they exist.

5.5.4 Spectral Analysis

In figure 5.16, the observed correlogram varies quite a bit around the line chosen to fit it. This does not necessarily imply that the fit is bad, because estimates $\hat{c}_{dd}(k)$ and $\hat{c}_{dd}(k+1)$ can be highly correlated [55]. In particular, fluctuations of individual coefficients will tend to be spread out and exaggerated in the estimated correlogram, making it difficult to interpret. A more reliable method of correlation validation is by comparison of spectra. We shall now describe such methods very briefly. Anyone intending to work with spectra is urged to consult the following excellent references: Koopmans [60], chapters 8-9, and Jenkins and Watts [55], chapters 6-7.

The **power spectrum** of a random process is the Fourier transform of its autocovariance function, and the **power spectral density** is the Fourier transform of its autocorrelation function. The two spectra are proportional by a factor equal to the variance of the process. Denoting the power spectrum by $C_{xx}^*(f)$, f being the frequency, we have:

$$C_{xx}^*(f) = \sum_{k=-\infty}^{\infty} c_{xx}(k) e^{-2\pi i f k}, \quad -.5 \leq f \leq .5 \quad (5.14)$$

where i is the square root of -1. The largest

5.5.4 Spectral Analysis

magnitude frequency f can have (according to the sampling theorem [60]) is 1/2, corresponding to alternation in successive values of $c_{xx}(k)$. Noting that $c_{xx}(-k) = c_{xx}(k)$, we can rewrite (5.14) as:

$$c^*_{xx}(f) = \sigma_x^2 + \sum_{k=1}^{\infty} c_{xx}(k) [e^{2\pi i f k} + e^{-2\pi i f k}]$$

$$= \sigma_x^2 + 2 \sum_{k=1}^{\infty} c_{xx}(k) \cos(2\pi k f), \quad -.5 \leq f \leq .5 \quad (5.15)$$

As an estimate of this, we can start by computing the <u>sample spectrum</u> $\hat{c}^*_{xx}(f)$, defined on the estimated autocovariance coefficients:

$$\hat{c}^*_{xx}(f) = \hat{\sigma}_x^2 + 2 \sum_{k=1}^{K-1} \hat{c}_{xx}(k) \cos(2\pi f k) \quad -.5 \leq f \leq .5 \quad (5.16)$$

where $\hat{\sigma}_x^2 = \hat{c}_{xx}(0)$. Of course, if the true autocovariance function is large for lags on the order of K-1 or greater, there will be an error which can only be reduced by examining longer data sequences. But as we shall see, it will rarely be necessary to measure $\hat{c}_{xx}(k)$ for very large k.

Although the spectrum is defined to be the Fourier transform of the autocovariance of x(t), it has direct interpretation in terms of the periodic behavior of x(t) itself. The following algebraic identity is well known (c.f. Jenkins and Watts [55]):

$$\hat{C}^*_{xx}(f) = \frac{1}{K} \left| \sum_{t=1}^{K} [x(t) - \hat{\bar{x}}] e^{-2\pi i f t} \right|^2 , \qquad (5.17)$$

for sample mean

$$\hat{\bar{x}} = \frac{1}{K} \sum_{1}^{K} x(t) .$$

In other words, the sample spectrum is the squared magnitude of the (complex-valued) Fourier transform of the original data. Peaks in $\hat{C}^*_{xx}(f)$ are directly interpretable as periodicities in the data, although their phase (polar coordinate angle) is deleted.

The spectrum also shows how the power of a process is partitioned among periodicities of different frequencies. In the case of random variables, the "power" is the _variance_, and it is easily shown that:

$$\int_{-1/2}^{1/2} C^*_{xx}(f) \, df = \sigma_x^2 \qquad (5.18)$$

for any random process $x(t)$.

The sample spectrum, being an estimate, is a random variable, whereas the actual spectrum is not. The two are related in a straightforward way:

$$C^*_{xx}(f) = \lim_{K \to \infty} E\{\hat{C}^*_{xx}(f)\} ,$$

but the expected value of $\hat{C}^*_{xx}(f)$ cannot be exactly measured, and the limiting operation has difficulties.

5.5.4 Spectral Analysis

From (5.16), we have:

$$\lim_{K\to\infty} E\{\hat{C}^*_{xx}(f)\} = \lim_{K\to\infty} E\{\hat{\sigma}_x^2 + 2\sum_{k=1}^{K-1} \hat{c}_{xx}(k)\cos(2\pi fk)\}$$

$$= \lim_{K\to\infty} (\sigma_x^2 + 2\sum_{k=1}^{K-1} c_{xx}(k)\cos(2\pi fk))$$

$$= C^*_{xx}(f) ,$$

since $\hat{c}_{xx}(k)$ is an asymptotically unbiased estimator of $c_{xx}(k)$. This appears simple enough, but consider $f=0$, for which:

$$C^*_{xx}(0) = \sigma_x^2 + 2\sum_{1}^{\infty} c_{xx}(k) .$$

There are many random processes (c.f. figure 5.16) for which $c_{xx}(k) > 0$ for all k, so it is possible that $C^*_{xx}(0) > 0$. However, a simple manipulation of (5.17) gives:

$$\hat{C}^*_{xx}(0) = \frac{1}{K}\left|\sum_{1}^{K}[x(t)-\hat{\bar{x}}]\right|^2$$

$$= 0 .$$

The limit is zero for any process x(t). The

difficulty is basically that:

$$\sigma_x^2 + 2 \sum_1^{K-1} \hat{c}_{xx}(k) = 0, \text{ for all } K < \infty,$$

but for any $\tau \ll K$,

$$E\{\hat{\sigma}_x^2 + 2 \sum_1^{\tau} \hat{c}_{xx}(k)\} = [\sigma_x^2 + 2 \sum_1^{\tau} c_{xx}(k)] \to c_{xx}^*(0) \tag{5.19}$$

which may exceed zero. Written this way, we see that the problem is attributable to correlations among the random variables $\hat{c}_{xx}(k)$, especially for large k. Subtraction of the sample mean (as opposed to the true mean) in (5.17) actually amounts to pre-filtering of the data to remove the sample spectrum value at f=0 (Blackman and Tukey [12], pages 139-146).

5.5.5 Practical Spectral Estimation

We have noted that values of the estimated correlogram are often highly correlated for nearby lags. The opposite is true for the sample spectrum --- fluctuations at nearby frequencies are nearly independent. Although this may not appear to be an improvement, it implies that an averaging (or smoothing) operation can lessen the effect of the fluctuations. By analogy, consider estimation of the mean of a process x(t) in the conventional way:

$$\hat{\bar{x}} = \frac{1}{K} \sum_1^K x(t).$$

If the autocovariance of x(t) is significantly positive at large lags, any deviation from the mean in

5.5.5 Practical Spectral Estimation

some x(t) will tend to be propagated to values x(t') for t' much different from t. Its effect will be magnified, confounding the attempt to estimate the mean. The averaging interval will have to be much longer than the largest lag of non-zero autocovariance. On the other hand, if successive values of x(t) are independent, the central limit theorem predicts that the sum:

$$\frac{1}{K} \sum_{1}^{K} x(t)$$

converges quickly to a normally distributed random variable with mean $\bar{x}$ and variance $\sigma_x^2/k \to 0$. This will in general be much faster convergence than for a correlated process.

However, independence of adjacent estimates is not sufficient to ensure that the smoothed sample spectrum and the true spectrum will coincide for long enough data sequences. The <u>variance</u> of $\hat{C}_{xx}^*$ (f) for any f can be shown to be <u>constant</u>, regardless of K. In other words, the expectation of the error $C_{xx}^*(f) - \hat{C}_{xx}^*(f)$ is not decreased in the slightest by taking more data points. This is not to say that it is useless to have large K: we shall see that the larger it is, the finer will be the <u>resolution</u> between spectrum values at neighboring frequencies. Consequently, the averaging procedure will be finer and more accurate. But mere volume of data alone will not produce a satisfactory estimate of the spectrum; a smoothing operation must always be applied.

The reason the sample spectrum $\hat{C}_{xx}^*$ (f) fails to converge to the true spectrum is that the autocovariance estimates $\hat{c}_{xx}$ (k) for k near K, being averages of few values, have large variances. The obvious improvement, indicated in (5.19), is to use only the first τ autocovariance coefficients for some $\tau \ll K$. This is called a __rectangular lag window__. We express this formally as follows: Define window $v_R(k)$ to be:

$$v_R(k) = \begin{cases} 1 & \text{for } |k| \leq \tau \\ 0 & \text{for } \tau < |k| < K \end{cases} \quad (5.20)$$

(The subscript R denotes "rectangular"). The spectral estimate is then:

$$\hat{c}_{xx}^{*R}(f) = \sum_{-(K-1)}^{K-1} v_R(k)\hat{c}_{xx}(k)e^{-2\pi i f k}$$

$$= \hat{\sigma}_x^2 + 2 \sum_{1}^{\tau} \hat{c}_{xx}(k) \cos(2\pi f k) . \quad (5.21)$$

However, we have introduced a perhaps unexpected source of error. Let operator $\mathcal{F}[.]$ denote the finite Fourier transform of its argument. Then, by the properties of Fourier transforms:

$$\hat{c}_{xx}^{*R} = \mathcal{F}[v_R \hat{c}_{xx}]$$

$$= \mathcal{F}[v_R] * \mathcal{F}[\hat{c}_{xx}] \quad (5.22)$$

where the asterisk denotes convolution. The Fourier transform $v_R^*(f)$ of the rectangular window is:

5.5.5 Practical Spectral Estimation

$$V_R^*(f) = \sum_{-\tau}^{\tau} e^{-2\pi i f k}$$

$$= \frac{e^{\pi i f(2\tau+1)} - e^{-\pi i f(2\tau+1)}}{e^{\pi i f} - e^{-\pi i f}}$$

$$= \frac{\sin[(2\tau+1)\pi f]}{\sin[\pi f]}, \quad -.5 \leq f \leq .5$$

Function $V_R^*(f)$, called the spectral window, is shown in figure 5.17 for $\tau = 10$. Since $V_R^*(f) = V_R^*(-f)$, only the portion for $0 \leq f \leq .5$ is shown. To estimate the spectrum, we have from (5.22):

$$\hat{C}_{xx}^{*R}(f) = (V_R^*) * \mathcal{F}[\hat{c}_{xx}(k)]$$

$$= \int_{-1/2}^{1/2} \hat{C}_{xx}^*(f) \, V_R^*(\emptyset - f) \, d\emptyset .$$

Clearly, $\hat{C}_{xx}^{*R}(f)$ depends on sample spectrum values $\hat{C}_{xx}^*(f')$ for f' very different from f, because of the side lobes of the spectral window. This will bias the estimate of the true spectrum. We would like to smooth the sample spectrum by using a weighted average of neighboring values --- this is accomplished by the main peak of the spectral window. However, the side lobes are undesirable and methods of reducing their amplitudes must be found.

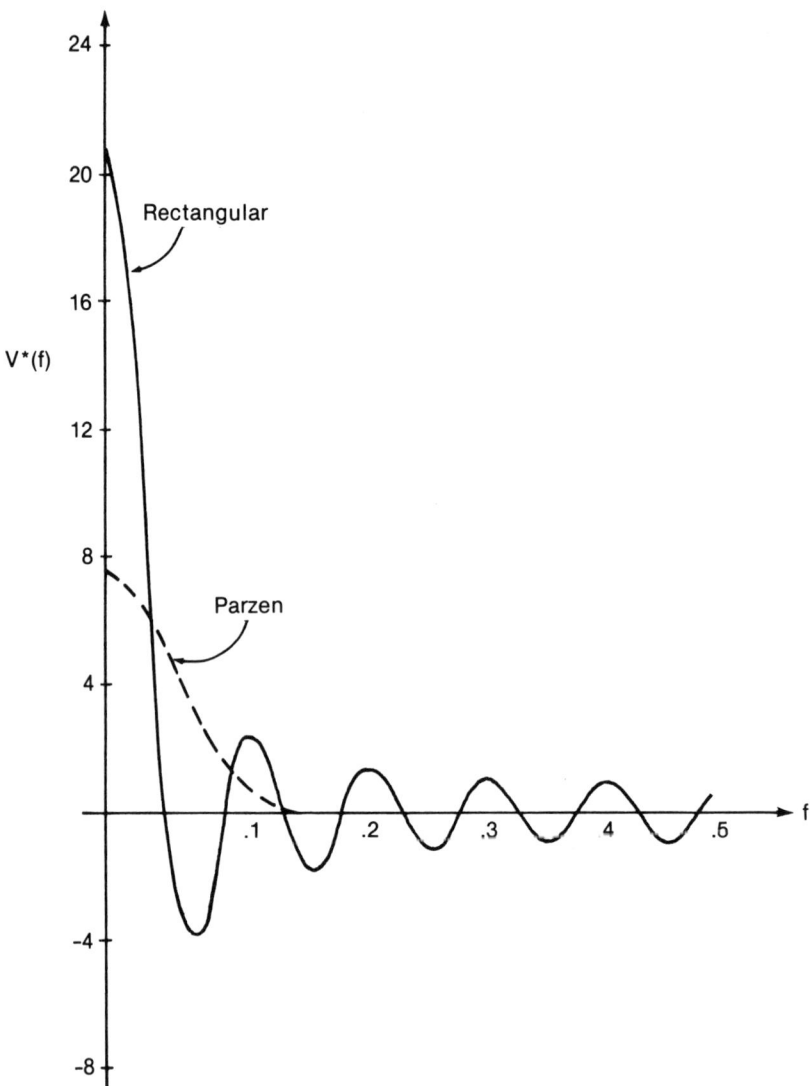

Figure 5.17 Rectangular and Parzen spectral windows

5.5.5 Practical Spectral Estimation

For this reason, the rectangular window is rarely used in practice. Other lag window functions have been proposed whose transforms have smaller side lobes. It is not our purpose to survey them here; there are several having good characteristics. One of the best is the **Parzen window** of lag τ:

$$v_P(k) = \begin{cases} 1-6a^2(1-|a|) & |a|<1/2 \\ 2(1-|a|)^3 & 1/2 \leq |a| < 1 \\ 0 & |a| \geq 1 \end{cases} \quad (5.23)$$

where

$$a = k/\tau .$$

As in the rectangular window, the Parzen window is symmetric for positive and negative lags, and it is zero for lags of magnitude exceeding τ. All lag windows have these properties. The spectral estimate is now:

$$\hat{c}_{xx}^{*P}(f) = \hat{\sigma}_x^2 + 2 \sum_1^{\tau-1} \hat{c}_{xx}(k) \, v_P(k) \, \cos(2\pi fk) . \quad (5.24)$$

(We sum only to lag $\tau-1$ because $v_P(\tau)=0$.) Note that only the first τ autocovariance coefficients need be estimated in order to compute the estimated spectrum.

Expression (5.24) can be used directly as the basis of an algorithm for computing smoothed estimated spectra. But the following algorithm (adapted from [55]) is faster, since it requires computation of only one cosine function per frequency point. The other $\tau-2$ cosine functions are computed iteratively:

Algorithm 5.6
begin;

  declare COS function, c(0:τ-1), vp(1:τ-1), C(0:nf);

  comment Estimated autocovariance coefficients c(0),...,c(τ-1) are input to the algorithm. These may have been computed using algorithm 5.5. The algorithm computes nf+1 spectral estimates in array C at frequencies 0, 1/(2*nf), 2/(2*nf), ..., 1/2. Jenkins and Watts [55] recommend nf ≈ 2*τ or 3*τ. Parzen lag window weights are stored in array vp as the first step in the computation.

  do k=1 to τ-1;
    a = k/τ ;

    if a < .5 then vp(k)=1-6*a*a*(1-a);
              else vp(k)=2*(1-a)**3;

  end;

  do i=0 to nf;
    d = COS(3.14159265*i/nf);
    x0=0; x1=0;

    do k= τ-1 to 1 by -1;
      x2=2*d*x1-x0+c(k)*vp(k);
      x0=x1; x1=x2;
    end;

    C(i)=c(0)+2*(x1*d-x0);
  end;
end;

Although the spectrum is computed at equally spaced frequencies in the above algorithm, this is not a requirement. Since the calculation of the spectrum at any given frequency does not depend on the calculations at other frequencies, it is straightforward to modify the algorithm to compute the spectrum at any arbitrary set of frequencies. This can be useful, as we will see, if one would like to test for a peak at a specific frequency value --- the spectrum can then be computed at many points near the desired frequency, but more sparsely over the rest of the frequency range. This saves computer time.

5.5.5 Practical Spectral Estimation

The <u>equivalent</u> <u>bandwidth</u> <u>EB</u> of a spectral window is roughly the width of its main peak. This is the range of frequencies over which most of the smoothing takes place. Only spectral peaks more separated than EB can be resolved apart, since peaks at closer frequencies will be smoothed into a single peak. The equivalent bandwidth of a Parzen window of lag τ is [60, 55]:

$$EB = 1.86/\tau \qquad (5.25)$$

so that to resolve apart two peaks at frequencies .21 and .22 requires:

$$\tau = 1.86/EB \gg 1.86/(.22-.21) = 186 .$$

Koopmans ([60], page 313) suggests that the relation $\gg$ above should be interpreted as "at least twice as large", so we might choose $\tau=400$. This will be expensive for large data counts K. Moreover, the larger the value of τ, the larger K must be to yield a stable estimate.

If there is a major peak in a spectrum at some frequency f, there will usually be peaks at <u>harmonics</u> 2f, 3f, etc., subject, of course, to the frequency limit of .5 . The peaks will tend to diminish in magnitude as the order of the harmonic increases. Many processes also have peaks at the <u>sub-harmonics</u> f/2, f/3, etc. Thus, to detect a peak at frequency f, and resolve it apart from a possible sub-harmonic at f/2, requires that the spectrum be computed much more often than at f/2, f, 3f/2, ..., at least in this frequency range. We must then have:

$$EB \leq [f - f/2] = f/2 .$$

For our purposes, we will often avoid these difficulties. We shall often just want to ensure that a model duplicates the basic spectral shape of an observed string. There will be little need to discern finely spaced peaks. If peaks exist, peaks will appear in the smoothed spectrum --- the smoothing process does not eliminate peaks; it simply merges them. (Although a single very narrow peak will be considerably flattened.) Of course, if there is a particular need to test for peaks at specific frequencies (we shall see an example in section 6.2.3), it may be necessary for τ to be large.

Jenkins and Watts [55] describe the method of <u>window closing</u> for choosing τ. An initial small value of τ (high degree of smoothing) is chosen, and the spectral estimate $\hat{C}_{xx}^{*P}$ (f) is calculated. The procedure is repeated for successively larger values, until the estimated spectrum appears unstable with many random fluctuations. The best estimate is usually just before the instability appears. (Of course, this is often subjective.) If the number of data points is very large, as is common in program behavior studies, the estimate may seem to converge and remain stable even for large τ. In this happy state of affairs, almost any τ will do.

Figure 5.18 shows the estimated distance string spectrum of reference string A, computed by algorithm 5.6. Lags τ of 20, 40, and 60 time units were tried, but only the results for lags 40 and 60 are displayed, because those for lags 20 and 40 were almost indistinguishable. Even the results for $\tau=40$ and $\tau=60$ agree closely enough for us to conclude that the estimates have more or less converged.

The spectrum is defined for all real frequencies f in the closed interval [-.5,.5], many of which are not reciprocals of integer periods. The spectrum in figure 5.18 is increasing above f=.3 or so, and the interpretation of this may not be clear. For example, what is the intuitive significance of the broad peak around f=.45, corresponding to a period of 1/.45=2.22 memory references? The answer is that if a random process contains a periodic effect, the period length itself may vary randomly. Consider the following example process x(t):

9, 0, 9, 0, 0, 9, 0, 9, 0, 9, 0, 0, 9, 0, 0, 9, ...

in which every pair of nines is separated by either one or two zeroes, with equal likelihood. Successive choices of the number of zeroes are independent. The process is strongly periodic, but its period-length is fuzzy, varying between two and three references. Thus, the spectrum of this process will have a broad peak between f=1/2 and f=1/3. An empirical spectrum appears in figure 5.19.

5.5.6 Spectra of Important Processes

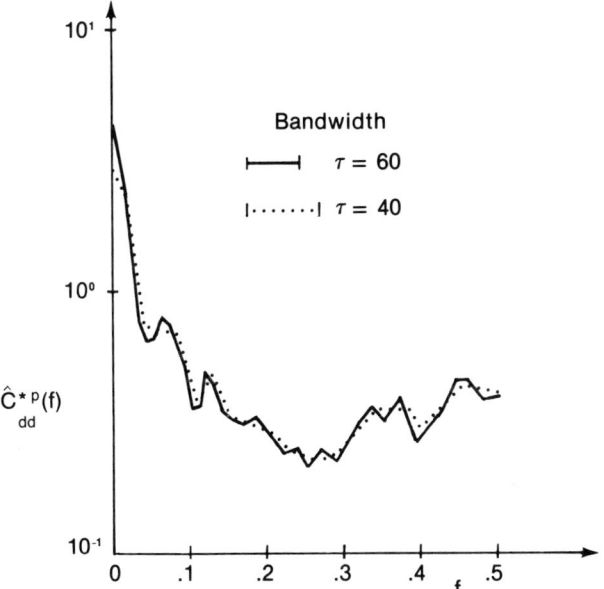

Figure 5.18 Spectrum of distance string A

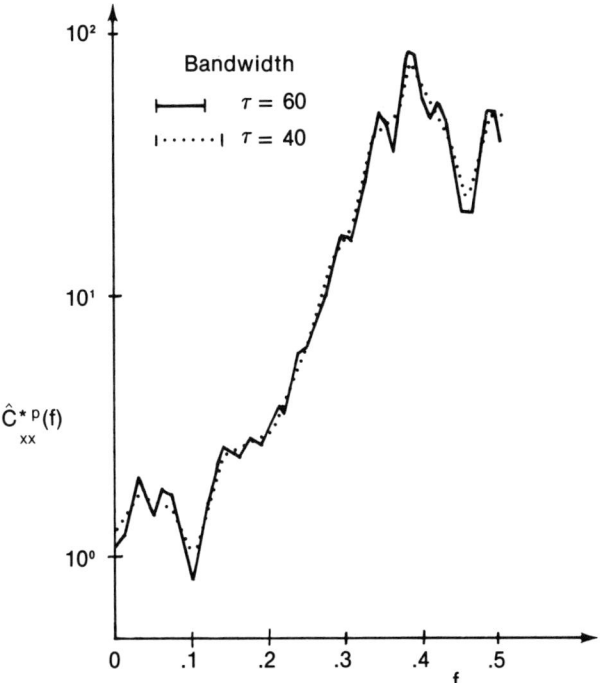

Figure 5.19 Spectrum of process $x(t)=9,0,9,0,0,\ldots$
K=379 samples.

5.5.6 Spectra of Some Important Processes

We can decompose a spectrum to some extent by knowing the spectra of some basic processes. A discrete-time process n(t) is called white noise[4] if:

$$c_{nn}(k) = \begin{cases} \sigma_n^2 & \text{if } k=0 \\ 0 & \text{if } k \neq 0 \end{cases} \qquad (5.26)$$

i.e. --- successive values are uncorrelated. The spectrum of a white noise process is then, from (5.15):

$$c_{nn}^*(f) = \sigma_n^2 \qquad -.5 \leq f \leq .5, \qquad (5.27)$$

a constant. Note that the distance string of an LRU stack model is an example of white noise.

Another useful process is the discrete-time impulse process h(t), defined as follows:

$$h(t) = \begin{cases} h & t=1 \\ 0 & 1 < t \leq K \end{cases} \qquad (5.28)$$

For this process, $\hat{h}=h/K$. Applying (5.17) this time, we have:

---

[4] More formally, this is band limited white noise, since the spectrum exists only for $|f| \leq .5$. True white noise is a continuous-time process having a constant spectrum for $|f| < \infty$.

5.5.6 Spectra of Important Processes

$$C_{xx}^*(f) = \frac{1}{K} \left| \left(h + \sum_{t=0}^{K-1} (-\hat{\bar{h}}) e^{-2\pi i f t} \right) e^{-2\pi i f} \right|^2$$

$$= \frac{h^2}{K} \left| 1 - \frac{1}{K} \sum_{t=0}^{K-1} e^{-2\pi i f t} \right|^2$$

$$= \frac{h^2}{K} \left| 1 - \frac{e^{\pi i f (1-K)}}{K} \frac{e^{\pi f K} - e^{-\pi f k}}{e^{\pi f} - e^{-\pi f}} \right|^2$$

$$= \frac{h^2}{K} \left| 1 - \frac{e^{\pi i f (1-K)}}{K} \frac{\sin[\pi f K]}{\sin[\pi f]} \right|^2 \quad (5.29)$$

The magnitude in expression (5.29) can be evaluated by resorting to vector addition and a little trigonometry, but for program behavior studies an asymptotic formula will usually suffice. If K is very large, the second term inside the vertical bars becomes negligible for $0<|f|\leq.5$, so that:

$$\hat{C}_{xx}^*(f) \approx h^2/K \qquad 0 < |f| \leq .5 . \quad (5.30)$$

Of course, we have already shown that $\hat{C}_{xx}^*(0)=0$ for any process. Note that the same argument (and result) holds for impulses at other than time t=1, since the sample spectrum depends only on the magnitude of the process's Fourier transform.

As a final example, consider the following transition probability matrix of a two-state Markov chain:

$$[p_{ij}] = \begin{bmatrix} a & 1-a \\ 1-a & a \end{bmatrix}$$

Let $x(t)=0$ if the Markov chain is in state 1, and $x(t)=1$ if the Markov chain is in state 2. By symmetry, the model is equally likely to be in either state in equilibrium, so that:

$$E\{x(t)\} = 1/2$$

$$c_{xx}(0) = \sigma_x^2 = 1/4$$

and for $k \geq 0$:

$$c_{xx}(k+1) = E\{x(t+k+1)x(t)\} - \bar{x}$$

$$= E\{[ax(t+k) + (1-a)(1-x(t+k))]x(t)\} - \bar{x},$$

since $x(t+k+1)$ equals either $x(t+k)$ or $1-x(t+k)$, with probability a or 1-a, respectively. Manipulating, and recalling that $\bar{x}=1/2$:

$$c_{xx}(k+1) = (2a-1)c_{xx}(k)$$

and thus:

$$c_{xx}(k) = (1/4) \cdot (2a-1)^k, \quad k \geq 0. \tag{5.31}$$

If $a>1/2$, that is, if $x(t+1)$ is most likely equal to $x(t)$, then all autocovariance coefficients are positive, and we say that this model has **positive serial correlation**. Noting that $c_{xx}(k)=c_{xx}(-k)$, we can, in this case, write the autocovariance in **exponential** form:

$$c_{xx}(k) = c\, e^{-d|k|}, \quad c,d>0; \ -\infty < k < \infty, \tag{5.32}$$

where $c=1/4$ and $d=-\ln[2a-1]$. Many other Markovian processes have an exponential autocovariance function.

5.5.6 Spectra of Important Processes

The spectrum of the above process, with positive serial correlation, can be computed as follows:

$$C_{xx}^*(f) = c \sum_{k=-\infty}^{\infty} e^{-d|k| - 2\pi i f k}$$

$$= c \left[1 + \sum_{k=1}^{\infty} \left(e^{k(-d + 2\pi i f)} + e^{k(-d - 2\pi i f)} \right) \right]$$

$$= c + \frac{ce^{-d + 2\pi i f}}{1 - e^{-d + 2\pi i f}} + \frac{ce^{-d - 2\pi i f}}{1 - e^{-d - 2\pi i f}}$$

$$= \frac{c(1 - e^{-2d})}{(1 - e^{-d})^2 + 2e^{-d}(1 - \cos 2\pi f)} \quad (5.33)$$

after a bit of manipulation. This is easily seen to be monotonically decreasing as f increases from 0 to 1/2. The calculated spectrum, for transition probability a=.99, appears in figure 5.20.

If a<.5 in the Markov model, the magnitude of the autocovariance function still decays exponentially, but with alternating sign. We then say that the model has <u>alternating serial correlation</u>. Note that consecutive values of x(t) also tend to alternate in this case. The spectrum for an alternating correlation model, with a=.01, also appears in figure 5.20. It is monotonically <u>increasing</u>; in fact, it is the reverse (with respect to the absicca) of the spectrum with a=.99 .

High spectral values at f=0 often arise in practice, but their intuitive significance may not be clear. Figure 5.20 may be helpful as an example to guide intuition. With transition probability a near 1, long runs of the same value tend to be generated, so the periods tend to be long. According to the positive-serial-correlation spectrum of figure 5.20,

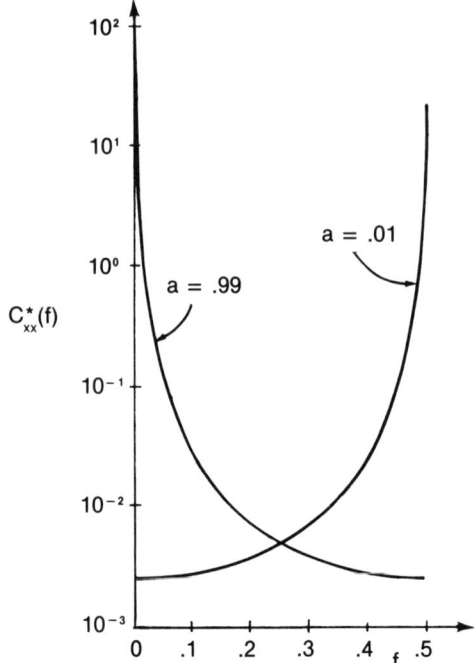

Figure 5.20 Spectra of Markov model, with a=.99 and with a=.01.

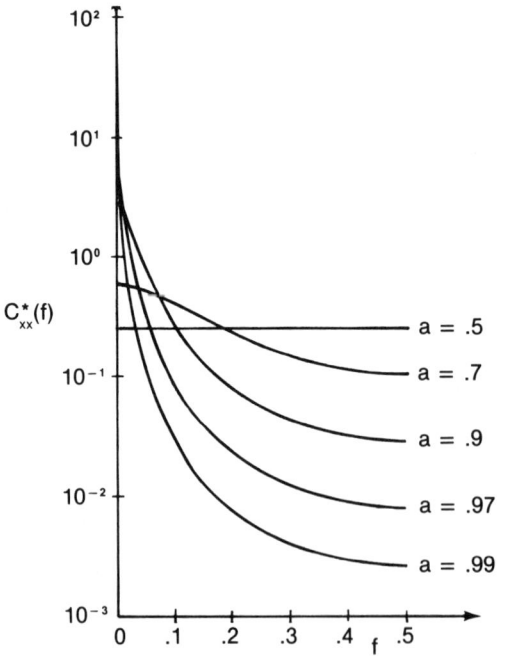

Figure 5.21 Several Markov model spectra, positive serial correlation.

5.5.6 Spectra of Important Processes

the largest contributions to the variance occur at the lowest frequencies (longest periods). To show that this is reasonable, let us consider the limiting behavior, with respect to parameter a, of the spectrum. As $a \to 1$, $x(t)$ becomes nearly constant[5], so that $c_{xx}(k)$ approaches σ_x^2, a constant, for all k. The Fourier transform of a constant is a Dirac delta function at f=0. We can see that with a=.99, the spectrum is beginning to take the shape of such a delta function. Similarly, as $a \to 0$, the values of $x(t)$ strictly alternate, as does $c_{xx}(k)$:

$$c_{xx}(k) = (1/4)(-1)^{|k|} e^{\ln[1-2a]|k|}$$

$$\to (1/4)(-1)^{|k|} .$$

The spectrum in this case would be a delta function at f=1/2, or period 2, and again we see a tendency towards this limiting behavior in the spectrum with a=.01 . A third case of interest is a=1/2, for which successive values of $x(t)$ become independent, so that the spectrum is flat. Thus, as a is made to approach 1/2, the peak at f=0 or f=1/2 will become smaller, and the spectrum will be flatter. Figure 5.21 shows several examples for values of a between 1/2 and 1.

5.5.7 Superposition of Spectra

If two processes $x(t)$ and $y(t)$ are uncorrelated, relation (5.15) implies that the spectrum of the sum process $z(t)=x(t)+y(t)$ is the sum of the two spectra. To show this, observe that:

$$c_{zz}(k) = c_{xx}(k) + c_{yy}(k) \qquad 0 \leq k < \infty$$

---

[5] We must be careful not to actually let a=1, or else the variance of $x(t)$ would vanish. This must be a limiting operation only.

if x(t) and y(t) are uncorrelated processes. Thus, we can predict the effect of additive signals on the spectrum. For instance, suppose process x(t) is specified with power spectrum C_{xx}^* (f), and let z(t) be similar to x(t) except for an inflated (larger) variance. One interpretation is to assume z(t)=x(t)+n(t), for some uncorrelated white noise process n(t), in which case, from (5.26):

$$c_{zz}(k) = c_{xx}(k) + c_{nn}(k)$$

$$= \begin{cases} c_{xx}(0) + \sigma_n^2 & \text{if } k=0 \\ c_{xx}(k) & \text{otherwise} \end{cases}$$

so that, using (5.27):

$$C_{zz}^*(f) = C_{xx}^*(f) + \sigma_n^2 \qquad -.5 \leq f \leq .5 \;.$$

The effect of the variance inflation is to increase all spectral components by the amount of the inflation.

Another example is the effect on the spectrum of isolated large values. Let D=d(1)d(2)...d(K) be an observed distance string containing a large distance of value h. To assess the effect of distance h on the spectrum of string d, we can model as follows: To the distance string we add an impulse process h(t). To ensure that the impulse process and distance string are uncorrelated, we assume that the impulse is equally likely to occur anywhere:

$$h(t) = \begin{cases} h' & \text{if } t=\tau \\ 0 & \text{if } t \in \{1,\ldots, \tau-1, \tau+1,\ldots,K\} \end{cases}$$

where τ is randomly chosen from the set $\{1,\ldots,K\}$. We choose the height of the impulse to be:

$$h' = h - \bar{d}$$

where $\bar{d}$ is the mean stack distance in D. This implies

5.5.7 Superposition of Spectra

that $E\{d(t)+h'\}=h$. Using result (5.30) for the impulse process:

$$C^*_{hh}(f) \approx (h-\bar{d})^2/K .$$

Thus, the large distance contributes an asymptotically vanishing additive constant to all spectral components.

Now, if a_h is the (time-average) probability of a distance of magnitude h, there will be an expected Ka_h such distances in the string. If successive distances are chosen independently, as in the LRU stack model, we can model the cumulative spectral contribution of all value h distances as a sum of contributions from uncorrelated impulse processes. Letting $C^*_{dd,h}(f)$ denote the spectral contribution of all distances h, we have:

$$C^*_{dd,h}(f) = Ka_h[(h-\bar{d})^2/K]$$

$$= a_h(h-\bar{d})^2 .$$

The total power spectrum can be obtained by summing over all h:

$$C^*_{dd}(f) = \sum_{h=1}^{n} a_h(h-\bar{d})^2$$

$$= \sigma_d^2$$

which we obtained previously as the spectrum of a white noise process. We have partitioned the power (variance) of the white noise distance string among distances of each value. Although we have reproduced the spectrum, it should be noted that we have not

really reproduced the distance string itself by our
model of impulses. For example, distances in the
impulse model can have almost unbounded magnitude
where many impulses happen to coincide, but real LRU
distances are bounded by n.

If successive distances are correlated, we cannot
partition in this way. For example, if a large
distance of magnitude h persists for more than one
time instant, its effect on the spectrum will not be a
constant, but a decaying periodic function having a
form like that of the rectangular lag spectral window
(figure 5.17).

Chapter 6
Two Modeling Examples

In this chapter, we shall apply methods of chapter 5 to suggest, and to validate, generative models of specific observed strings. The first example models page faults only. The second reproduces the distributional and correlational statistics of an observed distance string.

6.1 Modeling the Page Fault Process

The aim of the several program behavior models we have considered has been characterization, prediction, and in some cases generation of memory references of a single task. Although such models have many applications, we have used them primarily to compare paging algorithms and memory allocation strategies. However, if we wish to study the page fault behavior of a task (or entire system) given a scheme for memory management, we may not need information as detailed as individual memory references or stack distances. For instance, if a simulation model of a paging system has been constructed, we may drive it by generating page faults from one or more modeled tasks. The detailed behavior of the references is unimportant; only the page fault times are relevant[1]. Of course, an intrinsic reference string model can be used to compute page fault times, but the unneeded detail may complicate the problem of finding an adequate model. Moreover, computational speed will be enhanced in simulations using a page fault model, since it must predict many fewer events than a reference (or distance) string over the same period of virtual time.

Lewis and Shedler [62] and Gaver, Lewis, and Shedler [46] have proposed page fault models. Such

---

[1] In this section we assume a static, externally imposed memory allocation, so that a task's memory space demand is fixed and need not be a part of the model.

models generate an ordered sequence of virtual page fault times $t_1, t_2, \ldots$. In a good model, the sequence will be statistically similar to the sequence of page fault times of a real task, under a given memory allocation policy and paging algorithm. Although a paging algorithm is assumed a priori for such a model, it may be possible to fit the model to observed behavior under different algorithms by manipulation of model parameters. The same is true for memory allocation --- in fact, a convenient model might be explicitly parameterized by m (the memory allocation) or perhaps by T (the working set window size).

We shall discuss the Lewis and Shedler [62] model here. First let us consider, for comparison, the page fault model implied by the LRU stack model. We have already noted in section 4.3 that for a fixed memory allocation, page faults in the SLRUM occur at random, as a Bernoulli process. The lifetime --- the time τ between any two page faults --- has the geometric probability distribution:

$$F_\tau(x) = \Pr[\tau \le x] = 1-[1-f(m)]^x, \qquad (6.1)$$

where $f(m) = 1 - A_m$ is the fixed probability of a page fault. Successive lifetimes are independent and identically distributed random variables. The essential feature is the memoryless property of the geometric distribution. The probability of a page fault at time t is independent of the behavior of the task prior to t. This is a very strong property, since no matter how long the task has executed without a page fault, the distribution of the remaining time until the next fault is unchanged. But this is intuitively unreasonable --- if a task has executed for a long time without a page fault, we should expect it to continue to generate few faults. As we have noted, recent past behavior is the best extrinsic predictor of future behavior. It is probably more reasonable to assume that the longer the time since the last fault, the longer is the expected time until the next.

A similar analysis for the LRU stack model under working set memory management is more difficult. The instantaneous page fault probability depends on the

6.1 Modeling the Page Fault Process

instantaneous working set size:

$$f(t,T) = 1 - A_{w(t,T)} .$$

Since the working set size tends to stay roughly fixed over intervals of many references, it is clear that successive values of fault probability are correlated, but not necessarily equal. Extending this reasoning, the lengths of successive execution intervals (intervals between page faults) are also correlated. By comparison, lifetimes in the fixed-allocation case are uncorrelated for the SLRUM. Under working set allocation, the lifetimes are geometrically distributed with a time-varying fault probability (this is often called a doubly stochastic process [25]). If t is the time of a page fault, the time interval τ until the next fault has the (time-varying) probability distribution:

$$F_\tau(x,t) = 1 - \prod_{i=1}^{x} [1-f(t+i,T)] .$$

Note that between page faults, f(t,T) is monotonically non-decreasing --- it increases in jumps as pages leave the working set. This means that the tail of this distribution decreases faster than exponentially (section 5.5.1).

6.2 A Semi-Markov Page Fault Model

6.2.1 Preliminaries

Lewis and Shedler [62] applied some rather sophisticated statistical techiniqes to postulate a model for a particular task they had measured. They attempted to model only the page fault process, defined to be the sequence $V(1)V(2)...$ such that:

$$V(t) = \begin{cases} 0 & \text{if } d(t) \le m \\ 1 & \text{if } d(t) > m \end{cases} \qquad (6.2)$$

where m is a chosen memory allocation and d(t) is the LRU distance at time t. Lewis and Shedler reported results using three different memory allocations with the same measured distance string of length nearly 9 million references.

A process such as (6.2) above is called a _discrete_ (_time_) _point_ _process_. In general, such a process is based on the occurrence of events (in this case, page faults). Techniques for analyzing and modeling point processes appear in Cox and Lewis [25], and more recently in a collection of papers edited by Lewis [61]. In their attempt to construct a page fault model, Lewis and Shedler used several such techniques to gain insight into the measured process. It will be useful to review them here.

Two spectra will be important in this discussion. The power spectral density of the random process $V(t)$, defined in (6.2), is called the _count_ _spectrum_:

$$R^*_{VV}(f) = 1 + 2 \sum_{k=1}^{\infty} r_{VV}(k) \cos(2\pi k f), \quad |f| \le .5 . \qquad (6.3)$$

The highest meaningful frequency is $f = 1/2$, corresponding to page faults at alternate references.

Another way of describing a point process is by the sequence of _time_ _intervals_ (in this case lifetimes) between events. We denote the sequence of intervals as $\tau(1), \tau(2), \ldots,$ where the first page fault occurs at time $\tau(1)$, the second at time $\tau(1) + \tau(2)$, and so on. It is clear how to derive the process $\tau(i)$ from the process $V(t)$, and vice versa. The reader should keep in mind that $\tau(k)$ refers to _page_ _fault_ _number_ k, not to time k. The power spectral density of process $\tau(i)$ is called the

6.2.1 A Semi-Markov Page Fault Model 211

spectrum of intervals:

$$R^*_{\tau\tau}(f) = 1 + 2 \sum_{k=1}^{\infty} r_{\tau\tau}(k) \cos(2\pi k f) \, , \, |f| \leq .5 \, .$$

(6.4)

As before, the highest meaningful frequency is f=1/2, corresponding here to alternation on page fault number. For example, a peak in the spectrum at f=1/2 indicates that the lifetimes tend to alternate between large and small values.

Since the count and interval spectra depend only on the autocorrelations of processes $V(t)$ and $\tau(i)$, respectively, they are not equivalent for analysis. That is, each will generally contain information omitted from the other, since there are many different processes having a given autocorrelation function. Thus, both spectra are useful as characterizations of a measured page fault process.

6.2.2 Data Analysis

In this section, we summarize the procedures used by Lewis and Shedler to arrive at a model. These procedures are an example of careful statistical methodology applied in a practical situation. The general form of the method is in two parts. First, it is determined if any preprocessing should be done on the data. This includes characterization (and perhaps adjustment for) trends in the data. In the second part of the methodology, the gross features of the data are ascertained. These features, and intuition about the physical process, suggest possible models. Statistical testing may then eliminate some of the proposed models.

Several tests for trend are given in Cox and Lewis [25], chapter 3. One such test, based on the average of all page fault times, was applied by Lewis and Shedler. The data was found to be roughly stationary for the smaller two memory allocations (76 and 197 page frames) but not for the largest (512 page frames). Since memory was assumed initially empty and

loaded on demand, the long fill-up time of the size
512 memory may account for the non-stationarity in
that case. (A conceptually simple test for <u>linear</u>
trend would be to test the sequence of page fault
times $\tau(1)$, $\tau(1)+\tau(2)$, ... for fit to a straight
line --- see [25], page 3. But this test, by itself,
may be inconclusive.) No attempt was made to remove
the trend for the large allocation; rather, in the
subsequent analysis the data was assumed stationary.

The simplest models for a point process are a
(discrete-time) <u>Bernoulli</u> process or a
(continuous-time) <u>Poisson</u> process. These two models,
both zero-<u>th</u> order Markov, are analogous, and for time
scales of thousands of references (as in page fault
models) they are almost indistinguishable. Although
formal tests for a Poisson process were carried out
(c.f. [25] for a description of such tests), Lewis and
Shedler immediately eliminated the Poisson process as
a possible model, because of the large value of the
estimated lifetime coefficient of variation:

$$\hat{v}_\tau = \hat{\sigma}_\tau / \hat{\tau} .$$

The value of v_x for a Poisson process is 1, but values
estimated from the data exceeded 3 for all memory
allocations. Note that page faults in the LRU stack
model <u>are</u> a Bernoulli process; i.e. --- the
probability that $d(t) > m$ is constant, and serially
independent at successive references.

A slightly more complex model for a point process
is a <u>renewal process</u> [25, 38]. Here, the intervals
between events $\tau(1)$, $\tau(2)$, ... are assumed
independent and identically distributed. A test for
this [25] is to estimate the autocorrelation function
of process $\tau(i)$; the theoretical value for a renewal
process is:

$$r_{\tau\tau}(k) = \begin{cases} 1 & \text{if } k=0 \\ 0 & \text{if } k \neq 0 \end{cases} \qquad (6.5)$$

Unfortunately, the estimated value $\hat{r}_{\tau\tau}(1)$ from the
data was too high to be consistent with the

6.2.2 Data Analysis

possibility $r_{\tau\tau}(1) = 0$.

A renewal process is actually the first in a sequence of Markovian models of inter-event times. In an n-th order (Markov) model, the value of $\tau(i)$ depends directly only on the n previous values $\tau(i-n), \ldots, \tau(i-1)$. Since successive lifetimes are independent in a renewal process, it is a zero-th order model[2]. A point process model with n=1 will be called simply a Markov model; in such a model the values $\tau(i-2), \tau(i-3), \ldots$ influence $\tau(i)$ only to the extent that they influence $\tau(i-1)$. This is logically the next model to try.

Box and Jenkins [13] define the partial autocorrelation function $\phi_{xx}(k)$ as a means of testing for n-th order Markov dependence. Function $\phi_{xx}(k)$ has the following property: For an n-th order Markov process,

$$\phi_{xx}(k) > 0, \quad 1 \leq k \leq n$$
$$\phi_{xx}(k) = 0, \quad k > n .$$
(6.6)

A definition of $\phi_{xx}(k)$ for all k ([13], page 83) is difficult; however, the first two values are:

$$\phi_{xx}(1) = r_{xx}(1)$$
$$\phi_{xx}(2) = [r_{xx}(2) - r_{xx}(1)]/[1 - r_{xx}(1)]$$
(6.7)

The value found for estimate $\hat{\phi}_{xx}(2)$, obtained by substituting the estimated autocorrelation coefficients $\hat{r}_{xx}(1)$ and $\hat{r}_{xx}(2)$ into the above

---

[2] That is to say, it is zero-th order with respect to the sequence of lifetimes. There will, in general, be serial correlation in V(t), the page fault process.

definition, was close to zero. Thus a first-order Markov model was suggested for the sequence of lifetimes[3]. However, such a model would require very many states, one for each possible lifetime. One possible approach might be an autoregressive model (c.f. section 6.3), but this was not explored.

Another way of reducing the number of states is to model the sequence of execution intervals as being separated into classes, whose members have independent, identically distributed lifetimes. If this can be done, we choose the <u>class</u> according to a Markov process, so there is one state per class. In this way, a <u>semi-Markov</u> process is formed, in which the <u>ith</u> lifetime $\tau(i)$ depends on the class of $\tau(i-1)$, although not on the actual value of $\tau(i-1)$. Whenever a page fault occurs, the length of the next execution interval is chosen according to the probability distribution associated with the model state. Immediately thereafter, a new state is entered for the succeeding execution interval. Since the model state is not extrinsically observable, Lewis and Shedler used a <u>univariate</u> semi-Markov model [25] --- thus the state is assumed unknown, and knowledge of $\tau(i-1)$ does not fully determine even the distribution of $\tau(i)$. Although a semi-Markov model is not a true Markov model, it does approximately satisfy $\phi_{xx}(2)=0$, and is adequate to explain the data in this respect [62].

The following problems remain:

a) How many states should there be?

b) What should be the form of the lifetime distribution in each state?

c) How can the model parameters be estimated?

---

3) For completeness, $\phi_{xx}(k)$ should be evaluated for enough higher values of k to be reasonably sure that the function remains small for all $k \geq 2$. But if it is computationally infeasible to evaluate more than one partial autocorrelation coefficient, then $\phi_{xx}(2)$ is the most powerful test [62].

6.2.2 Data Analysis

Formal statistical methods now become less available, and Lewis and Shedler began to resort to empirical (even ad hoc) techniques.

The number of states of the underlying Markov process was chosen to be 2. This is the smallest non-trivial number of states (a one-state model is really a zero-th order model), and the gross features of the data were consistent with a two-state model. Physical intuition into the process also supports this choice, since stack distances (hence page faults under LRU paging) can be viewed informally as a two state phenomenon (section 4.3.1). One state (state 1) in the model is intended to represent slow locality variation with rare page faulting; the other (state 2) to represent complete (or nearly complete) changes of locality set with frequent faulting.

The form of the lifetime distribution in the low-fault-rate state can be estimated from the tail of the measured overall lifetime distribution. Figure 6.1[4], reprinted from the paper, shows the empirical lifetime survivor function $\hat{S}_\tau(x)$, defined to be:

$$\hat{S}_\tau(x) = \Pr[\tau(i) > x], \qquad (6.8)$$

as a dotted line. This is the curve for the smallest allocation, m=76. The dashed straight line represents the survivor function that would have been observed had the lifetimes been exponentially distributed with the same mean of 4781 references. This confirms the rejection of the Poisson process. Note that the measured curve is convex for small x and linear for large x (exponential tail). Models sufficient to predict this are the gamma and mixed exponential distributions. However, an anomaly appears in the curve at x=1024, which happens to be the page size, in words, used in the experiments. Many execution intervals of this length occurred, probably due to sequential references in a large array.

---

4) Figures 6.1-6.3 are copyright 1973 by International Business Machines Corporation. Reprinted courtesy IBM.

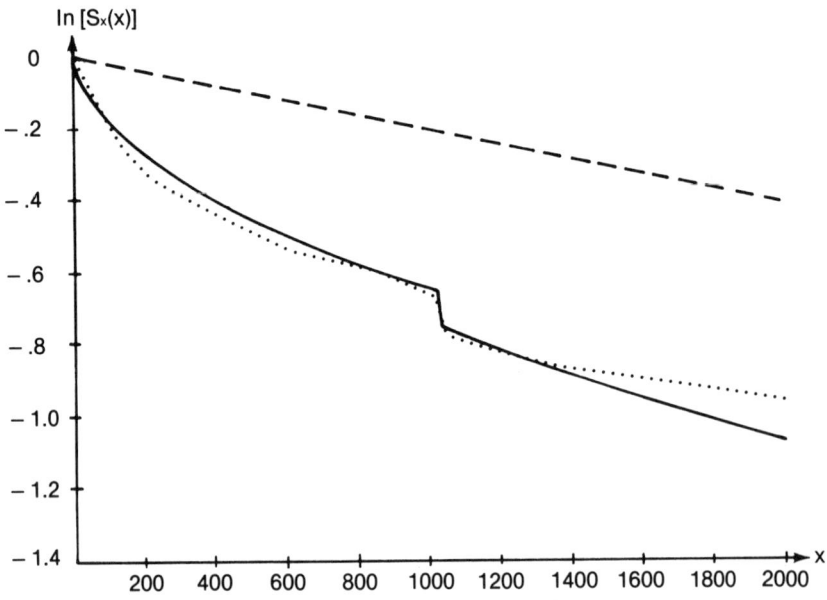

Figure 6.1 Empirical lifetime survivor function (dotted line) and model survivor function (solid line) [62].

6.2.2 Data Analysis

Returning to the semi-Markov model, if the lifetimes in each state were exponentially distributed, the overall lifetime density function would be:

$$f_\tau(x) = \lambda_1 \pi_1 e^{-\lambda_1 x} + (1-\pi_1)\lambda_2 e^{-\lambda_2 x} \qquad (6.9)$$

where π_1 is the equilibrium occupancy probability of state 1. Given the state transition probabilities of the Markov chain, it is easy to compute π_1 (c.f. Howard [53] or Kemeny and Snell [59]). Density function (6.9) is mixed exponential, so we can account for the basic shape (except at x=1024) of the measured survivor curve with a semi-Markov process having exponentially distributed interval lengths.

Actually, the measured lifetime distribution was highly skewed, with many very short intervals. Thus, Lewis and Shedler decided to use a distribution more skewed than exponential, with a decreasing hazard, for high fault rate, short mean lifetime, state 2. The negative binomial distribution, the discrete analog of the gamma distribution, was chosen arbitrarily for parsimony. The form of this distribution is:

$$p_2(x;a) = \Pr[\tau = x \mid \text{state } 2] = \binom{a+x-2}{x-1} p^{x-1}(1-p)^a \qquad (6.10)$$

$$0 < p < 1, \ a > 0$$
$$x = 1, 2, \ldots$$

The lifetimes from long-mean-lifetime state 1 were chosen to be geometrically distributed:

$$p_1(x) = \Pr[\tau = x \mid \text{state } 1] = q^{x-1}(1-q) \qquad (6.11)$$

$$0 < q < 1, \ x = 1, 2, \ldots$$

because of the exponential tail of the measured survivor function. Finally, it was decided on grounds of simplicity to lump the execution intervals of length 1024 into high fault rate state 2. The alternatives were to lump these intervals into state 1 (whose mean lifetime was much greater than 1024) or to create a third state (which would complicate the model and the estimation of its parameters). The final overall lifetime distribution of the model is thus:

$$\Pr[\tau = x] = \pi_1 p_1(x)$$
$$+ (1-\pi_1)[\gamma p_2(x;a) + (1-\gamma)\delta(x-1024)] \quad (6.12)$$

where $1-\gamma$ is the probability that a state 2 interval length is chosen according to probability mass function $\delta(x-1024)$, such that:

$$\delta(k) = \begin{cases} 1 & \text{if } k=0 \\ 0 & \text{otherwise} \end{cases}$$

There are several parameters that must be estimated from the data: parameter q from the geometric distribution, parameters a and p from the negative binomial distribution, parameter γ for the lifetimes equal to 1024, and the Markov transition probabilities. The method of estimation was fairly complicated and admittedly ad hoc; the interested reader should consult reference [62]. For memory allocation m=76 page frames, some estimated values of interest were:

6.2.2 Data Analysis

$$\hat{\mu}_1 = 45,715$$

$$\hat{\mu}_2' = 2023$$

$$\hat{\mu}_2 = 1973$$

$$\hat{a} = 0.45$$

$$\hat{\gamma} = 0.950$$

$$\hat{Q} = \begin{bmatrix} 0.458 & 0.542 \\ 0.038 & 0.962 \end{bmatrix}$$

where μ_1 is the mean of the state 1 lifetimes, μ_2' is the mean of the negative binomial distribution, μ_2 is the overall mean of state 2 lifetimes (including those equal to 1024), and $\hat{Q}$ is the matrix of Markov transition probabilities.

Parameter estimation was repeated for memory allocations 197 and 512. The general conclusion was that the estimated **structural** parameters $\hat{a}$, $\hat{\gamma}$, and $\hat{Q}$ remained roughly **constant** for allocations 76 and 197. Although the corresponding parameter values for allocation 512 differed by as much as 20 per cent, the apparent non-stationarity of the page fault process for this allocation may have been the cause. The primary difference among the allocations was in the **mean values** $\hat{\mu}_1$ and $\hat{\mu}_2'$ of the lifetime distributions. The structure of the model was relatively unaffected by changes in the memory allocation; only the scale changed significantly.

6.2.3 Model Checkout and Validation

Since this is a model of the page fault process rather than of internal task behavior, all statistical aspects of the model may be considered relevant in a functional sense. The model was tested for accuracy in two respects: distributional --- ability to reproduce the distribution of lifetimes, and correlational --- ability to reproduce dependencies among successive lifetimes.

The solid line in figure 6.1 is the computed survivor function of intervals generated by the model. The fit to the measured curve is reasonably good, although for lifetimes approaching 2000 references the model curve seems to be dropping below the measured curve. Figure 6.1 is only the beginning of the survivor function curve, since the maximum execution interval was over 300,000 references long. Since $\hat{\mu}_1 = 45,715$ and $\hat{\mu}_2' = 2023$, the portion of the curve shown is mostly from state 2. Parameter μ_1 was estimated from the slope of the tail of the measured curve, so the fit is actually quite good all along the curve.

Spectral analysis was used to test the correlational fit of the model. Figure 6.2 shows the spectrum of intervals, and figure 6.3 the spectrum of counts, of the measured process and the model. Both figures are reprinted from the paper. In spectral estimation, a smoothing operation must be applied for successful results (section 5.5.5). Two Parzen-window smoothed estimates of the measured process spectrum of intervals are shown in figure 6.2 --- the dots are a highly smoothed estimate (lag 50) and the triangles less so (lag 150). According to Lewis and Shedler, the dots seem to be the more reasonable estimate, but this is highly subjective.

The solid line in figure 6.2 is the computed spectrum of intervals of the model. Here, of course, the spectrum is exact and need not be smoothed. It can be seen that over the range $0 \leq f \leq .5$, the fit is good. However, Lewis and Shedler point out that the spectrum of intervals is a relatively weak test of fit, since it depends on probability distributions $p_1(x)$ and $p_2(x;a)$ only through their first and second

6.2.3 Model Checkout and Validation

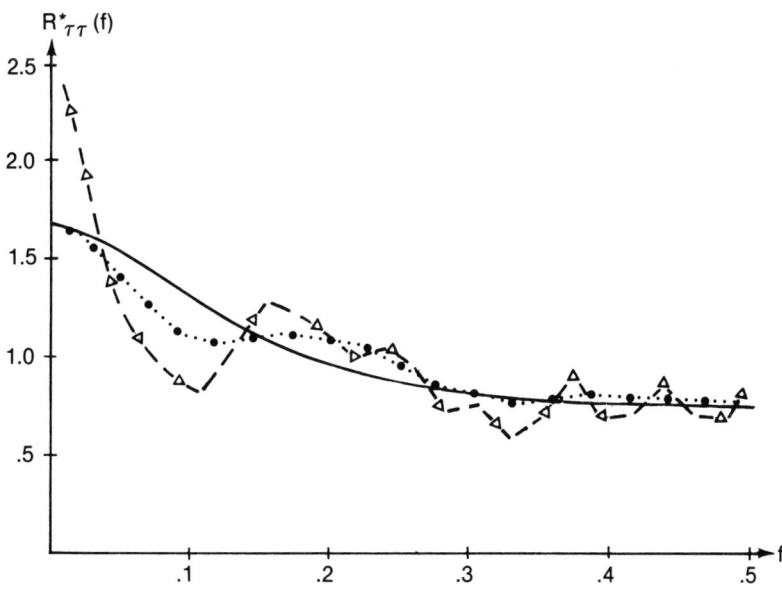

Figure 6.2 Spectra of intervals: empirical (dashed lines) and model (solid line) [62].

222   PROGRAM BEHAVIOR: MODELS AND MEASUREMENTS

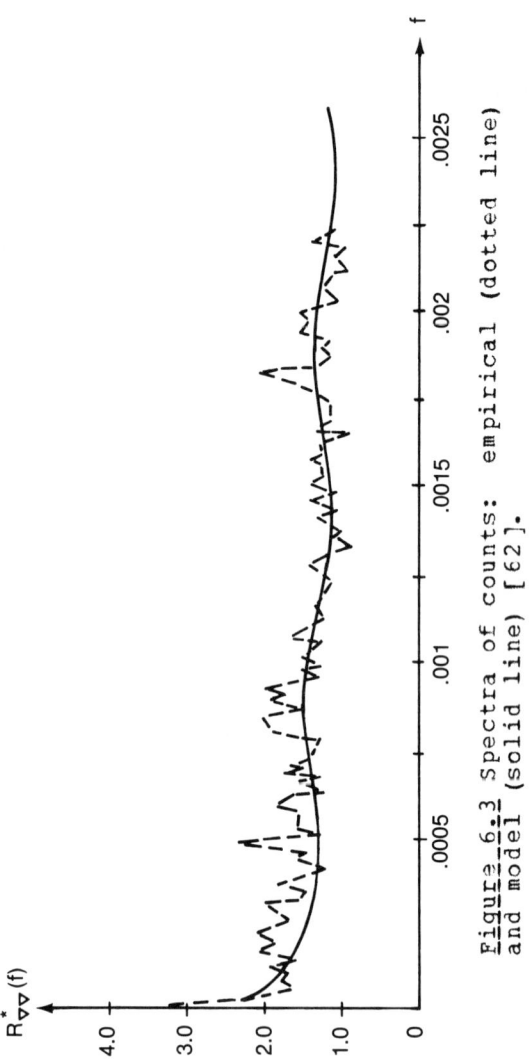

Figure 6.3 Spectra of counts: empirical (dotted line) and model (solid line) [62].

6.2.3 Model Checkout and Validation

moments. (This applies to this particular semi-Markov model, and is not true in general.) Any choice of two lifetime distributions having identical means and variances would produce the same model spectrum of intervals.

We have noted that the spectra of counts and intervals do not supply equivalent information. In this case the spectrum of counts depends on more detailed assumptions about $p_1(x)$ and $p_2(x;a)$. A difficulty (other than smoothing) in estimating the spectrum of counts in this case is that frequency here corresponds to page fault *time*; for instance, a frequency of 1/2 corresponds to a fault every other reference. Since the largest observed lifetime exceeded 300,000, there might conceivably be spectral peaks at any of the frequencies 1/2, 1/3, ..., up to 1/300000 or so. Of particular interest was the frequency 1/1024, since inclusion of the lifetimes of value 1024 into state 2 was on rather tenuous grounds. To resolve a peak of frequency 1/1024 from its harmonics and sub-harmonics requires evaluation of the spectrum much more often than at 1/512, 1/1024, 1/2048, etc., at least in this frequency range. Not only is this expensive, but there is doubt that the resolution can be accomplished at all unless the number of data points (page fault times) is very large.

Lewis and Shedler were able to obtain the required resolution by rather complicated methods, indicated in their paper, which are outside the scope of this discussion. The dashed line connecting the dots in figure 6.3 is the resulting estimated spectrum of counts of the observed page fault process. The solid curve is the computed spectrum of the model. To save computation time, the empirical spectrum was computed only for frequencies 0 through 1/449 references. Since the full spectrum goes to frequency 1/2, only about 0.4 per cent of the spectrum is shown; however, since most observed lifetimes exceeded 449 (the median was 1024), much of the important information is in this part of the curve.

The fit in figure 6.3 is good, but there are small peaks in the estimated spectrum at frequencies roughly equal to 1/512, 1/1024, and 1/2048. The conclusion drawn by Lewis and Shedler was that intervals of length 1024 should have been modeled as a separate state. The model spectrum has no peaks at frequency 1/1024 or its harmonics or sub-harmonics, so the model has no special tendency to generate page fault sequences 1024 references apart. Why does the model lack this tendency? The reason is found in the estimated value $1-\hat{\gamma} = 0.05$, which is (essentially) the probability that an execution interval from state 2 is of length 1024. This probability is small enough so that sequences of more than one or two successive intervals of this length are rare. No particular periodicity occurs. The peaks in the measured spectrum indicate that the lifetimes of value 1024 tend to occur in clusters, which is intuitively reasonable by their interpretation as sequential accesses through a large array. A more accurate model would have a third state to generate only intervals of this length, often several in succession. But this additional accuracy is probably not worth the complication of a third state, and the two-state model appears adequate for practical use.

Lewis and Shedler tested one other page fault trace, and found that the same model structure approximately held.

6.3 A Markovian Distance String Model

In section 5.5.3, we saw that the distance string correlogram of reference string A was reasonably well fit by an exponential function (at least out to lag 60). Many first-order Markov processes have exponentially decaying correlograms; hence they are potential models for this string. But as we noted in chapter 4, the general first-order Markov model has very many parameters. We shall presently obtain a model which is more parsimonious than even the LRU stack model. Since we intend this to be an example of model construction in practice, where a model is proposed, validated, and improved based on the validation results, the following discussion is rather long. For those interested only in the final model, it appears in a form suitable for simulation as algorithm 6.1, section 6.3.6.

The LRU stack model has n-1 freely chosen

6.3 A Markovian Distance String Model

parameters. To reduce this number requires an assumption about the functional form of the distance probabilities. In section 3.1.2 we showed that the distance distribution of reference string A was approximated adequately by Belady's lifetime function:

$$\Pr[d(t) > i] = 1 - A_i = (.213) i^{-2.88} . \qquad (6.13)$$

We shall design a model which predicts this Pareto distribution.

In like manner, we must also consider special cases of Markov models, to avoid an excess of parameters. For any random variable $x(t)$, define:

$$x^0(t) = x(t) - E\{x(t)\} . \qquad (6.14)$$

Of course, $x^0(t)$ has mean zero. The following linear differential equation is often used to model a physical process $w(t)$ in continuous time:

$$w^0(t) = b_1 \frac{d}{dt} w^0(t) + b_2 \frac{d^2}{dt^2} w^0(t) + \ldots + b_k \frac{d^k}{dt^k} w^0(t)$$

$$+ e^0(t) \qquad (6.15)$$

for parameters $b_1, \ldots, b_k$, and white noise process $e^0(t)$ called the <u>random shock</u> or <u>innovation function</u>. Successive values of $e^0(t)$ are independent; moreover, $e^0(t)$ and $w^0(t-1)$ are independent. The discrete-time analog of this can be written as:

$$w^0(t) = a_1 w^0(t-1) + a_2 w^0(t-2) + \ldots + a_k w^0(t-k)$$

$$+ e^0(t) . \qquad (6.16)$$

Either form above is termed an <u>autoregressive process</u> of order k, since $w(t)$ depends in Markovian fashion only on its k prior values. An autoregressive process is a k<u>th</u> order Markov chain, but not all Markov chains are autoregressive. While the idea of modeling stack distances by a differential equation may seem peculiar, it is a simple, parsimonious way to introduce Markov dependence.

Autoregressive process (6.16) has several features that make it apparently unsuitable for distance string modeling. One is that w(t) is continuous-valued; another is that w(t) may be negative. We may satisfy the first objection as follows: notice that the straight line fit in the correlogram of figure 5.16 is poor for lag zero, the variance. As a matter of fact, the line shown was obtained by linear regression on the logarithms of $\hat{c}_{dd}$ (1), ..., $\hat{c}_{dd}$ (60) --- the outlying variance at lag zero was ignored. One way to account for such an inflated variance is to assume the existence of a white noise <u>measurement error</u> process n(t), so that the stack distance actually observed is:

$$d(t) = w(t) + n(t) .\qquad(6.17)$$

Assuming processes n(t) and w(t) to be uncorrelated, we have:

$$c_{dd}(k) = E\{d(t+k)d(t)\} = \begin{cases} c_{ww}(0) + c_{nn}(0) & \text{if } k=0 \\ c_{ww}(k) & \text{otherwise} \end{cases}$$

(6.18)

Thus, the variance of the observed process is inflated by the variance of the measurement error. Suppose stack distances are inaccurate observations of a (fictitious) continuous-valued process w(t); in particular:

$$d(t) = \lceil w(t) \rceil \qquad(6.19)$$

where the notation $\lceil x \rceil$ denotes the smallest integer which is not less than x. Hence:

$$n(t) = \lceil w(t) \rceil - w(t) .$$

This is not quite in the form (6.17), since n(t) and w(t) are correlated, but we shall assume them uncorrelated as an approximation.

Ignoring the difficulty of negative values of w(t), an attempt was made to model the observed

6.3 A Markovian Distance String Model 227

distance string as an autoregressive process. The main problem in such an effort is to find the order of the autoregression, and there are several methods. Box and Jenkins [13] describe a scheme based on the partial autocorrelation function (section 6.2.2), but we applied an information-theoretic procedure due to Aikake [2] (or see Jones [56]). The procedure failed to terminate at order 30, indicating that this distance string d(1)d(2)...d(200000) is autoregressive of only a very high order (if at all).

Since a first-order model predicts the exponentially decaying autocovariance function, we decided to re-examine it. The autocovariance of a first-order autoregressive process

$$w^0(t) = aw^0(t-1) + e^0(t) \qquad (6.20)$$

is (c.f. Box and Jenkins [13]):

$$c_{ww}(k) = \sigma_\varepsilon^2 a^k / (1-a^2) , \quad k \geq 0, \qquad (6.21)$$

where σ_ε^2 denotes the variance of the innovation function $e^0(t)$. The best fit exponential function to the correlogram (figure 5.16) was found to be:

$$\hat{c}_{dd}(k) = (.113) e^{-.035|k|} . \qquad (6.22)$$

(Note the slowness of decay.) To predict this behavior, a first-order autoregressive process must have:

$$a = e^{-.035} \approx .9656$$

so the model is:

$$w^0(t) = (.9656) w^0(t-1) + e^0(t) . \qquad (6.23)$$

If a=1, the model becomes a <u>random walk</u> (with infinite variance), so this is very nearly a random walk. In particular, $w^0(t)$ will tend to "stick" at large positive or negative values for long periods of time, and very long runs of large distances will occur.

This is an unsatisfactory distance string model.

Model (6.23) can be improved by adding a restoring force; i.e. --- a mechanism for periodically resetting the value of $w^o(t)$. Define the restoring autoregressive model of order 1 as follows:

$$w^o(t) = \begin{cases} aw^o(t-1)+e^o(t) & \text{with probability } p \\ e^o(t) & \text{with probability } 1-p \end{cases} \qquad (6.24)$$

For this model, we have:

$$c_{ww}(0) = E\{[w^o(t)]^2\}$$

$$= pE\{[aw^o(t-1)+e^o(t)]^2\} + (1-p)E\{[e^o(t)]^2\}$$

$$= pa^2 c_{ww}(0) + p\sigma_\varepsilon^2 + (1-p)\sigma_\varepsilon^2$$

so that:

$$c_{ww}(0) = \sigma_\varepsilon^2 / (1-pa^2) . \qquad (6.25)$$

Similarly:

$$c_{ww}(k+1) = E\{w^o(t+k+1) w^o(t)\}$$

$$= pE\{[aw^o(t+k)+e^o(t+k)]w^o(t)\} + (1-p)E\{e^o(t+k) w^o(t)\}$$

$$= paE\{w^o(t+k) w^o(t)\}$$

$$= pa\, c_{ww}(k) . \qquad (6.26)$$

Combining (6.25) and (6.26):

$$c_{ww}(k) = [\sigma_\varepsilon^2 / (1-pa^2)](pa)^{|k|} , \quad -\infty < k < \infty .$$

Thus, the restoring autoregressive model has an exponential autocovariance $c_{ww}(k)$ proportional to $e^{|k|\ln[pa]}$

6.3 A Markovian Distance String Model

To fit reference string A with the restoring model, we must have:

$$pa = .9656, \qquad pa^2 < 1$$

which together imply:

$$p > .9656^2 = .932 \ .$$

Within these constraints, any value may be chosen. If we select p close to one, the model will have a tendency to generate long runs of (possibly large) distances before restoring. If we choose $p < .9656$, then $a > 1$ so that $w(t)$ [hence $d(t)$] will tend to increase steadily between restorals. There is no intuitive reason to believe that such behavior occurs in real strings. A compromise is to choose $a = 1$, for which we have a __restoring random walk__. Parameters in the resulting model are:

$$p = .9656$$

$$a = 1$$

$$\sigma_\varepsilon^2 = (1-p)\sigma_w^2 = .0039$$

using (6.22). The mean time between restorals is:

$$1/(1-p) = 29.1$$

The very small variance of $e^0(t)$ indicates that large distances, when they occur, will usually be generated repeatedly until restoral. This implies large distance clusters of expected length approximately 29.1, which is probably too long. Phase transitions will not usually involve as many as 29 pages. On the other hand, the smallest possible $p = .932$ implies a mean time between restorals of 14.8 references. Even if this is marginally acceptable, the model may be unstable in practice, since the denominator of the variance (6.25) will be very nearly zero.

There are two other problems with this model. First, as we have mentioned, negative values of $w^0(t)$ will arise. If these are simply thrown out, or set to zero, the autocovariance function shape will be disturbed. Second, we have not characterized innovation function $e^0(t)$, other than by its mean (zero) and variance. To produce Pareto distance distribution (6.13) in this model, we must be more specific. Most of the literature on autoregressive processes assumes normally distributed random variables and is not directly applicable. Let $f_{\epsilon^0}(x)$ and $f_{w^0}(x)$ be the probability density functions for random variables $e^0(t)$ and $w^0(t)$, respectively. To compute the probability $Pr[w \leq w^0(t) < w+dw]$ for any number w, there are two cases: If a restoral occurs, it is equal to $Pr[w \leq e^0(t) < w+dw]$; otherwise it is equal to $Pr[w \leq w^0(t-1)+e^0(t) < w+dw]$. Recall that $w^0(t-1)$ and $e^0(t)$ are independent, so that the latter probability can be obtained from a convolution. Thus:

$$f_{w^0}(w) = (1-p)f_{\epsilon^0}(w) + p\int_{-\infty}^{\infty} f_{w^0}(\phi/a) f_{\epsilon^0}(w-\phi) d\phi .$$

(6.27)

Because of the convolution, it is appropriate to invoke Fourier transforms. The Fourier transform of any function $g(x)$ is:

$$\mathcal{F}[g(x)] = G^*(s) = \int_{-\infty}^{\infty} g(x) e^{-isx} dx .$$

It is easily shown by a change of variable that:

$$\mathcal{F}[g(x/a)] = aG^*(as) .$$ (6.28)

Noting that convolutions map to products of the transformed functions, we have from (6.27) and (6.28):

$$F_{w^0}^*(s) = \mathcal{F}[f_{w^0}(x)]$$

$$= (1-p)F_{\epsilon^0}^*(s) + paF_{w^0}^*(as) F_{\epsilon^0}^*(s)$$

so that

$$F_{\epsilon^0}^*(s) = F_{w^0}^*(s) / [1-p+paF_{w^0}^*(as)] .$$ (6.29)

6.3 A Markovian Distance String Model

Although (6.29) looks simple, it is hard to find satisfactory density functions $f_{w^o}(x)$ and $f_{\epsilon^o}(x)$ which solve it. In the next section we shall obtain a solution, after making an important modification to the model.

6.3.1 The Restoring Log Random Walk Model (RLRWM)

We can solve the problem of negative values, and mitigate the problem of overly long distance runs, by defining autoregression on the _logarithm_ of a random variable. For analytical convenience, we shall assume a=1 in expression (6.24), so we have the following restoring random walk:

$$w^o(t) = \begin{cases} w^o(t-1) + e^o(t) & \text{with probability } p \\ e^o(t) & \text{with probability } 1-p \end{cases} \quad (6.30)$$

Define random variable $x(t)$ to be a (fictitious) continuous-valued stack distance, as follows:

$$x(t) = e^{w(t)} = e^{w^o(t) + \bar{w}}$$

$$d(t) = \lceil x(t) \rceil . \quad (6.31)$$

Note that $x(t) > 0$ for all real values of $w^o(t)$. Expressions (6.30) and (6.31) imply:

$$x(t+1) = \begin{cases} x(t)\,\delta(t+1) & \text{with probability } p \\ e^{\bar{w}}\,\delta(t+1) & \text{with probability } 1-p \end{cases} \quad (6.32)$$

where

$$\delta(t) = e^{\epsilon^o(t)} . \quad (6.33)$$

We call this the _restoring log random walk model_. Taking expected values of both sides of (6.32), and manipulating, we have:

$$\bar{x} = e^{\bar{w}}(1-p)\bar{\delta} / (1-p\bar{\delta}) . \quad (6.34)$$

The RLRWM predicts an exponentially decaying autocovariance for continuous-valued "stack distance" x(t). We show this as follows: using (6.32), we have for k>0:

$$c_{xx}(k) = E\{x(t+k)x(t)\} - \bar{x}^2$$

$$= pE\{\delta(t+k)x(t+k-1)x(t)\}$$
$$+ (1-p)e^{\bar{w}}E\{\delta(t+k)x(t)\} - \bar{x}^2$$

$$= p\bar{\delta}[c_{xx}(k-1) + \bar{x}^2] + (1-p)e^{\bar{w}}\bar{\delta}\,\bar{x} - \bar{x}^2 .$$

Substituting expression (6.34) and manipulating:

$$c_{xx}(k) = p\bar{\delta}\,c_{xx}(k-1)$$

so that

$$c_{xx}(k) = c_{xx}(0)e^{|k|\ln[p\bar{\delta}]} . \qquad (6.35)$$

Although this model is a random walk in $w^o(t)$, it is not a random walk in continuous-valued "stack distance" x(t). Since w(t)=log[x(t)], the larger the value of x(t), the greater will be the effect of changes in w(t). When the distances generated by this model become large, their variance also becomes large. High values of x(t) will often sharply decline even without restoral, so the expected length of large-distance runs is less than that of the ordinary restoring autoregressive model. Furthermore, such runs will consist of relatively more distinct values. Our physical intuition about distance strings indicates these to be desirable effects.

However, we make no claim at all that the model is intrinsically meaningful, except as a special case of a Markov distance string model. There is no reason to believe that successive distances of real tasks are generated in the intrinsic manner of the model. Recall that an autoregressive process, for our purposes, is nothing more than a parsimonious kind of

6.3.1 The RLRWM

Markov chain. An oddity is that the RLRWM has an uncountable number of states, corresponding to the possible values of $x(t)$ or $w(t)$.

We now consider a solution to Fourier transform equation (6.29). Belady's lifetime function implies a Pareto distribution of stack distances:

$$S_x(x) = ax^{-b}$$

so that

$$S_w(w) = S_x(e^w) = ae^{-bw}$$

$$f_w(w) = -\frac{d}{dw} S_w(w) = abe^{-bw}.$$

Note, however, that this form for $f_w(w)$ blows up for $w \ll 0$. For this reason, and for ease in solving (6.29), the following probability density was chosen for $w^o(t)$:

$$f_{w^o}(w) = (b/2)e^{-b|w|}. \qquad (6.36)$$

Straightforward integration shows the Fourier transform of this to be:

$$F^*_{w^o}(s) = b^2/(b^2+s^2).$$

Substituting into (6.29), we find:

$$F^*_{\epsilon^o}(s) = \beta^2/(\beta^2+s^2)$$

where

$$\beta = b/(1-p)^{1/2}$$

and thus:

$$f_{\varepsilon^\circ}(x) = (\beta/2)e^{-\beta|x|} \quad . \tag{6.37}$$

We have now characterized innovation function $e^\circ(t)$, so we can use the model to generate distance strings. From (6.31) and (6.36) we obtain:

$$F_x(x) = F_{w^\circ}(\log x - \bar{w})$$

$$= \begin{cases} .5(xe^{-\bar{w}})^b & 0 \le x < e^{\bar{w}} \\ 1-.5(xe^{-\bar{w}})^{-b} & x \ge e^{\bar{w}} \end{cases} \tag{6.38}$$

and thus:

$$f_x(x) = (b/2)e^{-\bar{w}} \cdot \begin{cases} (xe^{-\bar{w}})^{b-1} & 0 \le x < e^{\bar{w}} \\ (xe^{-\bar{w}})^{-b-1} & x \ge e^{\bar{w}} \end{cases} \tag{6.39}$$

We can find the mean of $x(t)$ by direct integration:

$$\bar{x} = e^{\bar{w}}[b^2/(b^2-1)] \quad .$$

Comparing with (6.34), we find:

$$\bar{\delta} = b^2/[b^2-(1-p)] > 1 \tag{6.40}$$

which means that there is a tendency for $x(t)$ to increase between restorals. To see that this tendency is slight, consider the expected multiplicative increase between restorals, which is:

6.3.1 The RLRWM

$$1(1-p) + \bar{\delta} p(1-p) + \bar{\delta}^2 p^2(1-p) + \ldots$$

$$= (1-p)/(1-\bar{\delta} p)$$

$$= [b^2 - (1-p)]/(b^2-1)$$

$$< b^2/(b^2-1) \approx 4/3 \text{ if } b \approx 2 .$$

This is a tolerable increase; in many cases it will not be enough to change the measured (discrete-valued) distance $d(t)$ at all during an inter-restoral interval.

6.3.2 RLRWM Parameter Estimation

There are only three freely chosen parameters in the RLRWM: p, b, and $\bar{w}$. All others can be computed from these three. Their estimation to fit a measured distance string is straightforward, as follows: b and $\bar{w}$ are chosen to fit the empirical stack distance distribution. We assume, of course, that the distribution can be adequately approximated by Belady's lifetime function. If the observed distance survivor function is plotted on log-log paper as in figure 5.15, b is the (negative of the) slope of the best fit straight line:

$$\log \Pr[d(t) > i] = -b \log i - \log a . \qquad (6.41)$$

To find $\bar{w}$, choose i such that $e^{\bar{w}} < i$ (usually $i=2$ will be sufficient, but the actual value of i will not enter into the result). From (6.38):

$$\Pr[d(t) \leq i] = \Pr[x(t) \leq i]$$

$$= F_x(i)$$

$$= 1 - .5(e^{\bar{w}}/i)^b .$$

Solving for $\bar{w}$:

$$\bar{w} = \ln i + (1/b)\ln[2(1-F_x(i))]$$

$$= \ln i + (1/b)\ln 2 + (1/b)\ln \Pr[d>i] .$$

Using (6.41), and manipulating:

$$\bar{w} = (1/b)\ln[2/a] , \qquad (6.42)$$

so that $\bar{w}$ is also estimated from the stack distance distribution.

Finally, we estimate p, the probability of no restoral, to fit the empirical decay of the autocovariance function. Suppose the autocovariance function is:

$$\hat{c}_{dd}(k) \sim e^{-\alpha|k|} .$$

Using (6.35) and (6.40), we have immediately:

$$e^{-\alpha} = p\bar{\delta}$$

$$= pb^2/(b^2-1+p) .$$

Solving for p:

$$p = (b^2-1)/(b^2 e^\alpha - 1) . \qquad (6.43)$$

For reference string A, the estimated parameters were:

$$p = .9611$$

$$b = 2.88$$

$$\bar{w} = -.296 .$$

6.3.3 Validation of the RLRWM

Correlational calculations for this model tend to be very difficult, largely because of the least-integer function used to convert x(t) to d(t).

6.3.3 RLRWM Validation

For this reason, simulation was used to test the model. A distance string of length 400,000 was generated by the model, and analyzed as though it had been measured from a real task.

Algorithm 5.5 was used to calculate the correlogram, and the result is shown in figure 6.4 as a dotted line. The model and distance string A autocovariance functions follow each other, except that the model inflates all coefficients by a multiplicative factor of approximately 2.8 . The correlation between d(t) and n(t) is probably not the cause --- such a correlation should have an additive rather than a multiplicative effect. The discrepancy is that the distance string A variance inflation is really too large to be explained as a "measurement error" n(t). Suppose, as an example, that n(t) were uniformly distributed[5] between 0 and 1. Its variance would then be easily computed as $1/12 \approx .083$. As can be seen in figure 6.4, the variance inflation of the modeled string is actually somewhat less, about .05 . [Recall that n(t) is in fact neither uniformly distributed, nor independent of x(t).] But the variance inflation of distance string A is about .35, which is much too large to be caused by n(t).

The spectrum of the model, obtained using algorithm 5.6, is shown in figure 6.5. The curve shown is for lag window $\tau=60$; it is so smooth that the estimates for smaller lags need not be considered. The model spectrum has the characteristic shape of a first-order autoregressive (Markov) process with positive serial correlation --- this is to be expected because of the nearly perfect exponential correlogram of the model in figure 6.4.

The fit of the model to the observed spectrum is poor. Much of the problem in the lower half of the frequency range reflects the model's failure to account for the measured variance inflation. In the frequency range roughly .05 to .25, the measured task and model spectra differ by an additive value of .3 or

---

[5] Of course, it doesn't really have a uniform distribution. Since the density of x(t) is monotonically decreasing, that of n(t) must be monotonically *increasing* between 0 and 1. The variance of such a process will be less than that of a uniformly distributed random variable.

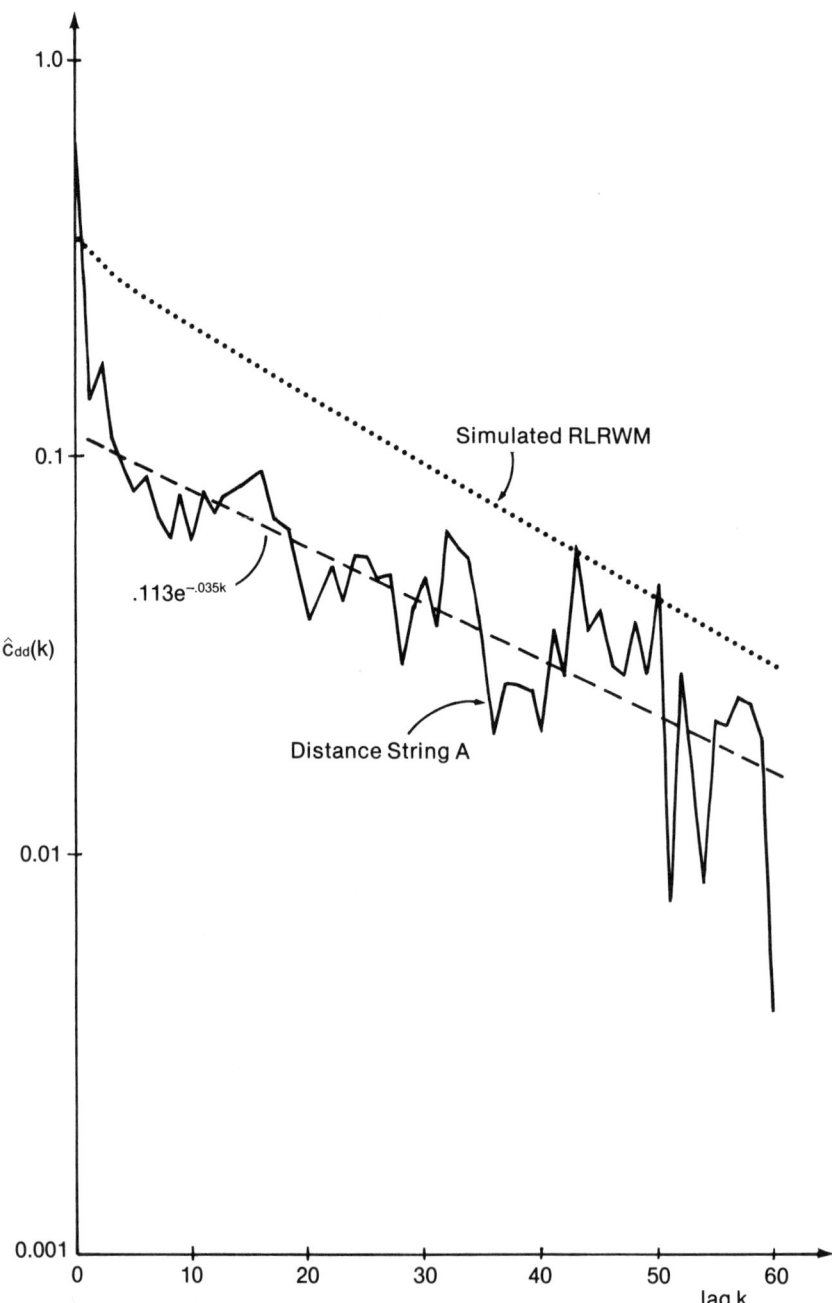

Figure 6.4 RLRWM correlogram (dotted line) and distance string A correlogram (solid line).

6.3.3 RLRWM Validation

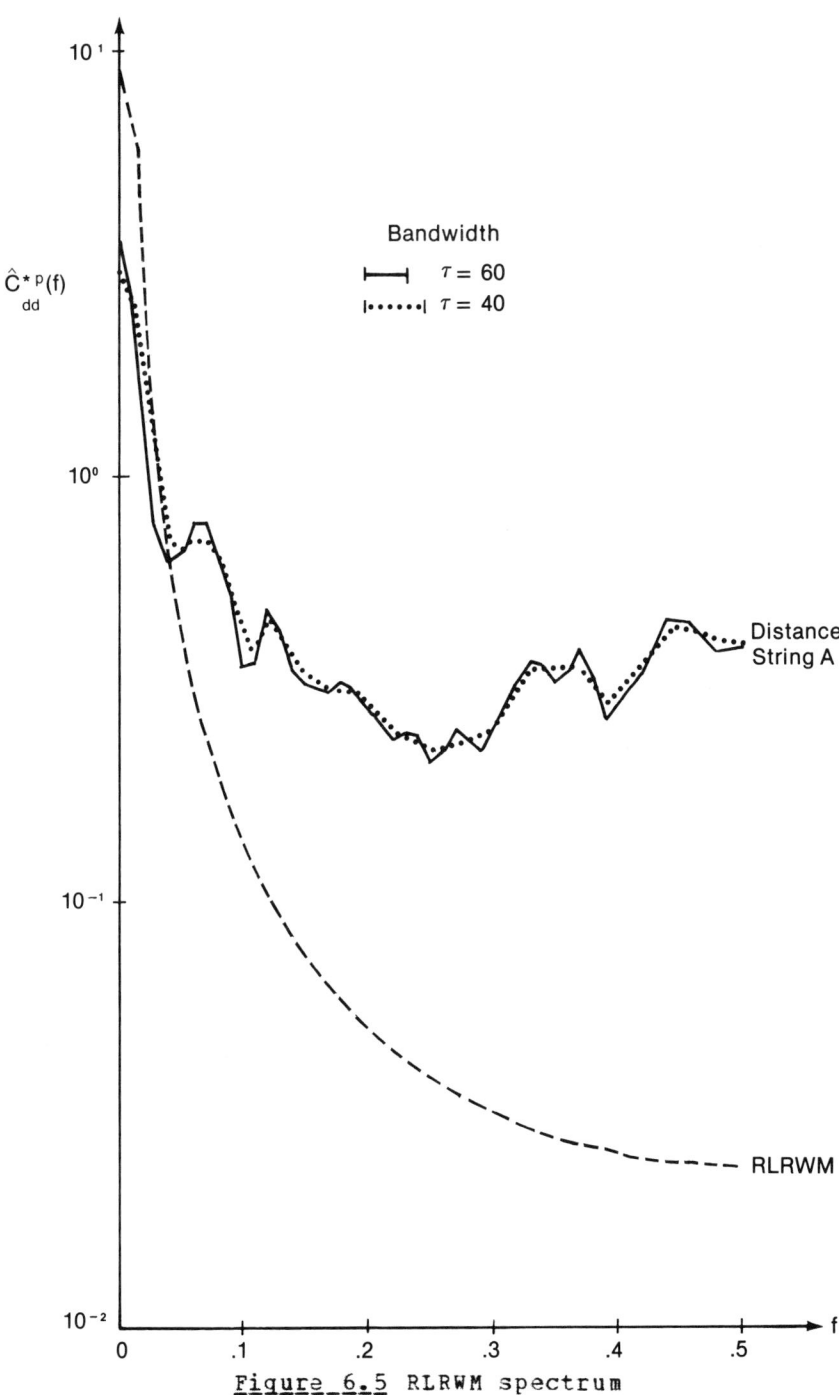

Figure 6.5 RLRWM spectrum

so, which is the unaccounted-for inflation.

The model also has too high a spectrum at frequency zero. This is an indication that the model tends to generate overly-long runs of distances. Recall the results of section 5.5.6 on the spectrum of a model with an exponential autocovariance function.

A final point of disagreement is in the higher frequencies, above .25, where the measured-task spectrum increases. These frequencies correspond to periods of 1/.25=4 references or less, so there are periodicities in the distance string of short duration which we have not attempted to predict in the model. These are probably of little functional consequence, since the period length indicates them to be oscillations of intra-locality distances. Thus, we shall make no attempt to model this effect.

6.3.4 A Noisy RLRWM

In principle, it should be straightforward to improve the model to account for the excess variance inflation of the observed distance string. We can add a white noise process, with a variance of .3, to the distance string generated by the RLRWM. But while this will inflate the resultant variance, it will also change the distribution of the generated distances. We would like to find a probability density which, when convolved with a Pareto density (as generated by the RLRWM), yields a Pareto density as a result. But to the author's knowledge, no such distribution exists[6].

Fortunately, we can also achieve variance inflation by taking the _product_ of the modeled distance string with an independent noise process. Consider independent processes $x(t)$ and $y(t)$, with $y(t)$ white noise. Let:

$$z(t) = x(t)y(t) \quad , \quad t=1,2,\ldots$$

---

6) except, of course, for the Dirac delta function; however this has variance zero.

6.3.4 A Noisy RLRWM

The variance of $z(t)$ is:

$$c_{zz}(0) = E\{x^2(t)y^2(t)\} - E^2\{x(t)y(t)\}$$

$$= E\{x^2(t)\}E\{y^2(t)\} - \bar{x}^2\bar{y}^2$$

$$= \sigma_x^2 E\{y^2(t)\} + \sigma_y^2 \bar{x}^2 . \qquad (6.44)$$

An appropriate choice of process $y(t)$ will yield $c_{zz}(0) > c_{xx}(0)$. On the other hand, for $k \geq 1$:

$$c_{zz}(k) = E\{x(t+k)y(t+k)x(t)y(t)\} - \bar{x}^2\bar{y}^2$$

$$= E\{x(t+k)x(t)\}\bar{y}^2 - \bar{x}^2\bar{y}^2$$

since successive values of $y(t)$ are uncorrelated, so that:

$$c_{zz}(k) = \bar{y}^2 c_{xx}(k) , \quad |k| \geq 1 . \qquad (6.45)$$

If $\bar{y}=1$, then $z(t)$ and $x(t)$ have identical autocovariance functions for $|k|>0$.

Recall that in the RLRWM, $x(t)$ is a continuous-valued "stack distance", and $w(t)$ is its logarithm. To multiply $x(t)$ by a noise process, we need only add the noise to $w(t)$. Let the probability density of $w^o(t) = w(t) - \bar{w}$ be, from (6.36):

$$f_{w^o}(w) = (b'/2)e^{-b'|w|} . \qquad (6.46)$$

Let $n'(t)$ be a white noise process, and let $n'^o(t) = n'(t) - \bar{n}'$ have probability density[7]:

$$f_{n'^o}(n) = (b/b')^2 \delta(n) + [1-(b/b')^2](b/2)e^{-b|n|} \qquad (6.47)$$

---

7) This density was found by solving a Laplace transform equation. The derivation is not difficult.

for some b<b', where δ(n) is the Dirac delta function. Then it can be shown, using Laplace transforms or by direct integration, that the convolution is:

$$f_{w+n'}(x) = (b/2)e^{-b|x-\bar{w}-\bar{n}'|} .$$

Since addition of n'(t) leaves the functional form of the density of w(t) unchanged, it will leave that of x(t) unchanged as well. Note that b will now be the Pareto exponent of the final generated string, so that the underlying RLRWM will have to generate a distribution with a larger exponent b'.

We call this the <u>noisy restoring log random walk model</u> (<u>NRLRWM</u>). We must determine the following

parameters: b, b', $\bar{w}$, $\bar{n}'$, and p (the probability of no restoral of the underlying RLRWM). Not all of these parameters are independent, however; we will show that only four are necessary to determine the model.

6.3.5 NRLRWM Parameter Estimation

We will now determine the five NRLRWM parameters, to fit a desired Pareto distance survivor function:

$$S_d(k) = (1/a)k^{-b} , k=1,2,\ldots \qquad (6.48)$$

and a desired exponential autocovariance function:

$$c_{xx}(k) = ce^{-d|k|} , k=\pm 1, \pm 2, \ldots . \qquad (6.49)$$

As in (6.38) and (6.39), we will actually obtain the following, "almost Pareto" survivor function for x(t):

$$S_x(x) = \begin{cases} 1 - .5(x/\alpha)^b & 0 \le x < \alpha \\ .5(x/\alpha)^{-b} & x \ge \alpha \end{cases} \qquad (6.50)$$

6.3.5 NFLRWM Parameter Estimation

where

$$\alpha = (2/a)^{1/b} .$$

The mean of x is found by direct integration:

$$\bar{x} = \alpha b^2 / (b^2 - 1) . \tag{6.51}$$

Parameters a, b, c, and d will be sufficient to determine an instance of the model.

To leave $c_{xx}(k)$, $k \geq 1$ unchanged after multiplication by noise, we stipulate that the product noise $e^{n'(t)}$ have mean $cne^{8)}$:

$$E\{e^{n'(t)}\} = 1 . \tag{6.52}$$

Thus:

$$\bar{x} = E\{e^{w(t) + n'(t)}\}$$

$$= E\{e^{w(t)}\} . \tag{6.53}$$

We already have a value for parameter b, to fit the observed distance distribution (6.48). To determine b' and $\bar{w}$, we first write:

$$\bar{x} = E\{e^{w(t)}\} = \int_{-\infty}^{\infty} e^w f_w(w) \, dw .$$

Using (6.46), and integrating:

$$b' = [\bar{x}/(\bar{x} - e^{\bar{w}})]^{1/2} . \tag{6.54}$$

---

[8] This is not really necessary; it is done for convenience. Even if multiplication by the noise does change all autocovariance coefficients, it does so by a constant for all $k \geq 1$. See equation (6.45).

We can obtain another equation in b' and $e^{\bar{w}}$ by fitting the observed correlogram (6.49) for $k \geq 1$. The "uninflated variance" is:

$$c = E\{e^{2w(t)}\} - E^2\{e^{w(t)}\}$$

$$= E\{e^{2w(t)}\} - \bar{x}^2 .$$

or:

$$c + \bar{x}^2 = E\{e^{2w(t)}\} = \int_{-\infty}^{\infty} e^{2w} f_w(w) \, dw .$$

Using (6.46) again, and integrating:

$$b' = [4(c+\bar{x}^2)/(c+\bar{x}^2 - e^{2\bar{w}})]^{1/2} . \tag{6.55}$$

Eliminating b' from (6.54) and (6.55), we have a quadratic equation in $e^{\bar{w}}$:

$$\bar{x} e^{2\bar{w}} - 4(c+\bar{x}^2) e^{\bar{w}} + 3\bar{x}(c+\bar{x}^2) = 0 .$$

It is easy to show that this equation has two real roots, one in the open interval $(0, \bar{x})$, the other exceeding $\bar{x}$. Since (6.54) implies $e^{\bar{w}} < \bar{x}$, we choose the smaller root. Thus:

$$\bar{w} = \ln\{[2(c+\bar{x}^2) - (4c^2 + 5c\bar{x}^2 + \bar{x}^4)^{1/2}]/\bar{x}\} . \tag{6.56}$$

Using (6.54), we then obtain b' immediately.

Since the underlying RLRWM should generate an autocovariance function with the same rate of decay as before, the estimation of p is identical to that in section 6.3.2. From (6.43), we have:

$$p = (b'^2 - 1)/(b'^2 e^d - 1) , \tag{6.57}$$

6.3.5 NRLRWM Parameter Estimation

for parameter d in (6.49).

Finally, we shall derive a value for $\bar{n}'$. Proceeding as above:

$$E\{e^{n'(t)}\} = 1$$

$$= \int_{-\infty}^{\infty} e^x f_{n'}(x)\, dx \ .$$

Using (6.47), and integrating, we have:

$$\bar{n}' = \ln\{(b'/b)^2 [\,(b^2-1)/(b'^2-1)\,]\} \ . \tag{6.58}$$

Since $\bar{n}'$ can be computed from b and b', the model is determined by only four independent parameters: $\bar{w}$, b, b', and p.

For distance string A, we have:

a = 4.69

b = 2.88

c = .113

d = .035

$\bar{x}$ = .846

and thus:

$\bar{w}$ = -.2277

b' = 4.128

b = 2.88

p = .9635

$\bar{n}'$ = -.0680

It may occur to the reader that nowhere in this

section have we explicitly set a desired variance inflation. We have done this implicitly, however, by fitting both the empirical distribution (hence, the variance), and the empirical autocovariance for $k \geq 1$.

6.3.6 Simulation and Checkout of the NRLRWM

The noisy restoring log random walk model is rather complicated, but it is easier to simulate than one might expect. We shall now give an algorithm to generate a distance string from the model.

Although we have treated the noise as additive to process w(t) of the RLPWM, it is more efficient to simulate the underlying RLRWM in its multiplicative form (6.32) and then multiply by the noise $e^{n'(t)}$. This saves one calculation of the exponential function per iteration. Note that noise process n'(t) has two components: a delta function component, and a component whose distribution has the same form as the distribution of RLRWM innovation process $e^0(t)$. Thus, we may use the same method to generate values of $e^{n'(t)}$ and of $e^{\varepsilon^0(t)}$, respectively.

6.3.6 NRLRWM Simulation and Checkout 247

Algorithm 6.1
begin;
   declare (UNIF, EXP, LN, ALMOST_PARETO) functions,
      d(1:K);
   comment "UNIF" is a pseudo-random number generator.
      Each reference to UNIF generates a new random
      number uniformly distributed in the interval
      (0,1). "EXP" is the exponential function. "LN"
      is a function to compute the natural logarithm.
      Function "ALMOST_PARETO" appears below.
      Variables beginning with the letter "e" denote
      the exponential of something. For example, en
      is a value of $e^{**n'(t)}$.

      read wbar, b, bprime, p;
      brat2 = (b/bprime)**2;
      nbar = LN(brat2 * (b**2 - 1)/(bprime**2 - 1));
      beta = bprime/(1-p)**.5;
      ewbar = EXP(wbar); enbar = EXP(nbar);

      ew = ewbar;
      do i=1 to K;

         delta = ALMOST_PARETO(beta);
         if UNIF<p then ew = delta*ew;
               else ew = delta*ewbar;

         if UNIF<brat2 then en = enbar;
                else en = enbar*ALMOST_PARETO(b);
         d(i) = $\lceil$ew*en$\rceil$;
      end;
end;

function ALMOST_PARETO(arg);
begin;
   comment this function returns a pseudo-random value
      with distribution:

$$F(x) = \begin{cases} .5x^{arg} & 0 < x \le 1 \\ 1 - .5x^{-arg} & x > 1 \end{cases}$$

   y = UNIF**(1/arg);
   if UNIF$\ge$.5 then y = 1/y;
   return(y);
end;

The primary overhead in the above simulation is exponentiation, which is performed either once or twice per iteration. Some efficiency can be gained by coding ALMOST_PARETO inline in the two places it appears in the main loop. This saves the overhead of subroutine linkage.

Figure 6.6 shows the empirical stack distance survivor function of 400,000 simulated NRLRWM references. Note the log-log scale. As expected, the distribution is an almost perfect match to the desired Pareto distribution.

Figure 6.7 shows the empirical correlogram of the same generated reference string. The variance inflation is now reasonably well modeled. (There is a slight remaining discrepancy, due to the fact that the variance of distance string A does not quite equal the variance of the best-fit Pareto.) For some reason, the correlogram of the model decays as $e^{-.040k}$ rather than the desired $e^{-.035k}$. This may be caused by the rounding up of x(t) to obtain d(t). It is actually the autocovariance of x(t) that should theoretically have the form $e^{-.035k}$. In any case, the model correlogram is a reasonably good fit to the observed correlogram of distance string A.

The empirical spectrum of the NRLRWM, computed using algorithm 5.6, appears in figure 6.8. The fit to the spectrum of distance string A is now acceptable. Note that the model spectrum is flat (with value about .27) above frequency f=.15 . This is hardly surprising, since most of the variance in the modeled string is now from the noise. The spectrum clearly shows the two components of the model's variance: a Markovian component with positive serial correlation and relatively long holding times, and a flat-spectrum noise component. Of the total model distance string variance of .39, the part

6.3.6 NRLRWM Simulation and Checkout

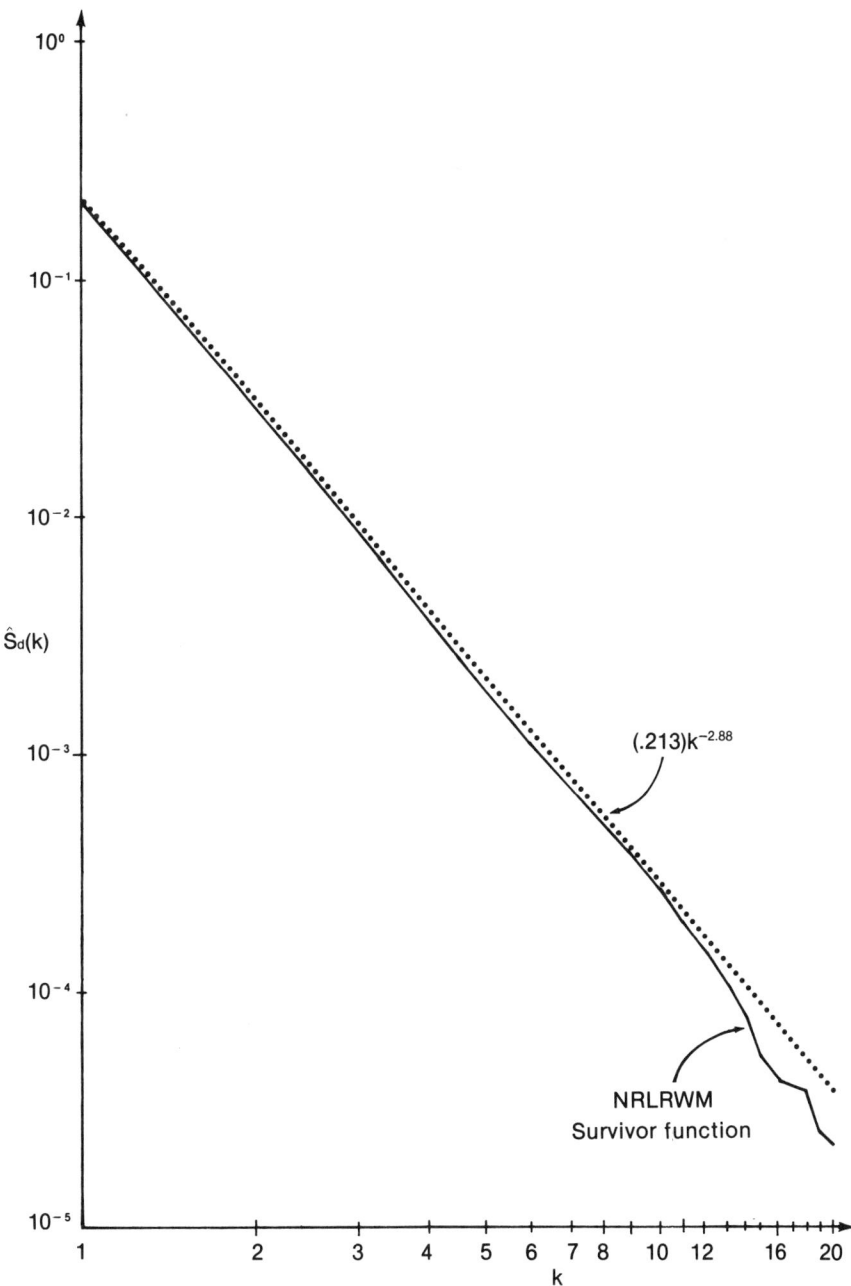

Figure 6.6 NRLRWM survivor function (solid line) and distance string A best-fit Belady lifetime function.

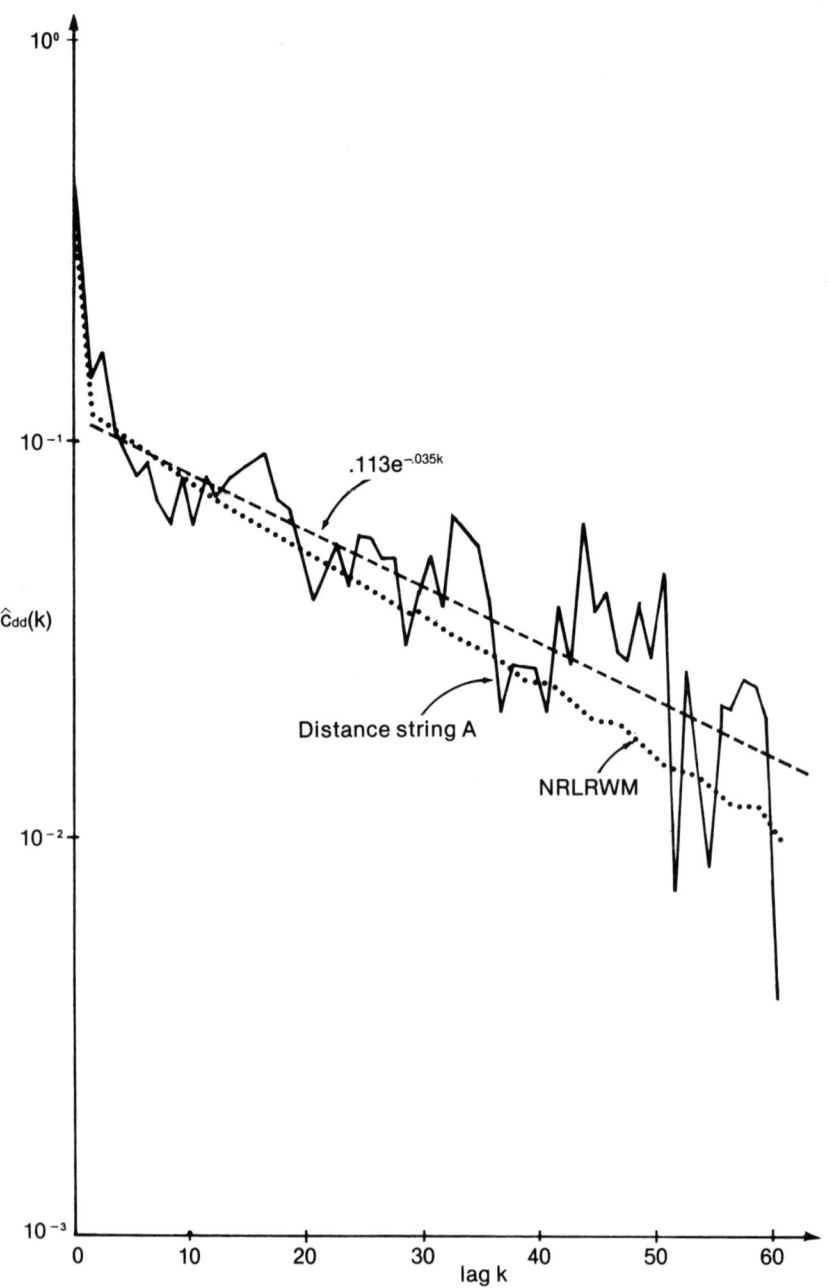

Figure 6.7 NRLRWM correlogram (dotted line) and distance string A correlogram (solid line).

6.3.6 NRLRWM Simulation and Checkout

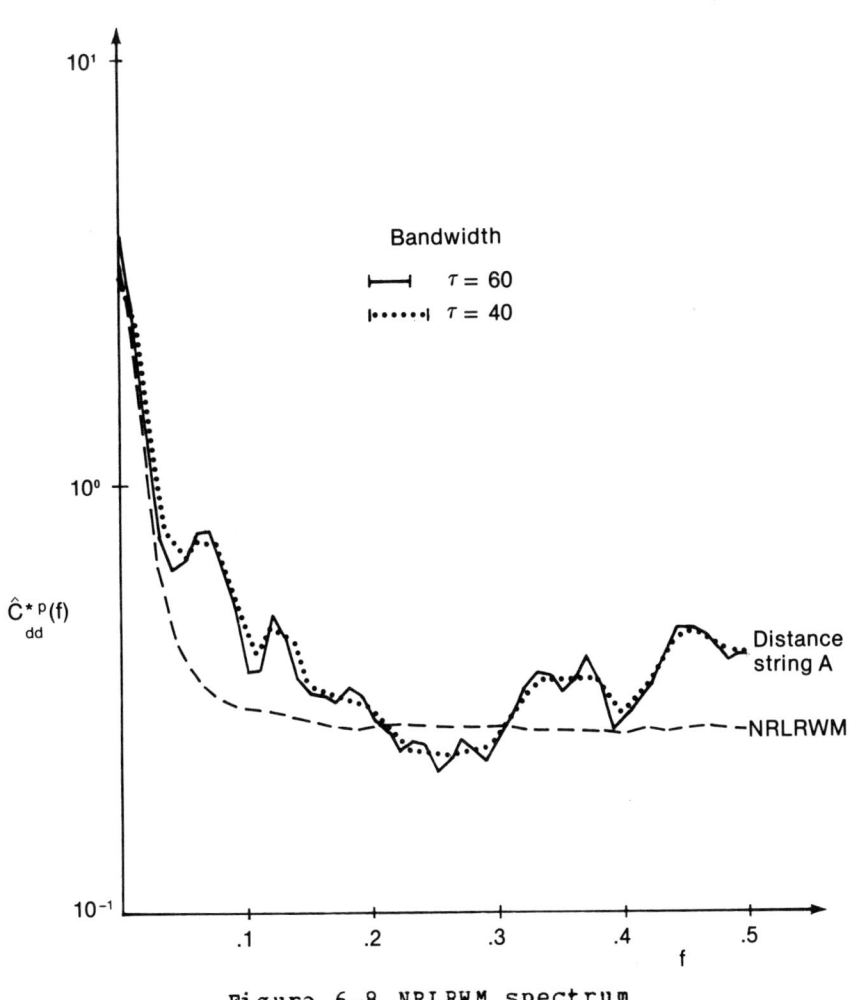

Figure 6.8 NRLRWM spectrum

attributable to the noise is about:

$$\int_{-1/2}^{1/2} (.27)\, df = .27$$

6.4 Summary

We have presented two principal models in this chapter: the Lewis-Shedler page fault model, and the NRLRWM distance string model. Both are quite complex, to the extent that their main application may be in simulation models of systems, rather than analytic models. Since neither program model has been validated against a large set of real reference strings, they should be considered largely experimental. Much work remains on further checkout, and possible improvement and/or simplification of each model.

Chapter 7

The State of the Art

We shall now conclude our survey of program behavior models and measurements by reviewing what we have done, and what remains to do. It should by now be obvious that the art is far from stabilized. The best program models are rather crude, at least by standards of other disciplines, although it is uncertain that we will ever construct tractable models of very high accuracy. This should not be discouraging, since such accuracy may be unnecessary. Programs, themselves, are so diverse that it is difficult to speak of "typical" ones (even though we have often taken the liberty of doing so!) Any reasonable program model will adequately reproduce at least some statistics of some programs. The important things to remember are the <u>limitations</u> of each model --- one should use a given model only where its deficiencies will not greatly affect the results. The program model should be matched to its parent system model.

Consider the case of the LRU stack model. There is an appreciable body of analysis based on it, as we have seen, and its particularly simple (Bernoulli process) predictions about page faults make it appealing for this purpose. There have been one or two SLRUM analyses, purportedly relating to practical memory management, which are in fact just reflections of the model's deficiencies. A typical error is to use the SLRUM to prove results about dynamic memory management; and theorem 4.22, on the "optimality" of static over dynamic allocation, is an example of the kind of thing that can result. The LRU stack model can predict average working set sizes with reasonable accuracy, but it cannot duplicate the serial distance correlation and phase-of-execution behavior that is necessary for more detailed working set analysis.

One can compound this kind of error by failing to validate properly the predictions of the resultant model. Some so-called "validations" have been nothing more than simulations of the system model <u>using the program model to generate reference strings</u>. It is hardly surprising that such validations usually succeed in confirming the analysis. Ideally, one should use at least one or two real reference strings to check a result based on a program model. In the present state of the art, this would be prudent for any program model.

7.1 Review of the Models

With only the exceptions of the (unrealistic) independent reference model, and the Lewis-Shedler page fault model, we have given sole consideration to models of distance strings. Even the Lewis-Shedler model relates to distance strings, in the sense that a distance string can be mapped many-to-one into a string of zeroes and ones, where $d(t) \to 0$ if $d(t) \leq m$, and $d(t) \to 1$ otherwise. The resultant binary sequence indicates the times of page faults. Most of the recent work on program modeling has dealt with distance strings, at least implicitly.

We began the study of distance string models with the LRU stack model. We then discussed extensions: multiple distance distributions, micro/macro models, and such Markovian methods as the Shedler-Tung model and the NRLRWM of chapter 6. The following summary presentation of the models may be helpful:

1) Independent Reference Model
   Advantages: Relatively simple for analysis. Parameters (the page reference probabilities) are easily measured.
   Disadvantages: Poor modeling accuracy.
   Analytical Results: There are many (c.f. Coffman and Denning [20]), but their real-world applicability is open to question.

7.1 Review of the Models

2) **LRU Stack Model**
   Advantages: Relatively simple for analysis. Parameters (the distance probabilities) are easily measured. The model is an adequate predictor of mean working set sizes and (less adequately) of page fault rates.
   Disadvantages: Does not model page fault clustering, phases of execution, distance string serial correlation. Hence, it fails to predict some dynamic effects.
   Analytical Results: LRU is an optimal paging algorithm, even under dynamic allocation (i.e., working set is optimal). Static allocation is better than dynamic allocation. See chapter 4.

3) **Multiple Distance Distributions**
   Advantages: Can exhibit phase and phase-transition behavior.
   Disadvantages: More parameters than the SLRUM, and the parameters are more difficult to measure. There is no empirical evidence of improvement over the SLRUM, but intuitively, some improvement is likely using the phase-of-execution concept.

4) **Micro/Macro Modeling**
   Advantages: Can model phases and phase transitions. Should be tractable for analysis.
   Disadvantages: Not well-developed as yet. There is little empirical data to validate actual models, although measurements [57, 65] have indicated that program behavior can be decomposed in this way.

5) **Shedler-Tung Model**
   Advantages: It models page fault clustering at phase transition times. Can be used in some analysis.
   Disadvantages: No validation data. It may be difficult to determine the best-fit model to a given real program. The locality set size is fixed.
   Analytical Results: Applied in a queueing analysis of a multiprogramming system with two active programs [83].

6) **Lewis-Shedler Page Fault Model**
   Advantages: Accurately models distributional and correlational statistics of the page fault sequence of a particular task.
   Disadvantages: In its current form, applies only to static allocation. Parameters are fairly difficult to measure. May be too complex for much analysis. Currently validated against only two reference strings.

7) **Noisy Restoring Log Random Walk Model**
   Advantages: Reasonably accurate model of the distributional and correlational statistics of a particular distance string. Very parsimonius. The parameters can be determined with relative ease from measurements.
   Disadvantages: May be too complex for analysis. Currently validated against only one real reference string.

The above are all generative models. We have also considered several descriptive models. These may be used directly in some analyses, or they may form part of a generative model. The important ones include:

8) **Belady's Lifetime Function:** An empirical approximation to the stack distance distribution of real programs.

9) **Working Set Model:** Gives a definition of "locality set". Relates the mean working set size and page fault rate, at various window sizes, with the interreference distribution of the reference string.

10) **Bounded Locality Intervals:** Provide a definition of phases and their transitions.

Denning [33] has shown some relationships between the size of the VMIN set (section 2.3.3), and that of the working set. Batson and Madison [6] have investigated the use of bounded locality intervals of levels other than 1.

7.1.1 What is Next?

It is always dangerous to anticipate the future, but we can at least suggest some potentially productive areas for research. The following represent miscellaneous thoughts, and are certainly not exhaustive. One open topic concerns those aspects of program behavior other than memory reference strings. Accurate, validated models of input/output activity, in particular, would be very valuable in system modeling. I/O measurements of individual tasks would be a necessary first step.

Distance string memory reference models should be further refined. The micro/macro concept, as applied to distance strings, is particularly attractive; by concentrating on only one level (the macro level, say), such models can often be conveniently analyzed. In general, Markovian models have potential for further development, with respect to accuracy and parsimony.

But there are alternatives to distance string models. High-level models, such as that of Lewis and Shedler, are less widely applicable, but convenient when they do apply. In a different vein, there are transformations, other than stack distances, that one might apply to the reference string for modeling purposes. For example, letting $\tau(t)$ denote the elapsed virtual time since the previous reference to page $r(t)$, we can transform a reference string into an _interreference interval string_ $\tau(1) \tau(2)...$, which might be the basis for a model. This string, like the distance string, is numerically significant, and should be relatively more stationary than the reference string. Since interreference intervals relate directly to working sets, such a model might be a superior working set predictor. More esoteric transformations are also possible, of course.

Belady's lifetime function has been around for quite awhile, and it is probably time for it to be challenged. For instance, there is some evidence [58 and private correspondence with R.Y. Kain] that certain lifetime functions are well-approximated by an exponential function. It may be possible to improve the accuracy of Belady's lifetime function by adding additional terms; for example

$$e(m) = a_1 m^{b_1} + a_2 m^{b_2} + \ldots + a_k m^{b_k}.$$

Of course, this adds more parameters. But the most serious defect in Belady's form is its failure to tail off. For instance, it has been shown [48] that if a tail-off does occur, it may be optimal to allocate the memory space at which the tail-off begins. In those cases where the tail-off is primarily due to first faults, it is not hard to modify a given lifetime function to cause it to exhibit tail-off (we have seen an example in section 4.2.4).

7.2 Measurement and Validation

We have considered methods of distributional and correlational validation, particularly as applied to distance strings. However, the methods are applicable to the validation of any type of numerically meaningful, reasonably stationary time sequence, such as the page fault and lifetime interval processes in connection with the Lewis-Shedler model. The details of such methods can be very technical --- we do not pretend to have reviewed the state of the art of statistical measurement and model fitting, nor could we attempt to do so. Rather, the methods given here have been selected for their practicality and relative simplicity.

In contrast with other methods we have presented, validation by use of the working set curve, and its derivative, the page fault curve, is designed particularly for use in program modeling. Although it is concerned explicitly only with **mean values** (of the working set size and page fault rate), it includes implicitly a form of distributional validation. Recall that the page fault curve is closely related to the interreference interval distribution. Serial reference string correlation will also affect the working set curve (although correlation among successive interreference intervals will not), so that this type of validation does check, perhaps weakly, for a kind of correlational fit. Recall the poor fits of the independent reference model working set curve; successive references in this model are uncorrelated. However, one should keep in mind that serial

7.2 Measurement and Validation

corelations among the references are dominated by the non-stationarities. It would be interesting to determine exactly how the distance string autocovariance function relates to the working set and page fault curves --- this would help in describing the power of working set curve validation.

An advantage of this type of validation is that it indicates directly some aspects of the model's performance as part of a system. In this sense, working set curve validation is more functional than direct distributional and correlational methods as used in chapter 6. It would be very useful to know how the measurable statistics of the distance string (or other reference string transformation) relate to functional measures such as the working set size or page fault rate. Such relationships are undoubtedly model-dependent, but perhaps there are general results, or results applicable to large classes of models. Thus, an analysis of the relationship between distance string and working set statistics would improve our understanding of both working set curve validation and distance string statistical validation.

Much of the remaining potential for research in validation, per se, concerns statistical methodologies; better spectral estimation procedures, for example. One question of more direct application to program modeling involves the power of correlational tests such as we have presented. Since the autocovariance function depends only on first and second moments, we have ignored third and higher moments when comparing modeled and measured distance string autocovariance functions. Whether or not this is a serious problem needs investigation. There may be alternatives for validation purposes to the distance string, having autocovariance functions which yield more powerful tests.

Appendix
Working Set Statistics of the LRU Stack Model

In this appendix, we shall obtain an expression for the working set size probability distribution of reference strings generated by the LRU stack model. From this we shall derive the mean working set size (working set curve) and working set page fault rate.

If $W(t,T)$ contains $w(t,T)$ pages, these will be the top $w(t,T)$ pages of the model's stack at time t. Suppose $w(t,T)=w$. If $r(t+1) \in W(t,T)$, with probability A_w, then $w(t+1,T+1) = w(t,T) = w$. Otherwise, $r(t+1) \notin W(t,T)$, with probability $1-A_w$, and $w(t+1,T+1)=w+1$. Using this idea, we can write, for $w, T \geq 1$:

$$\Pr[w(t,T)=w] = \Pr[w(t-1,T-1)=w-1](1-A_{w-1}) \qquad (A.1)$$
$$+ \Pr[w(t-1,T-1)=w]A_w .$$

Let the generating function $G_w(z)$, $0 \leq w \leq n$, be defined as follows:

$$G_w(z) = \sum_{T=0}^{\infty} z^T \Pr[w(t,T)=w] .$$

Function $G_w(z)$ gives the probability that the working set size is w for any window size T. Since $w(t,T)=0$ if and only if $T=0$, we have:

$$G_0(z) = 1 . \qquad (A.2)$$

From (A.1), we have for $w \geq 1$:

$$G_w(z) = zG_{w-1}(z)[1-A_{w-1}] + zG_w(z)A_w$$

or:

$$G_w(z) = G_{w-1}(z)[z(1-A_{w-1})/(1-zA_w)], \quad w \geq 1 . \qquad (A.3)$$

Appendix A

Combining (A.2) and (A.3), and manipulating:

$$G_w(z) = z^w \left(\prod_{1}^{w-1} (1-A_k) \right) \left(\prod_{1}^{w} \frac{1}{1-A_k z} \right)$$

If the A_i are all different (that is, if $a_i > 0$ for $2 \le i \le n$), it is straightforward to invert this generating function after taking a partial fraction expansion. We obtain:

$$\Pr[w(t,T) = w] = \left[\prod_{1}^{w-1} (1-A_i) \right] \sum_{i=1}^{w} A_i^{T-1} \prod_{\substack{j=1 \\ j \ne i}}^{w} \frac{1}{A_i - A_j}$$

$$w, T \ge 1 \qquad (A.4)$$

The working set page fault probability is then immediately found as:

$$\Pr[f(t,T) = 1-A_w] = \Pr[w(t,T) = w] \quad . \qquad (A.5)$$

Using (A.4), we can obtain an expression for $w(T)$, the mean working set size with window T. By definition:

$$w(T) = \sum_{w=1}^{n} w \Pr[w(t,T) = w] \quad .$$

Substituting (A.4) and manipulating:

$$w(T) = \sum_{i=1}^{n} A_i^{T-1} c_i \quad , \quad T \ge 1 \qquad (A.6)$$

where

$$c_i = \sum_{w=i}^{n} w \left[\prod_{1}^{i-1} (1-A_j) \right] \left[\prod_{\substack{j=1 \\ j \neq i}}^{w} \frac{1}{A_i - A_j} \right] \qquad (A.7)$$

Moreover, the page fault rate (for long reference strings) is:

$$f(T) = w(T+1) - w(T), \quad T \geq 0,$$

as was shown in section 3.1.1, so that:

$$f(T) = \sum_{i=1}^{n} A_i^{T-1} (A_i - 1) c_i, \quad T \geq 1. \qquad (A.8)$$

Obviously, the forms chosen to express (A.6) and (A.8) are designed to facilitate the computation of $w(T)$ and $f(T)$. The n values $c_1, \ldots, c_n$ need be calculated only once, after which each value of $w(T)$ or $f(T)$ requires $O(n)$ time to compute. Below is an algorithm to calculate curves $w(T)$ and $f(T)$ for the LRU stack model.

Algorithm A.1
begin;

    declare $w(1:J)$, $f(1:J)$, $A(1:n)$, $c(1:n)$, $cc(1:n)$, $T(1:J)$;

    comment We assume that $w(T)$ and $f(T)$ are to be calculated at some chosen set of window sizes $\{T_1, T_2, \ldots, T_J\}$, with $T_i \geq 1$ for all i. At the conclusion of this algorithm:

Appendix A

$w(i)$, $1 \leq i \leq J$, contains the mean working set size with window T_i.

$f(i)$, $1 \leq i \leq J$, contains the page fault rate per reference with window T_i.

Array A, input to the algorithm, is the cumulative stack distance probability distribution. Arrays c and cc are temporaries; $c(i)$ will contain the value of coefficient c_i in equation (A.7).

```
do j=1 to n;
  c(j)=0;  d=1;

  do i=1 to n;
    if j=1 then begin;
      if i=1 then cc(1)=1;
        else cc(i)=cc(i-1)*i*(1-A(i-1))/(i-1);
    end;

    if i≠j then d=d*(A(j)-A(i));
    if i≥j then c(j)=c(j)+cc(i)/d;
  end;
end;

do k=1 to J;
  w(k)=0;  f(k)=0;
  do i=1 to n;
    atc = c(i)*(A(i)**(T(i)-1));
    w(k) = w(k) + atc
    f(k) = f(k) + atc*(A(i)-1);
  end;
end;
end;
```

Clearly, the coefficients c_i are calculated in $O(n^2)$ time. After this initial step, the time to compute $w(T)$ and $f(T)$ at J window sizes is $O(nJ)$.

Bibliography

1. Aho, A.V., P.J. Denning and J.D. Ullman. Principles of optimal page replacement. *JACM* *18* 1 (Jan. 1971) pp. 80-93

2. Aikake, H. Automatic data structure search by the maximum likelihood principle. *Computers in Biomedicine*, supplement to *Proc. 5th Hawaii Int'l Conf. on System Sciences* (1972) pp. 99-101

3. Arvind. *Models for the comparison of memory management algorithms.* (Ph.D. Thesis) University of Minnesota Electrical Eng. Dept. (1973)

4. Baskett, F., K.M. Chandy, R.R. Muntz and F.G. Palacios. Open, closed, and mixed networks of queues with different classes of customers. *JACM* *22* 2 (April 1975) pp. 248-60

5. Batson, A.M. Program behavior at the symbolic level. *IEEE Computer* *9* 11 (Nov. 1976) pp. 21-26

6. Batson, A.M. and A.W. Madison. Measurement of major locality phases of symbolic reference strings. *Proc. Int'l Symposium on Computer Performance Modeling, Measurement, and Evaluation.* Cambridge, Mass. (March 1976) pp. 75-84. Available from ACM, New York

7. Belady, L.A. A study of replacement algorithms for virtual storage computers. *IBM Sys. J.* *5* 2 (1966) pp. 78-101

8. Belady, L.A. and C.J. Kuehner. Dynamic space sharing in computer systems. *CACM* *12* 5 (May 1969) pp. 282-88

9. Belady, L.A., R.A. Nelson and G.S. Shedler. An anomaly in the space-time characteristics of certain programs running in paging machines. *CACM* *12* 6 (June 1969) pp. 349-53

10. Belady, L.A. and F. Palermo. On-line measurement of paging behavior by the multivalued MIN algorithm. *IBM J. Res. Devel.* *18* 1 (Jan. 1974) pp. 2-19

11 Billingsley, P. *Statistical inference for Markov processes.* University of Chicago Press (1961)

12 Blackman, R.B. and J.W. Tukey. *The measurement of power spectra.* Dover, New York (1958)

13 Box, G.E.P. and G.M. Jenkins. *Time series analysis: forecasting and control.* Holden-Day, San Francisco (1970)

14 Brawn, B.S., F.G. Gustavson and E. Mankin. Sorting in a paging environment. *Comm. ACM* 13 8 (Aug. 1970) pp. 483-94

15 Brawn, B.S. and F.G. Gustavson. Program behavior in a paging environment. *Proc. FJCC* (1968) pp. 1019-32

16 Bryant, P. Predicting working set sizes. *IBM J. Res. Devel.* 19 3 (May 1975) pp. 221-29

17 Chu, W.W., N. Oliver and H. Opderbeck. Measurement data on the working set replacement algorithms and their applications. *Proc. Polytechnic Inst. of B'klyn Symposium on Computer Comm. and Teletraffic* (April 1972)

18 Chu, W.W. and H. Opderbeck. The page fault frequency replacement algorithm. *Proc. FJCC* (1972) pp. 597-609

19 Chu, W.W. and H. Opderbeck. Program behavior and the page fault frequency algorithm. *IEEE Computer* 9 11 (Nov. 1976) pp. 29-38

20 Coffman, E.G., Jr. and P.J. Denning. *Operating system theory.* Prentice-Hall, Englewood Cliffs, N.J. (1973)

21 Coffman, E.G., Jr. and T.A. Ryan, Jr. A study of storage partitioning using a mathematical model of locality. *CACM* 15 3 (March 1972) pp. 185-90

22 Coffman, E.G., Jr. and L.C. Varian. Further experimental data on the behavior of programs in a paging environment. *CACM* 11 7 (July 1968) pp. 471-74

23 Coffman, E.G. and R.C. Wood. Interarrival statistics for time sharing systems. *CACM* 9 7 (July 1966) pp. 500-503

24 Conover, W.J. *Practical spectral estimation.* Wiley, New York (1971)

25 Cox, D.R. and P.A.W. Lewis. *The statistical analysis of a series of events.* Methuen, London (1966)

26 Daley D.J. and D. Vere-Jones. A summary of the theory of point processes. In Lewis, P.A.W., Ed. [61] pp. 299-383

27 Denning, P.J. *Resource allocation in multiprocess computer systems.* (Ph.D. Thesis) MIT Project MAC Tech. Rep. MAC-TR50 (May 1968)

28 Denning, P.J. The working set model for program behavior. *CACM* *11* 5 (May 1968) pp. 323-33

29 Denning, P.J. Thrashing: its causes and prevention. *Proc. FJCC* (1968) pp. 915-22

30 Denning, P.J. Virtual memory. *Comp. Surv.* *2* 3 (Sept. 1970) pp. 153-89

31 Denning, P.J. On modeling program behavior. *Proc. SJCC* (1972) pp. 937-44

32 Denning, P.J. Comments on a linear paging model. *Proc. 2nd ACM SIGMETRICS Symposium.* Montreal (Sept. 1974) pp. 34-48

33 Denning, P.J. The computation and use of optimal paging curves. *Purdue Univ. Computer Science Tech. Report CSD-TR-154* (June 1975)

34 Denning, P.J. and G.S. Graham. Multiprogrammed memory management. *Proc. IEEE* *63* 6 (June 1975) pp. 924-39

35 Denning, P.J. and K.C. Kahn. A study of program locality and lifetime functions. *Proc. 5th ACM SIGOPS Symposium.* Austin, Texas (Nov. 1975) pp. 207-16

36 Denning, P.J. and S.C. Schwartz. Properties of the working set model. *CACM* *15* 3 (March 1972) pp. 191-98

37 Easton, M.C. and R. Fagin. Cold-start vs. warm-start miss ratios and multiprogramming performance. IBM T.J. Watson Rsch. Ctr. Report RC-5715. Yorktown Heights, N.Y. (Nov. 1975)

38 Feller, W. An introduction to probability theory and its applications. Vol. I. Wiley, New York (1957) (second edition)

39 Ferrari, D. Improving locality by critical working sets. CACM 17 11 (Nov. 1974) pp. 614-620

40 Ferrari, D. Tayloring programs to models of program behavior. IBM J. Res. Devel. 19 3 (May 1975) pp. 244-51

41 Ferrari, D. Program Behavior. IEEE Computer 9 11 (Nov. 1976) pp. 7-8

42 Ferrari D. The improvement of program behavior. IEEE Computer 9 11 (Nov. 1976) pp. 39-47

43 Fine, G.H., C.W. Jackson and P.V. McIsaac. Dynamic program behavior under paging. Proc. ACM Nat'l. Conf. (1966) pp. 223-28

44 Franklin, M.A., G.S. Graham and R.K. Gupta. Anomalies with variable-partition paging algorithms. CACM to appear

45 Freiberger, W.F., U. Grenander and P.D. Sampson. Patterns in program references. IBM J. Res. Devel. 19 3 (May 1975) pp. 230-43

46 Gaver, D.P., P.A.W. Lewis and G.S. Shedler. Analysis of exception data in a staging hierarchy. IBM J. Res. Devel. 18 5 (Sept. 1974) pp. 423-35

47 Ghanem, M.Z. Experimental study on the behavior of programs. IBM T.J. Watson Rsch. Ctr. Report RC-5460. Yorktown Heights, N.Y. (June, 1975)

48 Ghanem, M.Z. Study of memory partitioning for multiprogramming systems with virtual memory. IBM J. Res. Devel. 19 5 (Sept. 1975) pp. 451-57

49 Ghanem, M.Z. and H. Kobayashi. A parametric representation of program behavior in a virtual memory system. Proc. 8th Princeton Conf. on Info. Sciences and Systems. Princeton, N.J. (March 1974) pp. 327-330

50 Graham, G.S. and P.J. Denning. Multiprogramming and program behavior. Proc. 2nd ACM SIGMETRICS Symposium. Montreal (Sept. 1974) pp. 1-8

51 Hannan, E.J. Time series analysis. Methuen, London (1960)

52 Hatfield, D.J. and J. Gerald. Program restructuring for virtual memory. IBM Sys. J. 10 3 (1971) pp. 168-92

53 Howard, R. Dynamic probabilistic systems. Vol. I. Wiley, New York (1971)

54 Jalics, P.J. and W.C. Lynch. Selected measurements of the PDP-10 Tops-10 timesharing operating system. Information Processing 74. (Proc. IFIP Congress, Stockholm, 1974) pp. 242-46

55 Jenkins, G.M. and D.G. Watts. Spectral analysis and its applications. Holden-Day, San Fransisco (1968)

56 Jones, R.H. Identification and autoregressive spectrum estimation. IEEE Trans. Automatic Control AC-19 6 (Dec. 1974) pp. 894-98

57 Kahn, K.C. Program behavior and load dependent system performance. (Ph.D. Thesis) Purdue Univ. Computer Science Dept. (May, 1976)

58 Kain, R.Y. How to evaluate page replacement algorithms. Proc. 5th ACM SIGOPS Symposium. Austin, Texas (Nov. 1975) pp. 1-5

59 Kemeny, J.G. and J.L. Snell. Finite Markov chains. Van Nostrand, Princeton, N.J. (1960)

60 Koopmans, L.H. The spectral analysis of time series. Academic Press, New York (1974)

61 Lewis, P.A.W., Ed. Stochastic point processes: statistical analyisis, theory and applications. Wiley-Interscience, New York (1972)

62 Lewis, P.A.W. and G.S. Shedler. Empirically derived models for sequences of page exceptions. IBM J. Res. Devel. 17 2 (March 1973) pp. 86-100

63 Lewis, P.A.W. and P.C. Yue. Statistical analysis of program reference patterns in a paging environment. Proc. IEEE Computer Society Conference. Boston (1971)

64 Liptay, J.S. The cache. IBM Sys. J. 7 1 (1968) pp. 15-21

65 Madison, A.W. and A.P. Batson. Characteristics of program localities. CACM 19 5 (May 1976) pp. 285-94

66 Madnick, S.E. Storage hierarchy systems. (Ph.D. Thesis) Massachusetts Institute of Technology Project MAC Report TR107 (April 1973)

67 Mattson, R.L., J. Gescei, D.R. Slutz and I.L. Traiger. Evaluation techniques for storage hierarchies. IBM Sys. J. 9 2 (1970) pp. 78-117

68 McKellar, A.C. and E.G. Coffman. Organizing matrices and matrix operations for paged memory systems. CACM 12 3 (March 1969) pp. 153-65

69 Morris, J.B. Demand paging through utilization of working sets on the MANIAC II. CACM 15 10 (Oct. 1972) pp. 867-72

70 Oden, P.H. and G.S Shedler. A model of memory contention in a paging machine. CACM 15 8 (August 1972) pp. 761-71

71 Opderbeck, H. Measurement and modeling of program behavior and its applicati (Ph.D. Thesis) University of California, Los Angeles, Computer Science Dept. (1973)

72 Opderbeck, H. and W.W. Chu. Performance of the page fault frequency replacement algorithm in a multiprogramming environment. Information Processing 74. (Proc. IFIP Congress, Stockholm, 1974) pp. 235-41

73 Prieve, B.G. and Fabry, R.S. VMIN --- an optimal variable-space page replacement algorithm. CACM 19 5 (May 1976) pp. 295-97

74 Rodriguez-Rosell, J. Experimental data on how program behavior affects the choice of scheduler parameters. Proc. 3rd ACM Symposium on Operating System Principles (Oct. 1971) pp. 156-60

75 Rodriguez-Rosell, J. Empirical working set behavior. CACM 16 (Sept. 1973) pp. 556-60

76 Rodriguez-Rosell, J. Empirical data reference behavior in data base systems. IEEE Computer 9 11 (Nov. 1976) pp. 9-13

77 Saaty, T.L. Elements of queueing theory. McGraw-Hill, New York (1961)

78 Saltzer, J.H. A simple linear model of demand paging performance. CACM 17 4 (April 1974) pp. 181-85

79 Sayre D. Is automatic folding of programs efficient enough to replace manual? CACM 13 12 (Dec. 1969) pp. 656-60

80 Scherr, A.L. An analysis of time shared computer systems. (Ph.D Thesis) Massachusetts Inst. of Tech. Project MAC Report TR-18 (June 1965)

81 Schroeder, M.D. Performance of the GE-645 associative memory while Multics is in operation. Proc. ACM Workshop on System Performance Evaluation. Boston (April 1971) pp. 227-45

82 Schwetman, H.D. Analysis of a time-sharing subsystem: a preliminary report. Proc. 2nd SIGMETRICS Symp. on Measurement and Evaluation (Dec. 1974) pp. 65-75

83 Shedler, G.S. and C. Tung. Locality in page reference strings. SIAM J. Comp. 1 3 (Sept. 1972) pp. 218-41

84 Slutz, D.R. and I.L. Traiger. A note on the calculation of average working set size. CACM 17 10 (Oct. 1974) pp. 563-65

85 Spirn, J.R. Program locality and dynamic memory management. (Ph.D. Thesis) Princeton University Electrical Eng. Dept. (1973)

86 Spirn, J.R. Distance string models for program behavior. *IEEE Computer* **9** 11 (Nov. 1976) pp. 14-20

87 Spirn, J.R. and P.J. Denning. Experiments with program locality. *Proc. FJCC* (1972) pp. 611-21

88 Spirn, J.R., P.J. Denning and J.E. Savage. Models for locality in program behavior. *Brown Univ. Engineering Tech. Report* (June 1974)

89 Wilkes, M.V. *Time-sharing computer systems.* (3rd ed.) Elsevier-North Holland, New York (1975)

Index

activity set see bounded locality interval
address space 21
analytic model 2
associative memory 21-22
autocorrelation function 178
    (see also autocovariance function)
  partial 213-214
autocovariance function 177-184
  defined 177
  estimation 178-182
  implications 182-184
autoregressive process 225-226
  restoring 228
  log 231

Belady's algorithm see OPT
Belady's lifetime function 62-76, 80-81, 130-132, 174, 225, 256, 257-258
Bernoulli process 132, 208, 212
    (see also geometric distribution)
BLI see bounded locality interval
bounded locality interval 81-84, 256

change bit 45
change flag 19-20
concave/convex curve 56, 60, 64, 75-81
correlogram 178 (see also autocovariance function)

demand paging 23, 26-28
descriptive model 13-14
distance probabilities 93-94
distance string 34, 93
  measurement 166-168
  modeling 93-95, 132-142, 224-252
  validation 145, 169-206
distributional validation 170-177

equivalent bandwidth 195
execution interval 62
    (see also Belady's lifetime function)
expected forward distance criterion 32, 92-93, 119-123
exponential distribution 171-173, 175
external memory device 19, 22, 45
extrinsic model 10-13, 15 (see also working set)

fault flag 19

Index

FIFO algorithm 40-41, 44
functional model 15

gamma distribution 173-175
general locality model 88-91, 92, 95-97
generative model 13
geometric distribution 171-173
GLM *see* general locality model

hyper-exponential distribution
    see mixed exponential distribution

impulse process 198-199
inclusion property 33
independent reference model 13, 84, 86, 87-88, 91-93,
    96, 254
  parameter estimation 153, 154
  validation 154-155
informal principle of optimality
    see expected forward distance criterion
input/output model 8-10
interleaved memory 10-11
interreference distribution 60, 144, 152-153
  measurement 145-150
interreference interval string 257
intrinsic model 10-13, 15
IRM *see* independent reference model

Jensen's inequality 76

lag window 190-193
least recently used
  paging algorithm 36-37, 42, 44, 98
  stack 36-37, 112
least recently used stack model 111-134, 255
    (*see also* simple stack model)
  choosing distance probabilities 130-132
  and expected forward distance criterion 119-123
  extrinsic locality measurement 112
  multiple distance distributions 137-139
  parameter estimation 153, 154
  quasi-stationary distribution 139-140
  references asymptotically independent 118
  spectrum decomposition 204-206
  under dynamic allocation 123-127
  validation 154-165
  working set curve 260-263
  working set size distribution 118, 260-263
Lewis-Shedler model 211-224, 256

lifetime 62-64, 66-69, 142
    (see also Belady's lifetime function)
LIFO algorithm 42, 115-116
locality 16-17
   degree of 46, 131
   effect on lifetime curve 65
   extrinsic 16-17, 48, 88
   hierarchy 85-86
   improvement 50-55
   intrinsic 16-17, 49, 84-88
   list 85-92
   principle of 16-17
   properties of 45-49
   set 16-17, 26, 45, 85-86, 92, 94-95
   set formation time 81-82
   spatial 49-50
locality priority algorithm 86-88, 92, 96-97, 102-111
LPA see locality priority algorithm
LRU see least recently used

macro behavior 47-48
macro model 47, 140-142, 255
Markov model/process 139, 169-170, 213, 225
   autocovariance 200
   spectrum 201-203
memory allocation 25
   average 29-30
   fixed (static) 25, 126-127
   variable (dynamic) 2, 25, 28-30, 123-127
memory space 21
M/G/1 queue 3-5
micro behavior 47-48
micro model 47, 92, 94, 140-142, 255
MIN algorithm see OPT algorithm
mixed exponential distribution 174-175

name space see address space
nearness matrix 54
negative binomial distribution 176-177
noisy restoring log random walk model 240-252, 256
   parameter estimation 242-246
   simulation 246-248
   validation 248-252
NRLRWM see noisy restoring log random walk model

OPT algorithm 28, 33, 41, 44, 98

Index

page
   addressing 18-21
   definition 18-19
   frame 19
   table 19-21
page fault 21, 22
   characteristic function 58
   clustering 133-134, 137-139
   curve 58-62, 76-79
   first 64-66
   model 207-224
   process 208, 209-210
page fault rate/probability 58, 66-69
   of LRU stack model 132
   measurement 67, 145-165
   under working set 58-60
page fault frequency algorithm 43-45
paging algorithm 21, 23-45
   anomalies 33
   cost of 27-32
   demand 23, 26-27
   examples of 40-45
   non-lookahead 31
   optimal 28-32, 92-93, 107
   prepaging 23, 27-28
parameter - definition of 10
Pareto distribution 174-177
parsimonious model 10
PFF see page fault frequency algorithm
phase of execution 47, 83-84, 133, 137-139
Poisson process 2, 5, 212
     (see also exponential distribution)
Pollaczek-Khintchine formula 5
power spectral density 184 (see also power spectrum)
power spectrum 184-206
   definition 184-185
   estimation 185-196
   of important processes 198-203
   superposition 203-206
prepaging 23, 27-28
priority algorithm 33-40
priority list 35
program
   definition of 7-8
   graph 52-54
   restructuring 50-55
program trace 6-7
   how to do 166-168

random walk 227-228
   restoring 229
real time *see* time
reference string
   definition 25-26
   measurement 166-168
   problems in validating 144-145
   relation to distance string 34, 93-94
renewal process 212-213
restoring log random walk model 231-240
   parameter estimation 235-236
   as part of NRLRWM 246
   validation 236-240
RLRWM *see* restoring log random walk model

sample spectrum 185-196
   smoothing 188-194
semi-Markov model/process 91, 139, 140, 214
Shedler-Tung model 134-137, 255
simple LRU stack model
   see least recently used stack model
simple stack model 84, 86, 93-95, 98-111
    (*see also* least recently used stack model)
   lifetime distribution 109
   long-run cost 110-111
   optimal initial memory content 109-110
   optimal paging algorithm 102-108
   paging algorithm cost 100, 108-109
simulation model 2
SLRUM *see* least recently used stack model
spectrum *see* power spectrum
spectrum of counts 210
spectrum of intervals 210-211
stack 33-34
   algorithm 33-40
   distance 34 (*see also* distance string)
   LRU 36-37, 112
   properties 36
   updating 35-36
strong locality condition 94-95, 102-109, 121-123, 124-127

task - definition of 8
thrashing 22-23, 71-75
time
   real 25
   unit of 25
   virtual 7, 25
trace *see* program trace
trend - testing for 169, 211-212